For Reginald Stuart
with sincere thanks for
great cooperation in producing
of the Mountain Meadow

Bob Howard

THIS IS THE WEST

WILLIAM PAUL SCHENK

Where, Now, The West?

*There was a time when the West was a few moccasined steps
into the woods this side of Boston, New York, Philadelphia, and Charleston.
A little later, a page or two farther on in history books,
and the West was the smoky wall of the Alleghenies and the Blue Ridge.*

*There was a time when the West was a hunter's campfire or a lonely cabin
in Ohio, in Kentucky, in Indiana. Some sunsets, some sunrises,
a few pages more, and the West was a steamboat on the Mississippi
and the raw pine shanties in the mud of St. Louis and Chicago.*

*Wife and children, a skillet and some seeds, some chickens
and a plow inside his creaking wagon, a man would move ahead . . .
with a long rifle on one shoulder and a big chip of hope on the other.
But the West has a way of moving on, always ahead of a man.*

*The West moved to the Missouri, along the Plains, over the Rockies,
and on across the deserts . . . always ahead of the trappers, the miners,
the traders, the cattlemen, the sodbusters, the pony expressmen,
the overland stage, and the railroad.*

*Then, some say, the West came to an end, dissolved somehow
in the vast blue welcome of the Pacific. There are those who believe this.
Others know better.*

*They know the West never died. They know there was no ending
to its spacious story of sharp axes and willing hands, the comradeship
of horses and sky, daring in the night, and eager eyes on morning horizons.*

*They know the West lives on . . . in men and women . . . elusive
as the shadows on its mountainsides and the starlight in its valleys,
but eternal as the wind over its prairies
and the sunshine on its shores.*

Dedicated to Georgia M. Hilgers
of Sioux City—June 1949

THIS IS THE WEST

Edited by ROBERT WEST HOWARD

ILLUSTRATED

RAND McNALLY & COMPANY

New York   Chicago   San Francisco

ACKNOWLEDGMENTS *and* COPYRIGHT NOTICES

Grateful acknowledgment is made to the following for permission to reprint selections included in this volume:

American Music, Inc. for lyrics from the song "COOL WATER" by Bob Nolan, Copyright 1936 by American Music, Inc.

S. Omar Barker for "GRASS" and other verse.

E. P. Dutton & Company for the selection from *The Last Chance* by John Myers Myers.

Joe M. Evans for the anecdote from *A Corral Full of Stories.*

Houghton Mifflin Company for a selection by Archibald MacLeish from "GREEN RIVER" in *Time to Speak.*

Rinehart & Company, Inc. for the anecdote from *Conquest of the Missouri* by Joseph M. Hanson, Copyright, 1909, by A. C. McClurg & Company, renewed 1937; Copyright, 1946, by Rinehart & Company, Inc.

Library of Congress Catalog Card No. 57-12138

Printed in the United States of America
by RAND MCNALLY & COMPANY

To
the Members and Posse of
the Chicago Corral of THE WESTERNERS
who inspired, planned and co-operated in
the production of this book.

Acknowledgments

No MAN IS AN ISLAND—nor is a book-editing job. The list of people who aided in the genesis of THIS IS THE WEST from the notion stage is several times as long as the list of authors. A few who went out of their way to do favors are: Jack Fischer, editor of *Harper's Magazine;* C. L. Sonnichsen, Texas Western College, El Paso; Glen Randall, attorney, Phoenix, Arizona; Leslie Ernenwein, Western Writers of America, Tucson, Arizona, Lucius Beebe, author and editor of *The Territorial Enterprise,* Virginia City, Nevada, and John T. Amber, editor of *The Gun Digest.*

Victor Weybright of The New American Library caught the glimmer of the notion for "an overview book about the West" as tossed via mail by the Posse of the Chicago Corral. NAL financing and the patient work of Marc Jaffe, Associate Editor, enabled the project to get under way.

Herbert O. Brayer, 1956 president of the Chicago Corral, contributed much to the planning for the original outline. Leland Case, cofounder of the Westerners and currently editorial director of *The Christian Advocate* and *Together,* served as consultant on the selection of authors and used personal friendship to persuade several aboard. Don Russell, DeLoss Grant and Howard Euston of the Chicago Corral undertook extraordinary assignments in perfecting sections of the manuscript.

Special thanks go to David Vernon, of the Chicago Corral, for making available to Rand McNally his extensive collection of Western Americana from which the illustrations for this volume were selected.

Very special thanks go to the American Meat Institute and its executives, since their only hope of "return" on the book was through the development of a coherent report on the American West and the livestock industries born there. They not only granted me the time to contact authors and edit the manuscripts but underwrote travel and contingent expenses. Rita Lauer and Gwen Olmsted of AMI's staff did the final typescripts at home nights and week ends, to the detriment of family life.

Robert West Howard

Chicago
February 1, 1957

Contents

WALTER PRESCOTT WEBB

What is "The West"?

WHAT IS THE WEST?

Who but an editor would ask such a question? Who but a genius could answer it? Until the genius comes along, ordinary mortals will look at the West in uncomprehending awe and undertake to say what it is and what it means. Each sees something different and comes up with his own answer, but the answer never quite satisfies him for he cannot put in prose or in poetry or on canvas what the West makes him *feel*. All the arts combined cannot convey the full feeling that the West engenders.

The most definite and understandable thing about the West is this: It is a territory that can be marked off on a map, traveled to, and seen. Everybody who knows anything knows when he gets there. This territory begins in the second tier of states west of the Big River. A cord drawn from the southern tip of Texas to the farther boundary of central North Dakota marks its eastern limits. It stands almost in the tropics, and extends almost to the northern limits of the temperate zone. Its feet are warm, but its head is often cold.

From the eastern line the West extends to the Pacific Ocean, hemmed in by Canada on the north and Mexico on the south. It comprises half the area of the United States, all or part of seventeen states, and has a complete monopoly on the only boundary separating this country from Mexico, the only neighbor with a different language, tradition and civilization. Its length

I

will approximate 1500 miles, its width a thousand; an airline road around its border would be five thousand miles in length, one-fifth the distance around the world. This is the West, as distinguished from the other two regions, the North and the South.

Like Caesar's Gaul, the West is divided into three parts, three strips, laid one beside the other on a north-south axis: the Great Plains on the east, the Rocky Mountain chains in the center, the Pacific Slope on the west—three contrasting features encountered by any traveler moving by any route from east to west. Though these gigantic natural features give variety and part of the character to the country, combined they do not explain it. One can never understand the West—all of it—in terms of the rolling plains, the craggy mountains, or the slopes to the sea, for none of these is common to the entire region. They divide rather than bind the West to an inevitable destiny.

The overriding influence, the force that shapes more things in the West than all else, is the desert. That is its true unifying force. It permeates the plains, climbs to all but the highest peaks, dwells continuously in the basins and valleys, and plunges down the Pacific slopes to argue with the sea.

It is the guest that came to dinner, never to go away. It has stripped the mountains of their verdure, making them rocky; it has dried up the inland seas, leaving Death Valley completely dry and Lake Bonneville a briny fragment magnified by the name of Great Salt Lake. The desert has been the great designer of the American West, painting the landscape with gorgeous colors, chiseling the grotesque mesas and pinnacles, building the plains with the stripped-off soil laid down by perishing rivers. The desert shortened the grass on its borders before destroying it in the interior. It never permitted trees on the plains it built, and where it found them it beat them down to sage and shrub, reducing the leaves to thorns and the sap to grease and oil. Those it could not destroy, it shriveled, and those it could not shrivel, it petrified.

The Desert designed the animals as it shaped the land and made a grotesque joke of vegetation. It compelled them to conform to its colors, put horns on toads, made snakes that travel sideways to keep from sinking in the sands and grasshoppers that fly five miles to find a sprig of grass. One thing it required of all: that they be parsimonious with water. The rabbits require little if any; the antelope do without for long periods; rodents and plants, like the Joshua tree, manufacture their own; the horned toad requires none and can live long without food. The little prairie dog is one of the desert's jokes. He is a misnamed squirrel, because the Americans who named him could not believe that a squirrel would live in a dugout. As for water, the prairie dog will not touch the stuff. If he does pray for rain, as the folk verse would have us believe, he must do it out of sympathy for those who require water—

"The soapweed rolls over the plain,
    The brakeman rules over the train,
    The prairie dog kneels on the back of his heels
    As he silently prays for rain."

What is the West? asks the editor. It is many things, amazing, compli-
cated and confusing. Suppose we ask instead: What is *at the heart* of the
West? Where is the center from which force and power radiate? The
answer is simple if we will only see it. The heart of the West *is* a desert,
unqualified, unaltered, absolute. Draw a line from the eastern boundary of
the West to the Pacific, stand on its mid-point, and if you are not *in* the desert
you are near it, in a land with many of its characteristics.

One reason we do not understand the West is that we will not face a
fact; we do not want the desert to be there. We will not go to the heart of
it to make a beginning, to get our vantage point. We prefer to loiter on its
edges, approaching it from the outside rather than going to the inside, and
planting our mental feet in the center where the power of it is to be found.
Let us take our stand there, in the place of its greatest intensity, and measure
its radius and its circumference and influence. There it lies around us, palpitating in the sun, its sands shimmering in the distance, its mirages playing
tricks with our vision, its mountains etched against the sky, a crosscut saw
with missing teeth; by night it is a deceitful benediction, its breeze a sorcer-
ess, its heavens full of stars bigger than marbles or so small as to make the
Milky Way an unbroken powdery scarf of gossamer light. By day it throbs
and writhes in the sun—a live thing devoted to the destruction of all other
life. By night it is a mystery—

"O wilderness of drifting sand, O lonely
        caravan!
    The desert heart is set apart, unknown
        to any man."

Its radius is variable, its circumference uncertain, for the desert expands
and contracts as its enemy, rain, retreats or advances in eternal conflict.
Always at the margins there is dampness, at the borders moisture, at the
limits wetness. But at the center there is little of these. When the desert
pokes a hot finger into the border regions, the people speak of drought; when
it pulls the finger back, having touched rain, they like to think that their
country is "getting more seasonable." At the heart of the desert there is no
drought, only an occasional mitigation of the dryness. Drought comes only
where there is rain.

It is the desert, the dry mantle spread over all but the margins of the

American West, that contributes most to its unique character. It binds the plains, the mountains, and the slopes together, puts them in the same bed, under the same blanket.

The effect of the desert is expressed by the poet and song writer better than by the historian. Bob Nolan's song, "Cool Water" has caught the spirit of the thirst of the American West.

Cool Water

All day I've faced a barren waste without the taste of
water—cool water.
Old Dan and I with throats burnt dry and souls that cry
for water—cool, clear water.

Keep a-movin', Dan, don't you listen to him, Dan,
He's a devil, not a man, and he spreads the burning sand
with water.
Dan, can you see that big green tree where the water's
running free,
And it's waiting there for you and me.

The shadows sway and seem to say, "Tonight we pray
for water—cool water."
And 'way up there He'll hear our pray'r and show us
where there's water—cool, clear water.

Keep a-movin', Dan, etc. (1)

Dan and his rider suffered in the extreme what everyone in the West suffers in some degree, and all share with horse and man, the longing "to rest where there's no quest for water."

Under its desert influence the West exhibits many strange things. It is a place where nature tried her hand at the unusual, at making a show place. It has a spectacular quality which lures thousands to it yearly. They go there to see things they cannot see elsewhere in the nation, or the world. It is the only part of the country where the rivers run into both seas, the Atlantic by way of the Mexican Gulf and the Pacific directly. It is the region of the greatest extremes. It has the highest altitude, 14,495 feet at Mt. McKinley, and the lowest, 280 feet below sea level in southern California. It has no navigable streams, and only three big river systems. Many of its rivers, Lost River in Idaho and the Humboldt in Nevada, have no mouths in the ordinary sense, but simply disappear in the earth. It has the only volcano; its one body of water worthy of being called a lake has no outlet, and is so salty that the human can not sink. There is nothing to compare with its Grand Canyon, Painted Desert, Petrified Forest, and Yellowstone geysers. Its forests, scattered among its mountain tops, furnish the largest and oldest living things on earth, the Sequoias, which were saplings two thousand years before Christ appeared on earth. In the West dwell four-fifths of the surviving American Indians, four-fifths of the American Japanese, and three-fifths of the Chinese. Along its southern border live practically all the American people who speak the Spanish language. It is in some respects the most American of the three regions; in other respects it is the most cosmopolitan, having the largest contingent of world civilizations—the Indians, Japanese and Chinese.

It has registered the highest temperature in Arizona and the lowest in North Dakota, the highest annual rainfall in the Olympic Mountains and the least at Phoenix, Arizona. To go west is indeed like going to the circus, where all the extraordinary things are on display. It is the highest, the lowest; the hottest, the coldest; the wettest, the driest.

Once we are willing to grant the desert its sovereignty over the West, we are prepared to understand much of the life that goes on there, its history. A desert is a place acquisitive people put off taking until the last. To put it another way, the desert puts off the taker to the last, compelling him to occupy the more hospitable places first. The West remained a vacancy down to the time of the Civil War, and after. It was not left vacant because of its position, but because it hurled back the invaders. The Spaniards attacked it in the sixteenth century and were thrown back many times before they abandoned it in the eighteenth. One of their wisest officers, sent to inspect it, recommended that it be given back to nature and the Indians, who had it all along. The Americans began their attack early in the nineteenth century and recognized it for what it was and is. Lewis and Clark crossed it in 1803–06, Zebulon Pike penetrated it in 1807, and Stephen H. Long in 1819–20. They all described it as a desert, and Major Long made a map in which he laid down a white blotch and wrote in the middle of it in block letters THE GREAT AMERICAN DESERT. Jefferson Davis, when Secretary of War, was so convinced that the West was a desert that he imported two shiploads of camels to solve the transportation problem. Daniel Webster was so convinced of its aridness that he refused to exclude slavery in the territories, saying that God and nature had already decided that there could be no slavery in that arid land. "I would not," said he, "take pains uselessly to reaffirm an ordinance of nature, nor re-enact the will of God."

Behind the forerunners, the explorers and statesmen, came the land-hungry American pioneers. Their drive west was more like a response to instinct than to intelligence. They came with a great deal of pioneering experience but no experience with the sort of country they were approaching; they had never lived in a land without trees, where the spirit of the desert reigned.

They hit the first tier of the West, the plains, and were hurled back

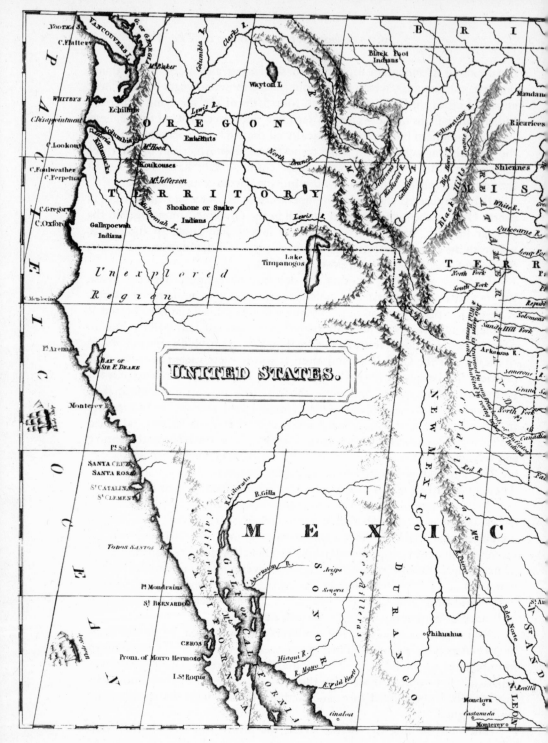

The semicircular lines of type on this section of an 1830 map of the United States advises that the desert is traversed by numerous herds of buffaloes and wild horses and roving tribes of Indians. From the *Malte-Brun School Geography Atlas*, 1834

to re-form and try again. Then they did a remarkable thing, they jumped almost two thousand miles to Oregon, to California, and to Santa Fe. They beat out the three trails that had been marked by Lewis and Clark, Pike, and Long. The Oregon Trail led them to water and trees; the California Trail led them to gold; the Santa Fe Trail to the Spanish settlements in the upper Rio Grande Valley. They made history, but they did not take the West. It lay almost unscathed between them and their homeland, gorgeous, spectacular and formidable, and at its heart lay the Great American Desert, palpitating, expanding, contracting, at the whim of the seasons. Over the plains and through the mountains roamed the most nomadic and ferocious tribes of Indians known on the American continent. A concerted attack was made on the heart of the West from its eastern and western borders, but for twenty years, 1850 to 1870, there was little progress.

By 1875 the army had rounded up the Indians, conquering them at last, but the pioneers had not occupied the land vacated. A few hunters roamed the plains to exterminate the buffalo herds; a few miners panned gold and dug silver in the mountains, but there were few permanent settlers. There had not yet appeared an American institution adequate for the job.

What is the West? To most people it is cattle on a thousand hills and bowlegged cowboys eating at chuck wagons, singing ballads, riding horses all day long, sleeping under the stars, and having a good time generally. But ranching is not an American institution; it did not come with the pioneers from the East. It came from the South, and with its coming the West was under attack from three directions. Ranching is a Spanish and Mexican institution, borrowed—horse, saddle, bit, spur and lariat—from Mexican neighbors who knew arid lands. The first longhorns were borrowed or stolen. The Americans in Texas learned the cowboy skills, and in Texas the cattle multiplied, but it was not until after the Civil War that they swarmed north, accompanied by cowboys and horses. By 1875 this Spanish institution of open-range ranching had covered practically the entire West, covered it sparsely but with some success. Aside from the Mormons in Utah and a few other islands of settlement, the cattlemen were the first permanent occupants of the vacant spaces.

Their tenure was brief because the American pioneers—the farmers—had learned something about living in the new country. They had invented a barbed wire with which to fence a treeless land, learned the principles of dry-farming which made agriculture less hazardous, and learned how to use the scanty waters for irrigation. Thus equipped, the farmers' invasion of the West was renewed and has continued to the present time. In reality, theirs has been a war on the desert. They plow up the grass in the wet years but the desert winds race in and take the soil away in the dry ones. They fight for water everywhere, take it from the rivers until they are dry, from beneath the surface until there is no more, and when all sources fail, as they do, the President is invited to make a tour of inspection of the ruin and the farmers go on government relief. They have occupied the desert but they have not conquered it.

What historically has the West been? It was the greatest challenge offered to the European nations in their attempt to take the present territory of the United States. It defied the Spaniards for two centuries. It held the Americans off until they had taken all else, hurled them back time after time, and never admitted them until they had changed many institutions and practices. The West demanded a new set of institutions and a new mode of pioneering of a people who thought they knew all about it. The necessity for this change of institutions was recognized by the first American who understood the West. In 1878 Major John Wesley Powell wrote:

"The physical conditions which exist in that land, and which inexorably control the operations of men, are such that the industries of the West are necessarily unlike those of the East, and their institutions must be adapted to their industrial wants. It is thus that a new phase of Aryan civilization is being developed in the western half of America."

The greatest social revolution that occurred in the history of American pioneering took place on the near edge of the West, and had to take place before the land could be occupied.

The West is one thing to the people who dwell there; it is another to people who live elsewhere. It thrills its occupants because it challenges them, makes them struggle and fight. People respond to a challenge, they love a fight. Even though they come out of it scarred up, they remember it with pleasure. The fact that they met the challenge, and survived, makes them come out thinking well of themselves, ready for the next round. They love the memory of their ancestors who crossed the country or stopped in it. They make grim and sardonic jokes of their own hardships, remembered and experienced. In their adjustment they made so many changes in their ways that they sometimes seem strange and even bizarre to those who do not know their reasons. They are unconventional because they could not make conventions work, found success only by defying them. They altered everything, would try anything, and were satisfied with nothing. They puzzled their neighbors, one another, and themselves.

John J. Ingalls tried to tell what the West did to normal people. Though he was speaking of Kansas, what he said applied to more than Kansas.

"For a generation Kansas has been the testing-ground for every experiment in morals, politics, and social life. Nothing has been vener-

able or revered merely because it exists or has endured . . . every inco-
herent and fantastic dream of social improvement and reform, every
economic delusion . . . every political fallacy nurtured by misfortune,
poverty, and failure, rejected elsewhere, has here found tolerance and
advocacy. . . . There has been neither peace, tranquillity, nor repose.
The farmer can never foretell his harvest, nor the merchant his gains,
nor the politician his supremacy. Something startling has always happened, or has been constantly anticipated."

What is the West? There it is: the place where something startling has
always happened. Where it is ever anticipated.

What is the West to the outsider, him who dwells beyond its greening
borders? It is mainly an imagination. Its extremes and its wonders—grand
as they are—never come quite up to what the outsider expected. Only the
distances and the magnitude of the plains and the mountains exceed expecta-
tions. But he goes there on vacation and drives from place to place in search
of what he is looking for.

What he is looking for, aside from the natural wonders, he does not
find. Indians, for example, and horses, cows, and cowboys. He sees mostly
miniatures in show windows, buys them to send home to prove that he has
been in the West. These tourists are today one of the best money crops, an
indestructible annual resource.

But those who go are as nothing to those who remain away, and visit
the West vicariously. They people it with imagination. The cowboy is their
darling, better dressed and more heroic than any cowboy ever was. He rides
ten thousand screens all over the world, albeit more concerned with his
heroines and villains than with his cattle. He becomes a peace officer because
everybody else is afraid to, and he kills more villains than ever swung from
ropes in the West or got off the train at high noon. He has a few horse races
with the Indians where there might otherwise be awkward pauses, and he is
almost sure to pull the gambler off that old stagecoach, do a kindness to a
small boy, make himself generally agreeable to all except evil men. He saves
more gold and girls than the U.S. Treasury and the Salvation Army combined. He has been known to fire thirty-seven shots from one six-shooter
without reloading. He does the most incredible things, the same things over
and over, and the world loves him.

He never existed. He is a myth. The West that he has created never
existed either. It is a myth too. But maybe the West created him and the
myth. There seems to be a kinship between the myth and the mirage, something where there is nothing, one the product of the human mind playing
over the desert, the other the product of human vision trying to perceive
what is on it, and both turning up with what was never there.

People love myths and preserve them in their affection. But real people—realists among people—do not love the desert. They live by it, around its borders, as close to its fire as they can, but they do not face it. They look the other way, towards greener country or at the high clouds, and let themselves think like small children that now the desert has gone away. And that too is myth, for the desert abides. It is the heart of the West. It makes the West what it is, keeps it from being what some would have it be.

Those who live in it or around its borders, as all Westerners do, should not avoid facing the desert, whose near presence gives them their chief problems, makes them Westerners.

If those who live within its reach were a primitive people, they would probably seek out the strongest force in nature operating on them. If in doing this they discovered that the desert was the supreme physical force, then as true nature worshippers they would devise rites and ceremonies designed to placate it, become supplicants. In such rituals, whatever the religion, the supplicant faces that which he implores. The Mohammedan faces Mecca five times a day in prayer; the Christian looks upward to heaven for his God; the primitive sun worshipper towards the burning orb in the sky. And so, if Western people who dwell around the margins of the Great American Desert were nature worshippers who had found the most powerful force affecting them, they would surely look inward, towards the desert, forming a huge concentric circle around that barren waste which is the glowing heart of the American West.

Western people are not nature worshippers; they are not going to bow down even to such a powerful force. But in their attempt to deal with the problems it creates, they should not deny the desert. They should face it more than they do. They should never forget that though it is neither god nor devil, it is their nearest and most disagreeable neighbor—more a devil than a man—and that it has no intention of going away.

Part 1

The LAND

A man said to the universe,
"Sir, I exist!"
"However," replied the universe,
"The fact has not created in me
A sense of obligation."

STEPHEN CRANE– "The Man"

ROBERT WEST HOWARD

The Setting

THE TRUCKEE BARTENDER didn't know what it was when he offered it to me—just a fistful of crystallized Hell gleaming sullenly in his right palm. Anyway, he had grown weary of it, and there were hundreds more back in the mountains. A $5 bill would buy it. I remember that my hand trembled as I reached into a pocket for the money. The egg-shaped rock had been sliced by a jeweler's wheel, and the inner face of agate polished. So the bark of reddish olive lava framed gray and amber shellfish and seaweed suspended in milky crystal. This was the jeweled half of a volcano bomb, once worshipped by the Pomos, Yuroks and other Pacific Slope tribes.

Thus I bought my "thunder-egg" a decade ago in Nevada. It has glowed from a corner of my desk since—sultry symbol of the birth of the American West. Here, in miniature, is the long torture that created the stage-set from Illinois to the Pacific . . . the eons of writhing below and above the oceans . . . the molten heave of mountain ranges two thousand miles long . . . the slow horror of the glaciers . . . the torrents of water and silt that created the eight hundred-mile hill between the Mississippi and Denver . . . the alchemy of hot winds, chinooks, northers and blizzards on the mile-high deserts between the ranges.

The West was born in gargantuan agonies. The gaunt terrain these produced influenced the men and women who finally ventured there. The Apache raider, the scout, mountain men, miners, cowboys, and honkytonk gals were but a reflection of the land itself. They reacted to nature's stage-set and built the American Saga as they went along.

13

The birth throes of the American continent were mainly an east-to-west process. All the descriptive powers of Dante would not do them justice. The upheaval of rock strata, blatant as Neapolitan ice cream or twisted taffy, gleams on every cliff in the Rockies and Cascades, just as it speaks from my thunder-egg, tossed molten into a flaming Pacific sky.

Somewhere in the paroxysms that seized the cooling earth, geologists now believe, an explosion sent nearly a quarter of the globe spinning back into space. And there that quarter spins today, the object of Indian prayers, cowboy laments, coyote screams and lovesickness. We call it "the moon." The hole it left was eventually filled by the Pacific Ocean.

Since ocean salts are created by the chloride sediments of soil and rock carried down by the rivers at an annual average rate, it is possible to estimate the ocean's age as one to one and a half billion years. The solid crust of the earth is believed to be about two billion years old.

We haven't the faintest idea of the landscape of that era. And it would make little difference if we did. Vast cataclysms went on for another billion years, at least, as the sphere cooled and adjusted to internal and external pressures. The rainbowed gouge of the Grand Canyon of the Colorado River was created above the ocean about 500,000,000 years ago. The Appalachians were hurled up along the Atlantic seaboard about 150,000,000 years ago. But the Rockies did not groan and break into lofty heights until 40,-000,000 years ago. And the Cascades, formed beneath the waters of the Pacific, were thrust upwards in a series of earthquakes and tidal waves 20,-000,000 years ago.

In the interims came the Reptilian Ages. The tiny disk- and star-shaped creatures within my thunder-egg passed on the life spark. Docile as Lincoln ewes, the forty-ton Brontosauri munched in the Dakotas' swamps. Tyrannosaurus crunched his grisly terror through the ferns and tall palms of Colorado and Oklahoma. Then, as though timetabled by a master plan, nature erased them—some by an Ice Age; some by parasites; some by the gleeful malice of the new races of fur-bearing rodents who crept into dinosaur nests and ate the eggs.

By the time the Rockies hurled up and the West took roughly familiar shape, the ancestors of most of earth's present animals roamed the continent. But they were dwarfs. Horses and camels were no larger than house cats and toy poodles are today. The rhinoceros was about the size of a marketable pig. The elephants were waist-high to modern man and, since they were vegetarians, would have been a fair match for a fox terrier.

Flesh-eating animals, called creodonts, had begun the split into two large families. The dog family also developed the wolves, coyotes, and bears. The cat family produced the lions, tigers, pumas and jaguars.

All of them adapted and grew larger. The Rockies shook, tumbled, and rose again. Rivers washed the debris east and west to build the smooth high plains and the long slope of the Big Hill up from the eastern flats. By the time the Cascades writhed into place, the horses of the West were the size of Shetland ponies. The rhinos were larger than a man. A huge hog, named the entelodont, was the bully-boy of the mountains—as tall as a grizzly bear and with a skull four feet long.

Still the West was not ready for Man. Step by patient step through each gigantic age nature had built the quick, pulsing life of the animal and the plant into higher forms. Each step seems to have been ideally suited to its eon. The tiny creatures in my thunder-egg belonged, unquestionably, to the dawn days of flowing, fiery continents, vast layers of poisonous gases and explosions that vaporized entire seas to searing steam. Somehow, down the ages, these creatures passed the flicker of life onward. Their descendants crawled out on the harsh, black beaches to become walking-fish and eventually Brontosaurus and Tyrannosaurus. The slimy algae took land root, mutated and changed, age by slow age, to grass and trees. Each plant and animal became more specialized, nestled down in a favorite corner where wind, rain and sunlight gave it the greatest comforts and ensured its survival. But the time of Man was not yet. One giant phase remained; the planers and levelers must do their work. That was the Ice Age.

Four eras of glaciation occurred on the continent after the Cascades were formed. No one knows how they came, or why they went away. The West suddenly became cold and froze up. The skies were dark with snow, almost endlessly, for centuries. The ice formed, mountain high. The horses, camels, rhinos, entelodonts, all perished, or fled south.

Eventually the heavens changed again. The sunshine came back. The glaciers slipped south, grinding and chipping the mountains smooth, crushing the rubble to gravel and sand and fine brown earth. The valleys became great lakes. The mountain passes were afoam with the black and brown sludge that would one day sell at $1,000 an acre as "prime prairie soil."

And nature, playing the long game with that pulsing awareness we call "life," introduced new animal and plant forms. The elephant reappeared, now almost as large as a dinosaur, clothed in heavy fur and armed with long, scoop-shovel tusks admirably suited to dredge frozen grass and moss and roots out of a snowbank. We call him "the mammoth" today. His bones have been dug up from the Arizona desert and have been found mingled with those of saber-tooth tigers, camels, horses, lions and tapirs in the black muck of the Rancho La Brea asphalt pits of downtown Los Angeles.

Under sun-warmth, the glaciers melted back toward the mountain valleys. But the immense water reserve of the runoff turned North America into inland seas. One body of water stretched from the Appalachians to the Rockies. It had numerous outlets to the Atlantic. Two of the principal ones were south into the Gulf of Mexico and east across New York. Today, in the hills south of Syracuse, New York, any amateur geologist can trace the great outlet channel and waterfall gouged by this glacial runoff. It is within a few miles of the sacred Council Fire the Onondagas kept burning at the headquarters of the Iroquois Confederacy. Perhaps there was a mystic connection, because the torrent roaring there carved out the Mohawk Valley as a "water-level route" between the Atlantic and the Midwest. Domination of this pass through the Appalachians made the Iroquois the most important Indian group of the Northeast, and held up white migration to the prairies and Rockies for 150 years.

The southerly outlet of the great lake of the prairie became the Mississippi Valley, with the modern Great Lakes as comparatively minor "ponds" on its northern fringe.

West of the Rockies other seas formed, without adequate outlets to the Pacific. As they evaporated, the chloride salts from the rock sediment intensified to densities heavier than those of the oceans. So when Jim Bridger came to the edge of Utah's Great Salt Lake, he whooped, "By God, I've hit the Pacific."

As the waters of the glacial floods receded, the West took its current shape. There were still earthquakes and volcanoes to produce minor change; but overall the pattern was set. The continent west of the Appalachians emerged as a plain of woodland and grass centered by the Mississippi's drainage to the Gulf of Mexico. West of this the land rose smoothly and evenly through the Great Plains until, at an elevation of four to five thousand feet, it met the tortured walls of the Rockies.

Beyond the Continental Divide, great valleys tilted south toward Mexico. They were slashed by cross ranges and buttes to the salty deserts of the Great Basin which sprawled before the Sierras. From the Sierras' peaks, the drop was sharp to the Pacific delta.

This was the skeleton stage-set of the American West when human beings first glided in from the North Pacific wings. But there were three conditioners of its vastness that would have profound influence on its human saga. These were The Weather, The Plants and The Animals.

THE WEATHER – The humid lands of the Atlantic coastal plain and Appalachians, averaging more than 40 inches of rainfall a year, were areas of great forests. West of them, from the Kankakee and Wabash mudflats and the wide trough of big brother Ohio rolled a flat, treeless country pounded hard by wind and rain.

This was the prairie. In summer it grew waist-high grasses. Sudden storms dipped the black fingers of tornadoes across its distances, or bashed the buck grass flat with hail that, spinning on straight lines from horizon to horizon, might be a hundred yards or five miles wide. Here, too, the wind found elbowroom from Thanksgiving to Easter. Blizzards howled a thousand miles across the brown and yellow floor until, at dawn, the creeks were tinkling silver and beasts stood with mouths half-open, frozen in their tracks. There it ran—a tilting plain a thousand miles wide from the Great Lakes to the edge of the blue-white Rockies; it was without the foreboding of the jungle, but the more frightening for its bland deceit.

The higher these Great Plains rolled up from the Mississippi's trough, the lower the rainfall. And the farther south one traveled on them, the longer the warm seasons; hence the higher the rate of water evaporation. The water evaporation rate is so high in west Texas, New Mexico and Arizona that—Walter Prescott Webb points out in his classic *The Great Plains*—the area would have to have 16 to 20 more inches of rainfall each year in order to equal the plant and grass potentials of the Dakotas. Thus, grass will grow in Montana with an annual rainfall of 14 inches, whereas central Texas needs 21 inches of rain to maintain the same grama or galeta grasses.

Only part of the evaporation is caused by the heat. The rest is "just blown away" by prevailing high winds, averaging from ten to fifteen miles per hour across all the high plains.

These winds fall into several types in the plains and mountain country.

"A Herd of Buffaloes at the Platte"–from the *Century Magazine*, volume XLI

The hot winds of the Southwest vary from a dry to an intense heat between June and September, blowing steadily in a "patchy" pattern that can be from a few yards to ten miles in width. The Chinook shows up west of Colorado as a steady warm wind that evaporates snow and ice and dries the ground rapidly. The blizzard is a snarling combination of high wind and snow that can create ten- and twenty-foot drifts overnight. (Some say "blizzard" comes from the old German word *blitzartig* meaning "lightning." Others contend it was coined by Davy Crockett and means "blast away.") Cold winds wreak another toll in the Rockies and high plains area with hailstorms. The rattling, shrieking "hailers" descend two, and sometimes three or four times a year during the growing seasons to raise general hell with crops and plants.

West of the Rockies, the dry plains lie in a great sheltered bowl cut off from storm clouds which come from either the Pacific or the Mississippi valleys. The country is essentially desert. Rainfall deficiencies average from twenty to five inches per year. The weather routine is wet summers and dry winters. The extremes of dry summers and wet winters prevail on the west side of the Pacific slope.

The Plants – Water, sunlight and soil minerals are as essential to a plant as its parent seed. The weather, then, is responsible for the landscape of the West—the tall grasses and tree-lined creeks to the Missouri and Red rivers, the short grasses up on "the big hill," the desert shrub and mesquite grass beyond the Pecos.

Draw a line along the south fringe of Canada's forest belt between the 98th meridian and the Cascade-Sierra chains, drop a north-south line from each end, and join the bottoms with a line tracing the north edge of the Mexican forest belt. The result is the "bowl" that holds the western plains and its plant life. There are no other regions like it on earth, except the steppes of Asia. The area makes up more than a third of the continental land of the United States but contains only ten per cent of our timberlands. Most of the forests that do exist are high in the mountains.

The Southwest, a unique empire of desert, black mountain and "Injun-colored" butte, has the most spectacular plant life. The short grass of the high plains gives way to tuft grass, mingling with sagebrush, creosote and greasewood. Crisscross through them creep the array of cacti—a plant family as amazing in its variety as the evergreen. Some cacti will grow only at high altitudes. So the saguaro, the family giant that looms like a pale green railroad semaphore above the slopes of Arizona, appears only in the narrow belt of the Sierra foothills south from Phoenix into Mexico.

Other cacti pop up anywhere in valley or desert—barrel-shaped, pot-shaped, big-eared, bushy, feathery—some armed with thorns long enough and tough enough to provide early man with stillettos and fishhooks. A few varieties hold from a quart to a gallon of brackish water. Others are fruit-bearers, hence a source of jellies and candies. Most are fragrant and flagrant flower-bearers, beautiful in pinks, rich reds and yellows after a spring rain.

Although the blossom of the giant saguaro was to become the official flower of the state of Arizona, a spiky member of the lily family would give all of the Southwest the nickname of "the Yucca Country." Soapweed, Spanish bayonet, or yucca, as it is variously called, grows rankly from the western slope of the Rockies to Arizona. It proved to be the "emporium of the desert" for Indians and early whites. The bright flowers, stalks, fruit and seeds are edible, raw or cooked. The leaf fibers, leached out, can be woven into fine linenlike cloth. The roots yield a detergent that will do a splendid job of sudsing the family laundry.

Northward the plains and mountain meadows developed other tree and plant families that were to become essential props of the West's stage-set.

The Larch, a mountain conifer, towers on slopes 2,000 to 7,000 feet above sea level, between Montana and Oregon. It is not an evergreen, so it sheds its needles each fall. The tough wood provided tunnel props for most of the West's gold, silver and copper mines.

Along the same slopes grew the rough and tough Bear Grass, unfolding lavender buds into a lilac bloom, and here and there grew a patch of the mountain man's true orchid, the Mountain Lady Slipper, gleaming like rubies.

The Mountain Alder arched rasping leaves toward the mountain snow-lines, uphill from the green bulk of Douglas Fir and Red Cedar forests. Spotlit by summer sun in the glades between shone the blue Camass, the yellow Glacier Lily and purple-blue plumes of Larkspur.

Farther west, in the moist glades of the Cascades' Pacific slope, reared earth's oldest living things, the redwoods. Before the glaciers, they grew in cathedral majesty across most of the continent. Some of the stumps in Arizona's Petrified Forest are extinct varieties of redwood and its cousin *Gigantea*, "the big tree." Living trees are known to be 3,000 to 4,000 years old. They reach a height of 325 feet, with 30- to 40-foot girth.

The name finally given them by naturalists is a saga chapter in itself, worthy of the West's inherent individualism. A Tennessee half-breed, Sequoyah, rumored to have been the son of a white trader and a Cherokee girl, developed the eighty-six syllable alphabet of the Cherokees in 1822. That achievement made possible the first Indian printing and reading. Sequoyah never saw the western deserts or the Cascades. He died on the Great Plains, in Oklahoma, in 1843. The redwoods and "big trees" were named "sequoia" in his honor a generation later.

The Great Plains, from June through September, became a patchwork quilt of lavender Pasque Flower, yellow and lavender Prairie Smoke, spined

"Prairie Dog Village"—from *North America*, by Hayden and Selwyn, 1883

Devil's Club, Prairie Aster, Woolly Arnica, the wild geranium called Cranes-bill (because of its beaked fruit), and passionate splashes of Mexican Poppy. Framing them in a vast, green sweep that seemed as limitless as the sky itself, arched the grasses. More than gold or silver, copper or oil or uranium, the grass would determine the future of the West and the eventual pattern of its conquest by man. Most of the wild animals that paced the retreating glaciers up the Big Hill and across the mountains were grass-eaters. And—shaggy, thundering prophecy—the most numerous animal of them all was a great-great-uncle of the beef cow.

THE ANIMALS – Somewhere, somehow, during the turbulence of earth's juvenile delinquencies, the shaggy, big family of *Bos* originated. They were grass-eaters, endowed with a series of stomachs; their young were nursed from four nipples of a milk pouch suspended beneath the cow's groin. The bulls were vicious fighters, trampling down small animals, gutting the larger ones with quick twists of their horns. The family divided and spread across the continents. The Asiatic branch became the water buffalo and hump-backed Brahman. An elephantine brute called Aurochs ambled through Asia Minor into Europe to become the ancestor of dairy and beef cattle. A third cousin's herds divided on some lost ridge of prehistory. One branch headed into Europe. The other branch worked its way west to find a natural home on the Great Plains. These were the bison. The European branch grew tall and rangy with rough brown coats. The Goths who hunted them called them Wisents.

The American bison, destined to become the symbolic animal of the West, finally bred out as a short-bodied, short-horned powerhouse with a coarse brown mantle growing across his shoulders, a black billy-goat beard, and a Hottentot hairdo. The grasses, the climate, the vast sweeps of the Great Plains were ideally suited to him. He bred into herds a million strong, whose charging hoofbeats matched the roar of the winter blizzard and the summer thunderstorm.

The bison was nearsighted and almost totally dependent on its sense of smell to locate enemies. Thus it became a food source for the members of the cat and dog families—the jaguars, pumas, wolves and coyotes. The meat was coarse. Provided you had never tasted a U.S. Prime or Choice sirloin, it would rate as moderately good beef.

The first white men to see bison—the Spanish in Mexico and the English on the shores of Chesapeake Bay—were still hipped with the notion that they were in India. So they harked back to the reports of Alexander the Great and Marco Polo, and called the bison a "buffalo." The name stuck—and always will: Buffalo, New York; Buffalo, Wyoming; buffalo nickel and even "buffaloed."

Outpacing even the bison in marital fervor was the jack rabbit. He, too, became a victim of the early white man's ignorance. He isn't a rabbit at all. He is a hare, capable of clocking thirty miles an hour on any prairie stretch. His back legs are geared like a kangaroo's. A clout from them will upend a young coyote. Because his ears are a third as long as his body, early settlers called the western hare the jackass rabbit, then slurred that to jack rabbit and plain "jack." Another grass-eater, and a burrower, the jack has breeding spurts that are still the despair of ranchers and truck-gardeners from Iowa to California. So the jack-rabbit drive, a sort of shotgun-and-dog adaptation of the cowboy's roundup, is still a periodic essential in western farm areas.

Just as prolific on the dry plains and in the Rockies was the prairie dog. He, too, is a victim of pioneer semantics. He isn't a dog. He's a squirrel who adapted to the plains. There weren't any trees, so he went underground. In the process, he developed a community pattern that may have given the early pueblo-builders some ideas. And he evolved a tail that labels him as a natural States'-righter. The prairie dog is plump, a foot to fifteen inches long, with brown or buff fur and a white underbelly. The ones who live on the dry plains from Saskatchewan south have black tails. Those who live in the Rocky Mountain area from Montana south have white tails. Nobody knows how or why this "Look where I'm from" appendage developed—or persists.

Ranchers never liked the critters. They ate as much grass as cattle. Their elaborate tunnels tripped both cattle and horses, and often broke their legs. The prairie dog is good eating, tastes like lean pork. Why nobody has ever raised him commercially is another mystery. He's a lot more efficient than the cow or sheep in turning grass into meat and hide. He doesn't need water holes or hay and grain crops.

Sharing the high plains, but avoiding wooded country and mountains, was the delicately beautiful antelope. Again—aah, those zoologists!—it isn't a relative of the antelope family of Africa and Asia but an American individualist and should be called the "Pronghorn" or "Prongbuck." The size of a small deer, the creature was the swiftest runner on the continent and capable of forty-five- and sixty-m.p.h. spurts. He has two unique signal systems. A prominent white patch along his reddish brown rump puffs up when he becomes startled. Scintillant on a clear day, it is actually a blinker-signal and can be seen for miles across the prairie. The action simultaneously contracts musk glands, so the entire herd is warned by both sight and smell.

Alongside the antelope and bison hooves, the white-tailed prairie dogs and the black-tailed prairie dogs, slithered treacherous death. Snakes, centipedes, tarantulas, Gila lizards and scorpions lurked on the high plain, mountain and desert. The rattlesnake, related to Europe's deadly pit viper, is the most arrogant serpent family of the West. King of the family is the diamondback of Texas and the Southwest, often arm-thick and eight to ten feet long. The timber rattler, five feet long and with brown hashmarks, clings to the woodlands and mountains. The deserts have the sand-hued, looping sidewinder; the high plains evolved the prairie rattler.

From Oklahoma south and west, the tarantula hulked blackly behind his hinged door in the grass banks, the centipede scuttled indoors and out waving his poison claws toward moths and bugs, the scorpion slunk with tail poised for the death-strike. And across the desert marches of the Southwest, the Gila monster watched unblinking from the rock crevices.

The jaguar and puma are the two largest cats of the West. Each reached a length of eight feet, and preyed on deer, bison and small game. The jaguar is tawny yellow with large black spots. His principal stalking grounds were Texas and across the Southwest. The puma, reddish or grayish brown with a fawn belly, covered most of the West and so had a variety of names. Puma is his Spanish name. The cougar, mountain lion, catamount and panther are all the same animal.

Both big cats slunk away if, on a mountain foray, they caught the scent of the hulking, gray-black boss of the Rockies. The grizzly was the only bear that couldn't climb trees. But he could climb anything that walked. Tall as a man and barrel-big, the grizzly weighed up to 1,000 pounds. His claws were adept at forking honey out of a tree, or, with one swipe, gutting a puma or a man. With typical fat-man personality, the grizzly rarely went out of his way to make trouble. His notion of a good time was to loll across a berry patch, with twenty or fifty other bears, lipping the ripe fruit off the bushes and gulping the tenderest roots. Any grasshoppers in the vicinity would be downed, too. Stones and old logs were thoughtfully explored for grubs, centipedes and similar protein titbits. The day's feeding would be a huge success if worker bees led the way to a honey tree and a creek provided trout, whisked out on the bank by the lightning dexterity of those foreclaws. When these supplies ran out, the grizzly would hunt for meat—any kind that happened by, and the gamier the better.

The grizzly was not a lone wanderer. Whole communities traveled the mountains together. Smith, Bridger and other mountain men reported seeing fifty to sixty on a hill slope and circling as many as two hundred during a morning's journey. Wounded, or crossed for any of a variety of reasons, the grizzly would track a man down with dog cunning and the sole intent of murder. The best escape, then, was a tall tree and a three- or four-day sit-out.

The black bears, not as ornery as the grizzly, averaged around three hundred pounds in weight. They weren't to be trifled with, though, and could climb trees as agilely as any man.

The beaver, master architect of the animal world, spread straight across the continent during the post-glacial periods. By the time man arrived, the beaver was as thoroughly at home in the Rockies, the Cascades, and the Sierras, as he was in the eastern mountains and river valleys.

On the peaks above his conical homes, a cousin of the antelope flitted like a bearded ghost from cliff to cliff. The Rocky Mountain goat isn't, of course, a goat but a zoological tie-in between the antelope and the Alpine chamois. The male stands three feet high at the shoulder. Roving with it, above the timber lines and across the deserts, was a true wild sheep, the bighorn. Both fed on lichens, larch and wiry grasses which grew from 6,000 feet up to the eternal snowlines.

Wolves and coyotes are cousins. Zoologists call the coyote the "prairie wolf." He is mongrel-sized with a personality that likes to whine about the hard life on the other side of the tracks. He lives on mice and prairie dogs, gangs up with other coyotes to tear down large animals, or hangs around on the edge of a big fight, waiting for the leavings. He has a howl like a small boy getting a first haircut. The gray wolf, who stays closer to woodlands and does most of his prairie-roaming in the winter, has more bulk and guts.

These, then, with a thousand bird families, with the trout and bluegills and great, splashing salmon, were the creatures of the West. Up from the south, one by one, they came in the wake of the retreating glaciers. Then, in slow process engineered by rainfall, by temperature changes and natural foods, each adjusted to a specific environment—the antelope to the open prairie; the grizzly to the hills and forest glades; the Gila monster and sidewinder to the desert. And each was as fixed to his pattern and range of operations as the grama grass, the redwoods or the cacti.

So the tortured westland, middle-aged now, soft-cloaked in greenstuff, teeming with creatures of its own conditioning, lay waiting for the arrival of Man. There would be only one more addition to this family before that fateful century when the European white burst across the Missouri to tame and destroy. Yet that last-comer, itself a refugee from the white man, would come very close to holding the West for the Indian for another century or longer. Indeed, if the horse had thundered back onto the Great Plains when the buffalo did, the whole human history of the West might have been different. The United States might still extend only to the Mississippi.

In all human history, the horse had known only one natural environment. That was the Kirghiz Steppe of Russia. And there, in the heydays of Greece and Rome, he trained endlessly with barbaric masters until horse-and-man became an inseparable team, a living centaur. Out of this teamship spawned the great cavalry hordes of Visigoths, Huns and Mongols, who terrorized Europe and Asia for a thousand years. So the Old World came to horsemanship and the horse itself entered Spain.

Another thousand years and the first Spanish horses landed in Mexico and Florida. From Mexico, they marched north as cavalry into Texas and the Southwest. Then, in 1545, Hernando De Soto died on the shores of the Mississippi. His followers built boats, sailed south toward Mexico—and turned their horses loose.

Nobody knows what happened after that. Did De Soto's horses, standing on Arkansas prairie, smell the west wind and shiver with delight? Did the Spanish explorer Coronado's horses grow frantic at the sight of the Great Plains, break their tethers and thunder away toward a call as urgent as the ones their ancestors felt on the Kirghiz Steppe 2,000 years before?

The fact remains that the Kirghiz and the Great Plains are twins in climate and in contour. They are the two best breeding places on earth for horses. Between 1550 and 1800, the small band of refugees from Coronado's and/or De Soto's troop multiplied to thundering herds that threatened to rival the bison.

And, as passionate evidence that history does repeat, the Comanche, Apache, Sioux, Cheyenne, Dakota, Crow and Blackfoot adapted as readily to the horse as did the Visigoths, Huns, Kassites, Mongols and Saracens. By the time the white man crossed the Missouri, the red man and the horse were developing into that same teamship that hurtled Europe into the Dark Ages. It is logical to dwell on the thought that, given another century or two of training, Indian cavalry might have raced *east* across the Missouri to conquer the United States!

But nature and time conspired to unfold the human drama of the West in another way. The red man tiptoed in from the Pacific, blended quietly with the land and remained, almost static, for 15,000, perhaps 20,0000, years. Then, in one smashing, violent century, the white man burst from his forest culture to the strange new world of the Great Plains. Came the Doers and the Doing.

Part 2

The FIRST WESTERNERS

*Every part of this soil is sacred in the estimation of my
people. Every hillside, every valley, every plain and grove,
has been hallowed by some sad or happy event in days
long vanished. The very dust upon which you now stand
responds more lovingly to their footsteps than to yours,
because it is rich with the blood of our ancestors and our
bare feet are conscious of the sympathetic touch. Even
the little children who live here and rejoice here· for a
brief season love these somber solitudes and at eventide
they greet shadowy returning spirits. And when the last
redmen shall have perished and the memory of my tribe
shall have become a myth among the white man, these
shores will swarm with the invisible dead of my tribe and
when your children's children think themselves alone in
the field, the store, the shop, upon the highways or in the
silence of the pathless woods, they will not be alone.*
—Oration by Chief Seattle.

ARCHIE BINNS– "Northwest Gateway"

MITZI ZIPF

The Fire Builders

MAN'S GREATEST CURIOSITY is about himself. There comes a time in a child's
life when he or she asks Mother, "Where did I come from?"

And the search begins again.

The delightful thing about it all is your guess may be as good as the
next. You may cut your cloth to your own pattern; you may fit the pieces
together to form your own picture. Science may present the known facts.
The individual can draw his own conclusion.

The age of man in the Western Hemisphere is controversial among
anthropologists. It is most probable man first came to the Americas in wave
after wave, or ripple after ripple, from west to east, or the northwest to
the southeast. This is a reversal of historic migrations.

All indications are that man came from what is now Siberia, across the
Bering Strait, a distance of less than 100 miles, into what is now Alaska. He
then probably traveled down the Pacific coast or fanned out across the bil-

27

lions of acres of North and South America. Some investigators say he may have come, too, in small boats across the southern Pacific in a technique called "island hopping."

There is nothing to say a few brave souls could not have invaded the east coast by crossing the North Atlantic by way of Iceland, Greenland, Baffin Island, thence down the coast. We know Norsemen did it later.

Taking everything into consideration, it is pretty well established man did not evolve in America, but migrated here.

There are, though, still those stubborn souls who say of evolution, "Why not?"

The best answer lies in the fact that no bones of primates (great apes) have been found in either North or South America. Monkeys abound in tropical and subtropical areas, but none of the big fellows.

This lack of primate bones has given rise to a standard joke among anthropology students. One student asked another, "What would you do if you found the skull of a great ape in the jungle in South America?" The reply: "I'd bury the damn thing and run like hell."

Only thirty years ago, the best-informed students believed man came to the Americas about the beginning of the Christian era or a little earlier. Since then, certain discoveries have pushed the horizon back 20,000 or perhaps 30,000 years.

Whence came these earliest peoples? Some say they came from a mythical lost continent of Mu in the Pacific. Some say they came from the mythical lost continent of Atlantis, in the Atlantic. But most agree on Bering Strait as the gateway.

When Columbus discovered the Americas instead of going around the world, he called the people he found "Indians" because he thought he had reached India. The name stuck. Scientists designated the North American Indian the *Amerind* to set him apart from the East Indian.

Establishment of the antiquity of man in America must depend not only upon the anthropologist but the geologist, paleontologist and a lot of other "ologists." The anthropologist cannot do it alone.

It is possible man migrated to the Western Hemisphere during the Ice Age. In fact, more and more deposits of extinct animal bones in association with fireplaces and man-made implements, are clinching it.

One of the first things to become clear to the early white men who explored from coast to coast was the difference in the physical characteristics among various native groups they met. Differences in skin coloring ranged from deep olive, through copper, to chocolate. Some had long pointed noses with high bridges. In others, the nose flanges were larger, broader. Some were tall; some were short; some were lean, others were fat. Some roamed the broad plains and hunted game. Some stayed at home and built permanent houses and tilled the soil. Some gathered seeds and grasses for food as well as wild berries. Others cultivated corn, squash and beans, grew cotton, dug irrigation ditches. Some wore only skins; some hardly any clothing at all. Others wove garments of vegetable fibers, including cotton. Their ways of life were as divergent as they are in the United States today.

To get a picture, consider our U.S.A. There is the "down Easterner," the "Southerner," the "Texan," the "Westerner." The dialect of each is full of colloquialisms—common to one section but not to another, and frequently not understood outside the area of origin.

So it was in ancient days.

The less ambitious migrants, especially on the Pacific side, remained along the seacoasts where living was easy.

What of those who ventured farther inland? Scientists believe they fanned out, taking no one major migration route into the interior, but many. Stage by stage, the wanderers made their way across what is now continental United States. They came across the Great Plains, into the Woodland area, down the Florida peninsula, into the Great Southwest, into Mexico, Central America. Some went to South America by way of the isthmus.

But in the Southwest, evidence shows they tarried a little on their southern trek. Then, after a while, they turned around and headed north again. In some places they stayed long enough to rest and to gather fresh food. In others they remained long enough to build homes and become a part of the land. In the Great Plains area they found great animals, primarily the bison. In the Southwest they found the woolly mammoth, the saber-toothed tiger, the bison, deer and smaller animals. Up to this moment evidence of the oldest man in America has been found only in the Southwest.

Sandia man is the earliest man in continental United States. No one knows what he looked like. He was a bad housekeeper, though, so he left ample evidence of having been here. Evidence of Sandia man was first found in Sandia Cave in Las Huertas Canyon in the Sandia Mountains east of Albuquerque, New Mexico. The geologist has deduced Sandia man lived on the lowest level of that cave about 15,000 B.C. Crude stone implements were found in association with bones of extinct mammals and fireplace trash.

The spear points used by Sandia man were crude and not too well shaped. Yet they did the job when it came to killing a gigantic mammoth. Points have been found embedded in the rib area of the mammoths.

There may have been other "men" between Sandia man and the next one to be named, "Folsom man." He got his name from the little town in New Mexico near which "Folsom points" were first found, in 1926, in association with bones of extinct animals, plus fireplaces.

Folsom spear points are finely worked, with a groove up the back and front in which the shaft of the throwing stick could be hafted. They show skill in workmanship and ingenuity in design. The spear to which the points were attached was the forerunner of the *atlatl*, used in later times by men of the Southwest. Folsom points, once identified, cropped up all over the Southwest.

Contemporary with Folsom was Yuma man. Since we have no skeletons of Sandia, Folsom or Yuma men, we cannot say what they looked like. We are sure they wore skins to keep themselves warm, built fires to cook their meat, and worked stone into implements to kill their game. Sandia, Folsom and Yuma men came across Bering Strait, no doubt. There is a long pause between the time of these men and later cultures which we can reasonably date.

Several ways of dating these groups have been devised. Fairly accurate dates may be established by means of radioactive carbon, the "Carbon 14" method. A machine similar to a Geiger counter counts the clicks the material gives off, and is said to be accurate up to plus or minus 250 years.

In the Southwest particularly, another method used is the study of tree rings, or the science of dendrochronology. Certain kinds of trees grow countable rings. Wide ones for wet years, narrow ones for dry years. A master pattern has been devised. Any datable wood may be fitted into the pattern, and the date of the last ring determined. This system originated at the Museum of the University of Arizona in Tucson. The giant log from which the system was deduced is on exhibit there.

Cross-dating pottery is a third method. If a certain kind of pottery found in a dated ruin is found in an undated ruin, it is possible the undated ruin is of the same time as the first.

Early peoples of North America can be classified in several ways. Head type is one—long head, broad head, round head. They can be classified by language groups, too. Then there is the geographic classification. Because persons live in a general area, they are related. Culture relationship is another and perhaps the best form of grouping.

The cultural unit first encountered by the Puritans and Virginians, on the east coast, is the Eastern Woodlands. Many tribes whose names have become well known to any small boy playing cowboy and Indian are included in this area. Many famous chiefs of the French and Indian War and Revolutionary times are among them. Hunters of sorts, they built (in the north) pens to capture caribou. They snared fish and small game, wore rabbit skins for blankets, had birchbark canoes and built conical skin or bark shelters. Utensils were of wood or bark. They made no baskets or pottery.

The Southeastern Indians, Florida to Texas, used many vegetables for food, although they were not vegetarians. They had intensive agriculture. Homes were rectangular with curved thatched roofs. They used dugout canoes, worked stone, bone and shell, and made baskets. Their robes were deerskin and buffalo, with ceremonial cloaks covered with bird feathers—a trait which seems to have come from Mexico or Central America. They were excellent potters. Ceremonial buildings were built on mounds—a possible connection with their neighbors to the west and north, the Mound Builders.

The Mound Builders reached a high cultural development. They built mounds for forts, for burials, and as bases for ceremonial houses.

Their less sedentary neighbors to the west roamed the plains and were dependent upon the buffalo for their living. They supplemented this diet with berries and roots but did not fish. They had no agriculture. Nomadic, they moved with the buffalo, the weather, the state of their hunger. Homes were movable tipis.

In prehistoric time, they moved their worldly goods on human- or dog-drawn travois—a platform of three long sticks tied in a triangle with a skin stretched across. Some tribes used smaller travois-type burden baskets, too, which were strapped to women's foreheads. They made no baskets or pottery and did not weave. Pottery would break when hauled long distances. Looms were hard to carry. Buffalo and deer skins were their most prized possessions. Highly skilled in working skins, they made marvelous rawhide receptacles. They did little or no work in wood, stone or bone.

There remain three other areas and a portion of a fourth, to cover the continental United States. The plateau area on the Northwest extended into Canada and not quite to the Pacific Ocean. Chief characteristic of the group that lived here was the use of salmon for food. They developed many culture traits found among no other Indians. They cooked with hot stones, placed in holes or in baskets. They pulverized dried salmon and roots for storage against the winter. Winter homes were circular pits with conical roofs. Movable summer homes were mats or rush-covered frames. The dog was used as a pack animal. Basketry was highly developed, but not pottery. They wore armor of reed-and-slat type, or heavy leather shirts.

The California area is south of the North Pacific area. It was a lazy culture. They lived on acorns, wild seeds, roots, small game or fish. Houses were the simplest shelters. They had no dogs, canoes or pottery. Basketry was highly developed.

The Southwestern area embraces Arizona, New Mexico, some of Eastern California, southern Utah, Nevada and Colorado, Baja California, and some of the more northern tier of states of the Republic of Mexico. There were striking differences within as well as without this area.

We know man has lived in Arizona and the Southwest since Pleistocene time, next door to some of the most highly developed culture patterns in the world—Aztec, Toltec, Inca patterns of Mexico, Central America and Peru in South America.

The Spaniards found a decadent civilization when they moved northward out of the valley of Mexico in search of the Seven Cities of Cibola. The development had reached its zenith and was declining. Even so, Fray Marcos de Niza, Coronado, and later Father Kino, were amazed at what they saw.

The people lived in villages, tilled the soil, watered their crops by irrigation, and had domesticated both the turkey and the dog. They knew how to store food from one harvest to another. They grew cotton, carded, spun and wove it into cloth which is beautiful even today, after several centuries of exposure. They were people who developed an architecture from a circular hole in the ground to many-roomed and many-storied apartment houses.

And they were the most superb potters on the North American continent.

But for all these developments, no Amerind learned to turn the circle up on its edge to make a wheel that would work for them.

It is astounding to look at a perfectly turned bowl and realize it was made without the potter's wheel, then to trace the design elements on a piece of pottery and realize they were drawn freehand with perhaps a cactus thorn, from a pattern carried in the head of the maker.

Most excellent weapons were made of various kinds of stone. Jewelry was created from stone, bone and shell.

People in the northern portion of the area buried their dead. Those in the southern portion cremated. There were groups within groups. There was a well-defined religion, with clans and ceremonial chambers we call kivas. The Southwestern area is more complex than any other one area in the United States.

All the people we have discussed are American Indians, just as all the people who live in the United States are called Americans. But, they are as divergent in origins and in culture patterns as are the people of today.

"A Sculptured Rock, River Gila"
—from *Bartlett's Personal
Narrative*, volume II, 1854

Here me, my warriors; my heart is sick and sad. Our chiefs are killed, the old men are all dead. It is cold, and we have no blankets; the little children are freezing to death. Hear me, my warriors; my heart is sick and sad. From where the sun now stands I will fight no more forever!

CHIEF JOSEPH, Nez Percé Tribe,
Late Nineteenth Century

O. K. ARMSTRONG

The Indians We Fought

WHEN I WAS A LAD there lived in our neighborhood an old soldier who was quite a hero to us boys because he had been an Indian-fighter. All we had to do to start him off on his exaggerated tales was to ask:

"What Indians did you fight, Grandpa?"

"Sonny, I fought 'em all!" he would say.

Grandpa represents the whole white man's world of the Old West, for we "fought 'em all." At first, of course, the West was just outside the settlements of Virginia and New England. As the explorers and pioneers pushed relentlessly westward, they encountered the native at every turn—and fought him.

The Indian was the native—the red man who could be both noble and treacherous, depending on whether he was peaceful or fighting for the lands on which he and his forebears had roamed, hunted and fished since prehistoric times. From the Adirondacks to the Alleghenies, through the great Northwest Territories and southern plantation states, we fought the natives and pushed them westward.

In the early 1800's a noble Shawnee warrior, Tecumseh, rose up with a vision of halting the white man's encroachments forever. He formed a confederacy of tribes, joined the British in Canada in the War of 1812, but was forced to battle with the soldiers of General William Henry Harrison, and in October, 1813, he was killed.

Still the expeditions and battles went on, until General Andrew Jackson,

33

who had fought more Indians than anyone else up to his day, decided it was time to herd the natives into big open stockades called "reservations." The "trail of tears" was the tragic result, as many tribes of Indians were uprooted and brought to wild areas beyond the Mississippi, some to be concentrated in Indian Territory and others in huge areas of the Great West. For those still leading the fight against the invading white man the mantle of leadership fell upon a worthy follower of Tecumseh:

BLACK HAWK, WHOM DEFEAT MADE FAMOUS – *Ma-kata-wimesheka-ka*, "Black Sparrow Hawk," was his full name. He was chief of only a small tribe of the Sauk in Illinois. But as a youth he had carried a rifle with those who joined the British and defied the Americans, and it was he who marked the last great resistance to the white man east of the Mississippi. Thus Black Hawk holds an honored place in the history of the West.

The Hawk was not a tall man, but he was sinewy and tough. He was fearless as a lion, and as determined as had been his hero, Tecumseh. He nurtured the hopeless plan of taking back the ancestral lands in the northern states bordering the Mississippi.

Actually, the matter had been settled, so far as the white man was concerned, when in 1804 General Harrison came to St. Louis, the town on the mud banks of the river, and signed a treaty with the tribes whereby they agreed to move west of the Mississippi in return for an annuity of $1,000 a year. But Black Hawk did not recognize this treaty. He said it was a paleface trick. The Sauks and other tribes had not been properly represented, he said, and besides, all who did sign were drunk.

The Hawk resolved to carry on resistance to the intruders and regain the "stolen" lands. There were the Winnebagos, the Potawatomi, the Muscoulins—all combined they could make a formidable force. So in the early summer of 1831 Black Hawk came back to the old Sauk village with a few of his warriors to repossess the land. He found white settlers plowing the ground. Troops came to rout him out, so Black Hawk retired to the mouth of the Iowa River. But he continued his plotting.

When the ice chunks stopped floating down the rivers and April breezes blew over the Iowa and Illinois prairies, the Hawk launched his invasion, back across the Mississippi. He commanded 200 warriors in all sorts of rough and rugged dress, with muskets, powder and ball, with their wives and children. Mostly they were Sauks, with a few Winnebagos and others. The governor of Illinois called for help and General Henry Atkinson came with his troops. The "White Beaver," as the Indians called the general, landed below Rock River and moved toward Black Hawk's band. It was not lack of courage that caused the Hawk to send out a flag of truce. As he later recorded: "When White Beaver came, I told my people we must go back."

"Indian Village"—from *Harper's New Monthly*, March, 1880

But the soldiers fired and killed two of the Hawk's warriors. The angered chieftain began a hit-and-run war that lasted until August of that year of 1832. Then the troops closed in for a real engagement, defeated the Indians decisively, slaughtered many of their people and took Black Hawk prisoner along with most of the guerrilla leaders.

Among the Illinois volunteers was a tall, rawboned soldier by the name of Abraham Lincoln. "It was just like fighting mosquitoes," Abe said.

The Indian prisoners were taken to Prairie du Chien and from there Lieutenant Jefferson Davis took them to Fort Armstrong. The matter was reported to the Great White Father, Andy Jackson.

"By the Eternal, any Indian as brave as that is a worthy foe," said the President. "Bring him to Washington."

So they brought Black Hawk to Washington and he saw Big Andy in the White House, and basked in the sun of heroic publicity—although still a prisoner. From Black Hawk's day, the Father of Waters marked the frontier where the West began. Beyond, the native could stay.

"Why not?" asked members of Congress, and the people. "Few white families would want to live out in that wilderness!"

But in the decade that followed, thousands of settlers did push into that wilderness. In 1849 gold was discovered in California, and that made the

West stretch from the Mississippi to the Pacific, with wagon trains moving like ants across the plains and over the mountains. And it brought out the most cunning fighter of all:

COCHISE—THE FIERCEST APACHE – California was now the Golden West. It was inevitable that the best lands of all the vast area of the plains and the mountains and valleys should become the battleground of settler against native for possession. It was certain that the Indian tribes, whether compressed into reservations or still roaming their open lands, should resist to the death. So the settlers "fought 'em all." They had to—or perish on the westward treks. Always they traveled prepared for trouble, and always they hoped the blue-clad, hard-riding troops of the U.S. Army were not too far away.

The Chiricahua Apaches in the southern area of the Arizona Territory were not exactly friendly, but neither were they dangerously hostile, until eleven years after the discovery of gold. Eleven years the big migration had gone on. In that region known as the Gadsden Purchase, some settlers had squatted to farm. Mostly they were single men when they staked their claims, soon to marry Mexican wives, as did John Ward. His wife had a son when John married her.

One day a reckless band of Pinal Apaches swooped down on Ward's ranch and made off with several cattle and the boy. A troop of the Seventh Cavalry came in, and Captain Bascom, new to Indian ways, sought out the man he heard was chief of the Apaches, Cochise, and asked him into his tent. Cochise came, with his brother, wife, son and two nephews. Once inside, Cochise was accused of stealing Ward's cattle and the boy. When he denied it, Captain Bascom told him all would be held hostages until the cattle and boy were returned.

Cochise slit the tent and escaped. In anger he and his braves seized three white men, whom he put to death when the soldiers refused to release the Indian hostages. Then, in misguided retaliation, the soldiers hanged the hostages near the graves of the three white men.

Cochise's fury knew no bounds. He vowed to exterminate every white family in Arizona Territory. Never was a threatened vengeance so relentlessly attempted. Never was there such ruthless raiding, murdering and plundering by the native, in all the history of the Great West. Never was an outlaw more vigorously hunted than this tall young Apache, and never was a quarry more cunningly elusive. For eleven years Cochise pinned down in the Arizona Territory more U.S. troops than any other warrior of any tribe.

Cochise was both fearless and clever. He engaged in no pitched battles. He took no undue risks. He was dedicated to the task of killing whites and he wanted to live long to do it. From his mountain strongholds he would sally out to attack wagon trains here, steal cattle there, murder the entire family of the settler at another point.

His favorite tactic was ambush. He taught his braves to lie in wait where they knew the white man would come: At springs, behind buttes along the wagon trails, beyond the ridges of hillocks, and on the bluffs. When the dread war whoop sounded and the hideously black-and-red painted warriors came rushing out—

"Apaches! Apaches!" the guides would shout, and that meant fight to the death. It meant that some of Cochise's braves would die, but almost always there died all the men they attacked. Women and children might be spared— for a time.

"Nobody knew, even if there was but a single enemy in the neighborhood, where they would strike next," wrote an early historian.

The War Between the States played into the hands of Cochise and his campaign of extermination, for most of the U.S. troops were withdrawn. By the time the war ended, the Apache Scourge was master of most of the territory. White settlers who escaped the bullets and flames had gathered in Tucson and a few other towns. Only one white man in all the region was given safe conduct by Cochise. He was Tom Jeffords, a red-whiskered stagecoach driver, as fearless as Cochise himself. Fed up with fighting the Apaches, he was escorted to Cochise's *wickiup*, placed his guns in the chief's hands and proceeded with the powwow in the Apache tongue. Cochise was fascinated by the courage of the man, called him "Chickasaw" (Brother) and instructed all his braves to leave "Taglito" (Redbeard) alone.

U.S. troops, seasoned from the war, tried to corner the Apache leader,

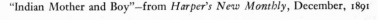

"Indian Mother and Boy"—from *Harper's New Monthly*, December, 1891

but they could never find him. They captured and executed a few of his braves, in their red-and-black war colors, stoically going to their deaths and saying nothing.

General Grant became Great White Father and resolved upon a "new policy" for the Indians. He would make peace with all the tribes, including these lawless Chiricahua Apaches. He assigned this seemingly impossible task to one of his favorite officers, General O. O. Howard. The general came out to Arizona Territory and hunted up Tom Jeffords.

"Can you take me to Cochise?" he asked. For several minutes the big red-whiskered man was silent. Then he answered:

"Yes, general. Leave your arms and soldiers behind."

After days of safe-conduct they found Cochise in his impregnable fortress. General Howard and Taglito stood facing the Apache Scourge. They sat down under a big oak and talked.

"No one wants peace more than I," Cochise said. "I have killed ten whites for every Indian's life taken. But the white man is increasing, while my tribe is growing smaller."

So peace it was, with a reservation for the Apaches covering the Chiricahua Mountains and San Simon and Sulphur Springs valleys. Cochise demanded one concession: Chickasaw Taglito must be their agent. Jeffords agreed, and ruled the Apaches for many years.

Meantime, far to the north, the tribes of the Sioux were gathering under the generalship of:

CRAZY HORSE—THE NATIVES' GREATEST COMMANDER – When President Eisenhower was visiting an Indian reservation one day he remarked to his hosts that if he were ever given an Indian name, he hoped it would be Crazy Horse.

"As a West Point cadet," said the President, "I learned that Crazy Horse was the greatest Indian cavalry tactician who ever lived."

He was an Oglala Sioux born in the year of the "Forty-Niners." A wild pony was seen dashing through the village just as he was born, so they named him "Tashuca-unitco." Fittingly named, for he grew to be a wild, restless young man, filled with hatred for the invaders upon the great open spaces of his forebears. Some Sioux might meekly accept reservation life, but not Crazy Horse.

At sixteen he began riding with Chief Red Cloud in three years of expeditions against the white settlements in Wyoming. There he proved himself to be a natural military genius. He perfected the tactics that made him feared and famous: how to deploy his riders to divide the enemy, how to cut off and encircle, how to use his reserves to best advantage against the superior forces and arms of rough-riding scouts or blue-coated troops.

Crazy Horse was also a diplomat. He married the loveliest of the Cheyenne Maidens, and welded that tribe as a firm ally to the confederation of the Sioux.

So through the early '70's Crazy Horse counseled his elders and their people to refuse longer to be confined on reservations. The Indian was made to be free, he said, and not even the great area stretching from Montana through the Black Hills of the Dakotas and into Nebraska should confine the Sioux. He raided the settlements and attacked the wagon trains. Even more ruthlessly he made war on the Crows, because they had so meekly yielded to white control.

Gold was discovered in the Black Hills, and in 1875, in violation of the Sioux treaty, the Indians were moved out to make way for the white prospectors.

"All roving bands of Indians must be back on their reservations by January 1, 1876," read the terse War Department order.

It was an order for the U.S. troops, but only a challenge to Crazy Horse. General George Crook was given the job of subduing Crazy Horse and all the rebellious Sioux and Cheyenne. In early spring of 1876 he raided and burned the Oglala village and captured the pony herd. Crazy Horse showed his bravery by pursuing and recapturing many of his ponies.

Now it was war, and Crazy Horse rallied his force to number 1,200 warriors. Encamped on the upper Rosebud, on June 17 they were attacked by General Crook's force of 1,300 men. Crazy Horse outgeneraled and outfought the troops, and Crook was forced to withdraw. Crazy Horse moved northward to join forces with the big medicine man, Sitting Bull, in the valley of the Little Bighorn.

Lieutenant Colonel (formerly General) George A. Custer, commanding the Seventh Cavalry, did precisely what Crazy Horse hoped he would do: He divided his regiment three ways, sending two battalions to scout for the Sioux warriors and himself leading a force of 264 men to a ridge overlooking the Little Bighorn. And there, one June 25, Crazy Horse staged his greatest battle, sending his almost naked riders circling the white men, firing, wheeling, retreating, while others came up circling and firing, until Custer and all his brave force fell.

It was almost a year later that the hunted Crazy Horse brought his people into the Red Cloud, Nebraska, agency and surrendered. Months later, the proud, unconquered chief was fatally wounded in an encounter with a soldier. His fearful victory at Little Bighorn marked the crest of resistance by the native. Never again was the challenge of the white man so fearlessly and clearly accepted. The reservation Indian became a part of the Great West.

"The Pony War-Dance"–from *Drawings by Frederick Remington*, 1897

*These lands are ours. No one has a right to remove us,
because we were the first owners. The Great Spirit above
has appointed this place for us, on which to light our fires,
and here we will remain. As to boundaries, the Great
Spirit knows no boundaries, nor will his red children
acknowledge any.*

TECUMSEH, Chief of the Shawnees:
to the messenger of the President
of the United States in 1810

BERT FIREMAN

Apache Electronics

AFTER THE LIGHTNING and mad drumming of the storm, the sunlight paints blue shadows upon the mesa again, the grass becomes a shimmering emerald carpet and the Great Plains are at peace. So the storm seems to be passing for the red men of the West, four generations after Custer, an old man's memory beyond Cochise. Far too many of our concepts of the modern Indian stem from Madison Avenue and Hollywood.

For the true picture of the warriors come to peace again, drive out to the Winslow, Arizona, or the Gallup, New Mexico, airport one day when the radio reports a forest fire somewhere in the West. Watch the snappiest fire-fighting units between Chicago and L.A., bright red helmets tilted over right eye, file into the Air Force planes flown over from March Field, California. Mescalero Apaches (the U.S. Forest Service's famous demonstration team of fire-fighters are Apache), Hopis, Navajos and Indians from the pueblos of Cochita, Taos, Jemez, Zia and Domingo are all in the regular force available.

They have great stamina, are handy with shovels and axes, subsist on little water and emergency rations without complaint, and are well-organized on the basis of clans and clan leaders.

Firefighting is an important source of revenue for several villages. In one year the Zuñi pueblo realized $250,000 from this source—more than the clan earned by farming.

The communication system used to recruit the fighters is unique. A

42

radio at Gallup crackles out the message of a forest fire. At the Zuñi pueblo an Indian records the message, then runs to the top of the highest building as village criers have done there for centuries. In the piercing song-talk of the Zuñis he announces that "the Red Hats" should assemble. In a few minutes they are on a bus, and shortly they roll up to the airport in Gallup. "Fighting fire," one of the Indians said during a coffee break at a blaze near San Diego in the tinder-dry fall of 1956, "is one thing the white man does that makes sense to the Indian."

The electronics factories at Flagstaff, the ranches around Zane Grey's old hangout near Natural Bridge ($250 a month plus keep for a skilled cow-hand), the new oil field in the San Juan Basin, the irrigated truck gardens of the Colorado River basin—all of these join with the fire-eater Red Hats in spelling a new day for Navajo, Apache and all the Pueblo Indians.

The Japanese, who thought they were prepared for every emergency in World War II, were among the first to realize that this new day was dawning. They cracked American codes with ease. Their soldiers at radio listening posts were trained to interpret messages in every borrowed tongue the polyglot American soldiers might use on walkie-talkie sets. Even pig-Latin was quickly untwisted. Battlefield communications were demoralized.

Then somebody remembered the 3,500 Navajo soldiers with Uncle Sam's forces. They spoke a language that no more than a few dozen out-landers had ever learned. Only a few religious books had been published in their tongue. Soon radios were crackling with orders in Navajo. The happiest soldiers in the U.S. forces were these usually-reserved young men from the mountains. They prattled on with mounting glee at the utter confusion they created in Japanese listening posts. The American advance pushed forward, aided by orders in a language—maybe the only one in all the world—that no Japanese had ever learned.

Later, in the hand-to-hand combat, there were grunts of astonishment from Navajo and Apache as well as the Japanese. For the two races look enough alike to be neighbors. Japanese Americans are still mistaken for Navajos or Apaches in the streets of Tucson and Phoenix, just as tribesmen in civvies are mistaken for Japanese-Americans in L.A. They tend to be of the same size, their skin is soft brown, their hair black and straight, their eyes Oriental in appearance. Here may be an anthropologic clue, since both Navajo and Apache arrived in the land of the turquoise sky less than 1,000 years ago.

The Navajos and Apaches are an Athapascan people whose dialects stretch from the northern interior of Alaska down into Sonora and Chihuahua, Mexico, a linguistic line of more than 4,000 miles in length.

The Navajos dwell mainly in the uplands of Arizona and New Mexico. South of them, along the western flank of the Rockies, are the Western

Apache tribes, sturdiest and fiercest warriors of all. Beyond the Rio Grande River, overlapping the Sioux country to the north and reaching south almost to the Gulf of Mexico, were the Lipans, cousins of the Western Apaches and Navajos, but not nearly so handy.

They had many words in common, some ceremonials and tribal beliefs that were similar, and the same basic social unit in an extended family or clan with descent traced through the mother. None was a closely-organized nation. All tended to be divided into warring bands. Only pressure from white immigrants forced them together.

An Apache of the Nineteenth Century
—from the *Century Magazine*, July, 1889

Oliver La Farge, outstanding Southwestern novelist who has become a pamphleteer for the Indian cause, pointed out in *American Heritage* (October, 1956) that Athapascans "did not glorify war. They made a business of it. Killing enemies was incidental; in fact, a man who killed an enemy had to be purified afterwards. They fought for profit, and they were about the only North Americans whose attitude towards war resembled that of the professional soldier. This did not make them any the less troublesome."

Traditionally both tribes were farmers and seed-gatherers. They cultivated small crops by means of elementary irrigation or the overflow from spring floods. The Navajos gathered acorns and piñon (pine) nuts. The Apaches additionally cooked a matted preserve called mescal, roasting the tender shoot of the agave, or century plant. Both hunted, but did not live in regions well-endowed with game.

The Apaches never progressed beyond a primary basket culture, but the Navajos took full advantage of their neighbors to learn weaving and silversmithing, with pleasant results. Living within the Navajo territory were the Hopi Indians, one of the Pueblo tribes. They were growing cotton and weaving it into ceremonial garments and blankets before the arrival of the Navajos. Early in the nineteenth century the Navajos, too, began developing skill as weavers. Among the Hopis, men did this work. It is likely that the intermarriage of Hopi maidens with Navajo men brought the skill to the Navajos. But the tedious task of carding, spinning, and weaving was never accepted by the war-inclined males.

Early rugs often were rewoven from clothing or blankets taken on raids. Using native vegetable dyes and later aniline dyes acquired from traders, the Navajos developed a blanket of great durability and beauty. The Navajo rug—although originally a horse blanket—became one of the most refined native arts in the nation.

From Spanish and Mexican craftsmen the Navajos learned to work with metal, first with iron, which was useful, and later with silver which was both ornamental and negotiable. Navajo silver, mounted with turquoise, became a measure of wealth along with the number of horses and sheep a family owned. Production of jewelry and blankets became main sources of cash income as the tourist traffic increased. This was particularly true in years when drought curtailed the lamb crop.

A Navajo weaver earned very little, perhaps no more than five cents an hour. By the time the wool was clipped, washed, carded, spun, dyed, and then woven into a rug or blanket on a primitive loom set up in the open near the family hogan, the weaver had invested hundreds of hours in her art. Navajo weavers rarely worked from an established or repeated pattern. Every rug was different, the design conceived in the weaver's mind as work progressed. As the fame of Navajo rugs spread because of their brilliance and durability, folk tales that may be apocryphal developed around the skill of the weavers.

A visitor to Navajo country wanted to order a rug made in a special design. He could not communicate clearly with the husband of the weaver—since half of the Navajos over fifty still cannot speak English—so he drew the design on a handy piece of paper. The Navajo nodded. Through an interpreter he said he would take the order to his wife. He was certain she could weave the rug. "Come next year," he said, "it will be ready." So the tourist returned at the appointed time. The Indian unrolled the finished rug. It was an accurate reproduction of an Arbuckle Coffee label. The tourist had penciled the design on the back of a label. Somehow the Navajo neglected to impress upon his weaver that the desired design was on the opposite side. The same story is told, with only slight variation, of an Elks Club that wanted the familiar elk head and clock woven into a Navajo rug.

Today, hands that were adept at throwing the cedar shuttle back and forth across the loom are turning to more profitable pursuits. The Navajos are scattering throughout the West in search of employment. Men work as railroad gandy-dancers from Chicago to the Golden Gate. Bunches of carrots for the tables of the nation are tied by Navajo men, women, and children in sun-bathed valleys of Southern Arizona. They trim sugar beets in Colorado and plant potatoes in Idaho. Tribesmen who once belittled Hopis for menial cultivation of cotton, now find cotton-picking in the Southwest more profitable than tending sheep.

As a harvest worker, the Navajo is recruited by the U.S. Employment Service and private labor contractors. After centuries of semi-starvation he makes no great demands for housing accommodations and accepts relatively low wages. Entire families work in the fields. Nobody has very seriously attempted to force Indian children into schools away from their reservation.

There are extremes in the postwar Indian uprising more startling than the changes Rip Van Winkle found after his long sleep. In Flagstaff, Arizona, an electronics assembly plant recruits weavers from the Navajo reservation. The dexterity of the women is put to use assembling complex gadgets for aircraft radio and navigation equipment.

The largest compact Navajo community has been built up at Bellmont, west of Flagstaff on U.S. 66, where during the war the federal government built a permanent ordnance depot, staffed largely by Navajos. They have no fear of the munitions they handle. Their wages soon enable them to replace the cayuse-drawn wagons with Ford and Chevrolet trucks.

At Kingman, still farther west toward Las Vegas, is a metal fabricating plant where Navajos and tribesmen from the Hualpai reservation find work. The search for new supplies of labor has brought other firms to the Southwest. Near Casa Grande, Arizona, a garment mill has been built to utilize the labor of Pima and Papago women.

During 1956 the Navajo Tribal Council signed contracts that will bring the tribe's communal funds $33,000,000 for rental of oil and gas lands in the San Juan Basin of Northwestern New Mexico. Navajo gas is being pumped to the Pacific Northwest and Los Angeles. Almost at once a half-million dollars was set aside to lure new industries to the reservation. The Navajos are prepared to finance construction of plants that will provide jobs for their people.

This means a steady loss of the tribe's two great art forms—weaving and silverwork. But how can the 5 cents an hour earned by the weaver stand the competition of 75 cents an hour earned thinning sugar beets, or the pay of $2 an hour as an oilfield worker?

Economically the Hopis and other Pueblo Indians have shared the backwardness of the Navajos. A few of their young people are employed at Harvey Houses as waiters and bellhops, some adults find employment selling and making souvenirs for tourists, but for most Pueblo Indians their living is still wrested from the thin soil.

In Southern Arizona, the Apaches struggle towards self-advancement. Their reservation is largely grazing country. Once white ranchers rented Apache lands while Indian cowboys were paid inferior wages to do the dirty work. Now the Apaches' chief source of income on the vast San Carlos-White Mountain reservation is from their own cattle.

Their industry started as a federal handout. During the 1870's belligerent Apache clans were driven onto a parched reservation. Two forces more or less kept them there—military pressure and hunger. They were hunted down and some of their number slaughtered by troops after nearly every outbreak. They were bribed to stay peaceful by weekly or twice-weekly handouts of flour, sugar, coffee, beef, and unwanted soap. Each native who answered roll call was given something like five and a half pounds of freshly-slaughtered beef, four pounds of flour, and supplementary rations.

Men with large families were issued live animals, thus easing the Indian agent's work. The Apaches ate everything, including the offal. One day an old Apache was issued a scrawny black cow for his family's ration. Instead of killing the critter, Altahas and his son roped the animal and put their brand number on her. A few months later they branded her heifer calf. Whenever the family was issued butchered beef, they traded it to some less ambitious Indian for a live animal.

Thus the family herd grew, and with it the wealth of Wallace Altahas, son of the old Apache. Others copied the plan. Wallace became best known in Apacheland as R-14, the ration number issued to him when he was a prisoner during the Apache Indian wars. At the time of his death in 1937 his wealth was estimated at half a million dollars. He once owned 10,000 head of cattle. They roamed a range of 150,000 acres of tribal land under supervision of his white foreman, Johnny Moore. When R-14 died, many colored silk shirts were placed in his casket, as were $1, $5 and $10 silver certificates, plus a sack of corn to make *tulapai*, the crude Apache brew on which he had spent many happy days.

At the present time the semiannual Apache cattle sales can't support the growing tribe, nor is income from their leased asbestos mines and timber lands enough to provide the social services they believe are needed to supplement private family income and government facilities.

In 1955 the Apache tribal council engaged the Stanford Research Institute to make an economic survey of tribal lands and other resources, and to make recommendations for economic development of the mountainous reservation. Implementation of the recommendations rests with a group of tribal leaders chosen in a democratic way.

Leader of the drive to develop new income and to bring industry to the reservation has been Jess Stevens. One of his brothers is employed in the Indian Service's area office; another supervises use of cattle lands for the tribe. Their grandfather was a white man born in Massachusetts. After the Civil War he came to Arizona as a trader and married a Coyotero, or White Mountain Apache, maiden. He was a trader, mail carrier, agent, sheep and cattle raiser, and the first sheriff of Graham County. Geronimo and Victorio raided his herds. They spat on the ground at mention of a white man becoming an Indian; it was not so; it was a trick. Yet Stevens was loyal to his bride and to the people he had chosen as his own. His grandsons are leaders in the tribe now, and they're looking everywhere on the horizon—at industry, uranium, and education—to lead their people to self-sufficiency.

These days—in Tucson, Phoenix, Albuquerque and L.A.—every "exclusive" woman's shop features the Squaw Dress. They are lovely, billowing things, sensuous in intimation, agleam with braid, rickrack and geometric designs. They are, the salesladies announce, "an adaptation" of the huge skirts of Apache women.

Where did the Apache women get the style? They were nearly naked, by habit and choice, in the late 1860's, when the Army established posts in the Southwest. The officers' wives took one look at the squaws, gasped and retreated to quarters. Thereafter, meals were served with lectures—until the husbands gave in. Then post headquarters announced—with *hrmphs* and *ahems*—that Apaches would be denied rations until their womenfolk donned "civilized" attire. After that, the beneficent white ladies collected all of their outmoded mutton-shoulder, early Victorian dresses—and pressed them on the benighted heathen. Off swirled the squaws rigged for an 1850 soiree at Whitehall. And they never deviated from the style.

So full circle in time for full-circle skirts. The Squaw Skirt is straight from Buckingham Palace, after a century of mesa detour.

Otherwise, Navajo and Apache adaption to industry is changing the patterns of tribal life. The old ways are passing. Dig those Apache firemen and Navajo electricians!

Part 3

The DOERS and the DOING

REGINALD R. STUART

The Mountain Men

THE ROCKY MOUNTAIN FUR TRADE depended upon a combination of fantastic factors. There was the whim of fashion, which decreed that well-dressed Europeans and Americans wear high-crowned, beaver-trimmed hats. There was a musky secretion which immunized the fears of naturally shy and timid creatures. There was a breed of men who daily faced death from a dozen different sources. Add to these a fourth dimension, time—forty years from 1806 to 1846. Never again would be possible another such combination.

During the years, many a person has been called the typical "mountain man." There were Mike Fink and his buddies, Carpenter and Talbot. By all accounts they were toughs from the dives and saloons along the waterfront of old St. Louis. Their favorite pastime was shooting cups of whisky off each other's heads at seventy paces. It took something akin to courage to trust the marksmanship of a half-drunk companion.

They were the brawling, boasting kind that kept the camp continually stirred up. One day Fink and Carpenter quarreled over a girl in St. Louis, a thousand miles distant. There were threats and accusations, but eventually matters were patched up. To reseal their friendship, Mike proposed their favorite shooting stunt. The coin was tossed, and Carpenter lost.

"He's going to kill me," he confided to Talbot.

Even so, he put the cup of whisky on his head.

"Don't shake so," Fink called tauntingly. "You'll spill the liquor and I'll need a drink when I've finished this job."

At the shot, Carpenter fell over on his face.

"Oh! You spilled the whisky!" Fink chided, as he calmly reloaded.

The others turned the dead man over to find a hole drilled through the center of his forehead two inches below the hairline. Talbot swore it was plain murder. Nothing was done about it . . . then.

A few weeks later during a drunken brawl, Mike boasted of killing

51

Carpenter. Talbot whipped out his gun and shot him through the heart.

To even up matters, Talbot was drowned in the Teton River a few weeks later.

To many, Mike Fink and his cronies were the typical "mountain men."

Then there was Hugh Glass who met up with a grizzly. After the encounter, poor Hugh was a horrible sight. The bear had torn his clothes and flesh into bloody streamers. His companions did the best they could to make him comfortable. Any thought of recovery was out of the question. They could only wait for Glass to cash in and give him a decent burial.

But Hugh refused to die. The Indians who had been threatening the party for several days were likely to discover their plight at any time. Things look bad. So Major Henry called for volunteers who would remain with Glass until he died. He even promised half a year's wages. John S. Fitzgerald and Jim Bridger (then only a boy) volunteered for the task.

The party went on its way. A few days later Fitzgerald and Bridger caught up. The former carried Hugh's gun; the latter sported the "dead" man's knife. Their tale of Hugh's death and burial was plausible.

But Glass had not died. Furthermore, he swore by all that was holy he would not die until he had evened up some scores. He had been in a sort of coma, but he had seen his protectors divide up his property and heard them discuss his inevitable fate. Eventually, he crawled, inch by inch, to a spring. A scraggly bush of wild cherries hung above the water hole. Buffalo berries were abundant. These furnished him nourishment while his wounds were healing.

Days passed and Hugh added up his chances of escape. He still had his razor. When at last he could crawl about, he started for the settlement downstream, pitting his life and a razor blade against the hard realities of hundreds of miles of travel in a hostile country. It was the season when buffalo calves were being dropped. These, to large extent, sustained him during this terrible trip.

"Beavertown"—from *Marvels of the New West*, by W. M. Thayer, 1887

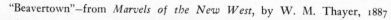

At last he met and joined a party of trappers headed for the upper Missouri. Indian attacks wiped out his companions. Other wild and unbelievable adventures held him back, but in time he found his way to his party's camp on the Bighorn.

Scarcely more than a skeleton, gnarled and scarred from his bear fight, he looked more like a ghost than a living man. Only in his eyes could be seen the indomitable hate and determination.

A few days earlier Fitzgerald had left camp for the settlement. Jim Bridger was still there. Because of his youth, Glass forgave him, but with stinging epithets he drove home the lesson of faithlessness.

After a short rest, he was off again to track down Fitzgerald. Once more he faced adventures, hardships, and privations which would kill a half-dozen strong men. At last, at Council Bluffs, Hugh found his quarry—now a soldier in Uncle Sam's army. From him he recovered his gun and heaped on the coward's trembling head the scorn and curses of a wronged man. "I heard the bargain—your shameful perfidy and heartless cruelty—but, again I say, settle the matter with your own conscience and your God."

To many, Hugh Glass was the typical "mountain man."

Then there were the tall-tale tellers—some of them trappers turned scouts, who came too late for beaver, but who could still guide parties across the plains and deserts. Around the campfires in the comparative safety of numbers and arms, they spun fantastic, improbable tales that have grown with the years. To many, these were the typical "mountain men."

There was still another sort of "mountain man." Jedediah Strong Smith was of that kind. To a lesser extent, perhaps, Major Andrew Henry, William L. Sublette, David E. Jackson, James Clyman, Thomas L. Fitzpatrick, George C. Yount, and Harrison G. Rogers might be grouped with this more rational type of Rocky Mountain trappers.

Born January 6, 1799, in the Bible-named community of Jericho, County of Chenango, New York, young Jed Smith was raised on the tales of Lewis and Clark. When he was fifteen, a Dr. Simons gave him Paul Allen's classic account of that great expedition. Ever after, it was Jed's criterion for camping procedure.

The tide of western migration which ran at flood during the years following the War of 1812 swept the Smith family to Erie County, Pennsylvania, then along northern Ohio to the Western Reserve, and finally dumped them—about the time of Jed's majority—in Ashland County. In national affairs, it was the "Era of Good Feelings" engendered by John Quincy Adams, the adroit and scholarly Secretary of State.

The next year Jed was on his own in northern Illinois. By the spring of 1822 he had reached St. Louis. This capital of the trans-Mississippi West was in its prime. Craft of all kind plying the waters of the Mississippi, the Missouri, and the Ohio, charted their courses from the docks of St. Louis. An advertisement in the local paper for "Young Men of Enterprise" caught his eye. He was quickly snapped up by General Ashley and Major Henry, who were gathering together a trapping party for the upper Missouri.

A boat wreck and an attack by the Arikarees, in which Smith received his baptism of fire, held up the expedition for weeks. Finally, sent in charge of a small trapping party to the upper Bighorn, Smith was almost killed by the sudden attack of a grizzly. The great beast sprang on him and attempted to crush his head in its massive jaws. In the process, Jed was almost scalped— the flesh was cut to the bone and one ear was partially torn off.

Without a leader, his men stood about, uncertain and helpless. Finally, the wounded man himself took charge. "Get some water," he directed, "and you"—pointing to Jim Clyman—"sew the skin together."

When the painful task was done, Jim announced, "I can't do anything for your ear."

"Oh! You must try. Do something with it!"

So Clyman put it in place the best he could and sewed it on. Smith was soon able to travel. Though scarred for life, it affected Jed in only a single particular. From that day on, he wore his hair long.

In appearance Smith was tall, thin, and clean-shaven, with brown hair and blue eyes. According to all accounts, he also kept himself clean morally. He was not a squaw man, and he neither used tobacco nor profanity. He partook of intoxicants only on state occasions. Like other travelers of his day, he carried a Bible, and once, at least, as recorded by one of his men, he offered a "powerful" prayer at the burial of two companions. He was kind, sympathetic, and optimistic. At the same time, he was determined and persevering. There is no indication that he indulged in wit or humor, but when he spoke, his words carried conviction.

Smith soon learned that though there were many other fur-bearing animals in the West, the beaver was, by far, the most important. The average mature beaver weighed about thirty-five pounds and his pelt from one and one-half to two pounds. The price for prime fur in St. Louis varied from four dollars to six dollars per pound. Prices current in the mountains were one-half the latest quotation from the Fur Capital.

Beavers were found throughout the West, particularly along waterways lined with cottonwood, willow, birch, alder, and aspen, which, in the main, constituted their food supply. They lived in burrows in the banks, with entrances several inches below the low-water mark of September.

Each member of a party was able to handle from four to six of the heavy traps. They were set at twilight and raised at the break of dawn. The most successful procedure was to place the trap in about four inches of water near the entrance to a burrow. The bait, a pleasantly scented secretion of the

"A White Trapper"—from *Harper's New Monthly*, May, 1891

beaver's castor gland, was placed on a leaf suspended directly above the trap. So tantalizing was the scent that the beaver stood up on his hind legs and walked directly into the trap. When it sprang, he dived into deep water and was usually drowned by the weight of the trap before he could gnaw off the imprisoned foot.

The game was usually skinned on the spot. A lengthwise slit was made down the belly and four transverse cuts down the inside of the legs. At the camp, the pelt was stretched on a frame, scraped, and dried. Later it was folded up, the fur side in, for packing. Besides the fur, the tail—a camp delicacy—and the castor glands were saved.

No longer a raw recruit, Smith became successively a trusted messenger, an efficient lieutenant, and finally the respected senior partner of the firm of Smith, Jackson, & Sublette. Smith and his associates brought two innovations to the fur trade. They introduced the American principle of free enterprise; no longer were the men servants or *engagés*, but independent trappers whose earnings depended upon their skill and energy. Then, too, the annual rendezvous took the place of the company's fort. The former made for efficiency, the latter for economy.

The rendezvous was the forerunner of all the modern "Wild West" carnivals. For the company, it brought in the past year's fur catch, and for the trappers and the Indians it provided the next year's supplies. The rendezvous was the great social event of the year. Here the trapper met all his friends, swapped tales of adventure, formed new partnerships, and competed in games of skill and chance.

Smith's first contact with the Pacific Coast came when he led a trapping party via the Colorado River and the Mojave Desert to the Mission San Gabriel during the summer and fall of 1826. Detained and restricted by the padres, he was forced to spend the winter of 1826-27 in almost endless negotiations with Governor Echeandia at San Diego. Even so, the trip gave him intimate knowledge of southern California and, by reports, of all the coastal area. With this difficulty ironed out, he came north through the San Joaquin Valley and camped in the tules on the lower Stanislaus.

In conformity with plans made during the previous summer, it was imperative for Smith to reach the trading rendezvous of his company in Utah by July 4, 1827. In April, Smith and his entire party, carrying some 1500 pounds of fur, attempted to cross the mountains up the American River canyon. The snow was too deep and several horses were lost. Ever after, the river was known to the Spaniards as *Los Americanos*. Changing his plans by leaving most of his men and all the furs in California, Smith and two companions crossed the Sierras in the vicinity of present Ebbetts Pass and plowed across the barren deserts of Nevada and Utah, suffering terrible privations from thirst and hunger, but reaching Cache Valley a day in advance of the appointed time.

That fall, with a party of eighteen, he again entered California by the southern route. In 1826 the Mohaves had been friendly and co-operative. This year, without cause they fell upon his company at the Colorado River crossing. Ten men were killed. All the horses and provisions except fifteen pounds of dried meat were taken. Nevertheless, on September 18, Smith reached the camp of the men he had left in California in late spring. He had promised to return not later than September 20. .

Regretfully, Smith faced the necessity of again negotiating with the Californians. On his arrival at Mission San Jose, he was promptly thrown into jail by Father Durán. Once more his detention proved a valuable asset. A forced trip to Monterey, where he was assisted by John Rogers Cooper, a former Bostonian, and a sail up the coast to San Francisco, gave him first-hand knowledge of the economy and geography of the Bay area. Finally, he was permitted to sell the accumulated beaver pelts and to buy horses and supplies. On December 30, 1827, he took "French leave" of the Mission.

This time he headed north with his company, trapping as he went. When at last he reached the northern end of the Sacramento Valley, he turned off northwest to the coast. All that spring and a part of the summer he fought his way through the uncharted area of coastal California and Oregon.

Years later an Indian boy told his teacher about Smith's journey up the coast. His every movement was watched by natives hidden in the bushes. In keeping with the attitude of primitive people, strangers were considered enemies. There was no doubt about an attack. The question was, "When?"

By July 13 the party had reached the mouth of the Umpqua River. Already they were within the trapping area of the Hudson's Bay Company. The Indians whom they encountered had proved annoying, but were not thought to be dangerous. The next morning, taking two men and a native guide with him, Smith scouted ahead for a road through the tangle of under-brush and swamps. The camp was left in charge of Harrison G. Rogers, his trusted lieutenant, who was instructed to permit no Indians to enter.

Several hours later Smith's scouting party returned down a small tribu-tary, now known as Smith River, which enters the Umpqua near its mouth. Suddenly a shot rang out from the shore, and the guide tipped over the boat, spilling men and guns into the river. Escaping the fusillade from the shore, Smith and his companions hid in the brush until night. Satisfying himself that his entire camp party had been massacred, Smith and the other survivors now began a month's struggle, without arms or supplies, through the Coast Moun-tains to the Hudson's Bay fort at Vancouver. The day before their arrival,

"Native Californians Lassoing a Bear"—from *Picturesque America*, volume II, 1874

Arthur Black, the only survivor of the party which had been left at the camp, also found his way to the Fort.

Dr. John McLoughlin, the Hudson's Bay factor, immediately dispatched an armed party to the Umpqua, which was accompanied by Smith and his three men. The route was up the Willamette, across the Calapooya Mountains, and down the Elk and Umpqua to the scene of the massacre. It was a tragic sight. Skeletons were strewn about the camp—the mortal remains of Smith's closest friends. In the end, most of Smith's goods were recovered and sold to the Hudson's Bay Company.

The next spring Smith and Black set out on the return up the Columbia, on to Fort Colville, and then via Lake Pend d'Oreille to Flathead Lake, where they met Smith's partner, D. E. Jackson.

By August, 1830, Smith had sold his interest in the partnership and was headed for St. Louis and a visit home. This last year's hunt had grossed the three partners $84,499.14. After all expenses had been paid, there was still $53,920.92 to be divided.

During all these years Smith had kept journals of his activities. His maps of the West were the most comprehensive in existence. It was his plan to have them published in the near future. Only one area seemed inadequately covered. That was the Southwest.

There were eighty-three in the combined party of Smith, Jackson and Sublette who left St. Louis for Santa Fe on April 10, 1831. It was on a barren plain near Cimarron that the party made a desperate effort to locate water. Springs were all dry. Smith and Fitzpatrick headed south. Again the supposed water hole was disappointing. Leaving his companion to advise the oncoming party, Jedediah continued alone into a broken country beyond.

Just what happened is not known. Apparently, Smith was shot from the back by Comanches as he was drinking at the water hole he found.

No man of his time had a clearer idea of the West than Jedediah Smith. He had effectively shown that South Pass was an open corridor for an Overland Trail. From the Great Salt Lake he had traveled three different routes to the Pacific—for two of which he had been the pathfinder. In addition, he was the first to make the journey from California to Oregon and the first to cross the Sierra Nevada Mountains. He was not only the greatest Western traveler of his day, but, by careful inquiry, had been able to map much of the region he had not traveled.

It has been said: "If Smith's maps and journals had been published in 1830, they would have advanced the conquest of California by a score of years."

He was the "door opener" for all Americans who came overland to California. To many, Jedediah Strong Smith was the typical "mountain man."

The bones of fallen fighters lie
Along far lonely trails:
The coyote howls, nose to the sky;
The shifting west wind wails.

Upon low hills a million cows
Have seen Time's moonlight pass—
Look! See the little blades they browse
Are bloodstained swords *of Grass!*

S. OMAR BARKER—"Grass"

DON RUSSELL

The Scouts

THE RATTLESNAKE slithered out of the buffalo skull, down into the wallow toward them. Stillwell and Trudeau couldn't shoot, or even whisper. The Cheyenne were searching only 100 yards away. Slowly, Trudeau raised his face a few inches from the muck, rolled the tobacco wad against his tongue, puckered and aimed. The quid hit the rattler square in the left eye. It hissed and turned tail. Three days later, Stillwell and Trudeau stumbled into Fort Wallace. The relief columns rode off toward General Forsyth's beleaguered Scouts Company within the hour.

No one word more immediately envisions romance and adventure of the Indian-fighting days of the American West than "scout." The military manuals have another word for him—a long word: "Reconnaissance." It was military intelligence that the scout sought. But military experts in the early days were confused about the matter.

In 1776, the generals were responsible for military intelligence. If General Washington wanted to hire Nathan Hale or Harvey Birch as a spy, that was entirely a matter between the general and his expense account. Spy companies took the field against Black Hawk in the war with the Sac and Fox Indians. Scout companies and battalions were raised for the War with Mexico a decade later. The change probably occurred when the Americans' march west reached the French towns of the Mississippi Valley. Scout is the Old French word for "spy." The Army's shift in terminology could well have been a St. Louis or New Orleans influence.

59

In time, the Army got its services of reconnaissance and information regularized. Pointing the way were the experiences of the numerous exploring parties sent out to mark routes for highways and railroads across "the Great American Desert" west of the Missouri. As Frémont, Marcy, Cooke, Mullen, and other army officers organized these expeditions, they needed guides who knew the way across the plains and mountains. Fortunately, at about this time, the beaver trappers and mountain men were unemployed. Kit Carson, Jim Bridger of the tall tales about the wonders of Yellowstone, Tom Fitzpatrick of the Broken Hand, Old Bill Williams, Jim Beckworth, and others signed on as Army scouts.

Scouts were hired by the month, as needed, by the Quartermaster Department of the army. The pay varied from $60 to $150 a month. Their duties were to guide expeditions through unfamiliar country, to carry dispatches, to follow trails, and to contribute their knowledge of Indian ways and tactics. They were not hired primarily as fighters; the soldiers presumably could take care of that end of it. But Indian warfare resembled present-day warfare in that no one was neutral. When there was a fight anyone could get into it, and he had better do so.

The quartermasters were authorized to hire civilians not only as scouts or guides—the distinction was not entirely clear—but also as teamsters, packers, interpreters, clerks, carpenters, blacksmiths, laborers, and in other occupations as needed. Consequently around every army post gathered frontiersmen seeking jobs. Most aspired to be scouts, garbed in buckskin, with shoulder-length haircuts, mustache, and goatee.

Buffalo Bill Cody received his first important recognition as a scout in the fall of 1868. Arriving at Fort Hays, Kansas, with a message for Lieutenant General Philip H. Sheridan from Fort Larned concerning an Indian outbreak, Bill was asked if he could take a necessary dispatch to Fort Dodge. None of the other would-be scouts hanging around Hays City were willing to risk their necks in the Indian country. Bill went to Fort Dodge, was sent from there with another message back to Fort Larned, and then carried a report on to Sheridan at Fort Hays, a total of more than 300 miles in less than sixty hours. This was typical of Buffalo Bill's service as scout. There are several other instances on record of his lone dashes through country overrun with hostile Indians.

Sheridan thought so much of Buffalo Bill's exploits that he named Cody chief of scouts of the Fifth United States Cavalry. With that organization, Cody took part in seven expeditions and was engaged in nine Indian fights. Another of his great assets was his uncanny sense of terrain. In December, he successfully trailed a column commanded by Brevet Brigadier General William A. Penrose after a blizzard that had stopped the Fifth Cavalry for a day and a half. When the command's wagon train came to a steep bluff,

"Government Scouts"—from *Drawings by Frederick Remington*, 1897

Buffalo Bill recalled his experience as a teamster and showed the army drivers how to roughlock the wheels and "run down, or fall down—any way to get down." This gained a week in catching up with the snowbound and short-rationed Penrose expedition. When the relief was accomplished, another of Buffalo Bill's frontier talents came into play. He was sent out with twenty wagons and killed enough buffalo to supply the combined commands.

Buffalo Bill was retained continuously on the payroll for four years, a record equaled by few scouts. Officers of the Fifth Cavalry agreed that his greatest exploit during this period came during the pursuit of Tall Bull of the Cheyenne, who had raided settlements along the Solomon River and carried off two women captives. Instead of following the trail of the Indians, Buffalo Bill led Brevet Major General Eugene A. Carr's command across country to get ahead of them.

The attack on their village came as a complete surprise to the Indians. One of the women was rescued; the other was tomahawked before the troops could reach her. The regimental history records that Scout Cody "guided the Fifth Cavalry to a position whence the regiment was enabled to charge upon the enemy and win a brilliant victory." Whether Tall Bull himself was killed by Buffalo Bill or by Captain Frank North of the Pawnee Scouts in this fight is of no great importance.

After four years' continuous service as scout, Buffalo Bill knocked off to try his luck on the stage. During two following summers, between theatrical seasons, he returned to scouting. The second of these summer jobs was in 1876, again with the Fifth Cavalry. It was then that Buffalo Bill led some half-dozen scouts and soldiers to the rescue of two couriers and killed a Cheyenne called Hay-o-wei, or Yellow Hand, perhaps more correctly translated Yellow Hair. This was the "first scalp for Custer," for Custer's command had been killed in the Battle of the Little Bighorn only a few days before. After the fight at Hat (or War Bonnet) Creek the Fifth Cavalry joined the expedition commanded by Brigadier General George Crook. Buffalo Bill was named chief of scouts for the entire expedition.

Some twenty civilian scouts were employed on General Crook's Bighorn and Yellowstone Expedition. Some became notable in the annals of the West. There was Baptiste Pourrière, known as Big Bat; Baptiste Garnier, known as Little Bat; Jonathan White, called "Buffalo Chips" because he so closely imitated Buffalo Bill; Louis Richaud; Ben Arnold; and many more. One of the most remarkable was Frank Grouard, often called Crook's favorite scout. He was born in 1850 on the island of Ana in the Paumoto group of the Friendly Islands. His father was Benjamin F. Grouard, a missionary from an old New Hampshire family, who had married the daughter of a Polynesian chief of Ana. Frank was brought to California at the age of two and went to school in San Bernardino. When he was nineteen he left home and took a job carrying mail between Fort Ellis and Fort Hall. He was captured by the Sioux. His Polynesian features caused them to believe he was an Indian from some strange tribe. Frank lived with the Sioux six or seven years, and came to know Sitting Bull and Crazy Horse intimately before he escaped. His knowledge of the Sioux was of great value when he became scout for the campaigns against them in 1876 and 1877.

Buffalo Bill left the expedition to return to the stage. He was succeeded as chief of scouts by John Wallace Crawford, known as Captain Jack Crawford, the Poet Scout. Captain Jack was neither the greatest of poets, nor the greatest of scouts. He probably won his promotion because of his sobriety.

Captain Jack is credited with carrying dispatches to General Crook on a highly perilous route of four hundred miles. He also brought with him from Colonel Jones of Cheyenne a bottle of whisky as a present for Buffalo Bill. Buffalo Bill gave him high praise, saying, "Jack Crawford is the only man I have known that could have brought that bottle of whisky through without accident befalling it." Jack had promised his dying mother he would never take a drink. Apparently he never did. Buffalo Bill made no such promise. (Tall tales are told of Bill's tall drinking. He took his whisky seriously. Yet no officer ever complained that he was out of action on that account. And it is of record that in all his years of show business he never missed a performance because of liquor.)

Jack Crawford was born in County Donegal, Ireland, came to America as a boy, and, at fourteen, enlisted in the 48th Pennsylvania Volunteers for the Civil War. While in a hospital wounded, he was taught to read and write by a Sister of Charity. There are those who doubt if this was a very charitable deed; as a result Captain Jack produced some very bad poetry. He wrote four or five volumes of verse, ranging from paper-backed pamphlets that he sold himself from Chautauqua lecture platforms to the leather-bound and handsomely printed *Broncho Book* produced by Elbert Hubbard's Roy-crofters. He also wrote plays and acted in them, struck gold in the Black Hills, served as scout in Apache campaigns, wrote numerous magazine articles, went prospecting in the Klondike, and generously recited his verses whether or not called upon to do so.

Indians were employed as scouts, too, although their terms of service were usually short. Among the Arikarees with Custer was Bloody Knife. He had been Custer's scout in several expeditions and was killed on the Little Bighorn while standing beside Major Marcus A. Reno. Custer also had a group of Crow scouts, among them Curley, sometimes called the only sur-vivor of the Last Stand. More definite is the claim that he was first to bring the news of the disaster.

Crook's column had Crow scouts, and a group of Shoshones under Chief Washakie. They left at about the time Buffalo Bill did, not to appear on any stage, but, according to one authority, "several of them urge additional reasons indicative of the fact that the ladies of the tribe are not regarded by their lords as above suspicion in times of such prolonged absence."

Most reliable were the Pawnee Scouts, raised for several Indian cam-paigns by Captain Frank North. Frank was a clerk in a trader's store at the Pawnee Agency in 1864 when Major General Samuel R. Curtis came that way on a campaign against the Sioux and Cheyenne. He asked for a company of Pawnee Scouts. It was raised, with Joseph McFadden, another clerk at the store, as captain, and North as lieutenant. General Curtis was so impressed with North's ability in handling Indians that he asked North to raise a second company. The following year Frank North's Pawnee Scouts were called out again for Major General Patrick Connor's campaign to the Powder River. Thereafter Captain North was usually in the field with a battalion of two to four companies of Pawnee Scouts for every summer's Indian campaign down to 1877. Frank North had unusual influence with the Pawnees. Left to their own resources they were invariably defeated by the Sioux and Chey-enne; under North's leadership they fought these tribes to a standstill.

The Indian Scouts were used more for fighting than for scouting. On occasion, the army took advantage of its authority to employ scouts to recruit fighting men. In 1868 Brevet Major General George A. Forsyth, assigned to General Sheridan's staff, obtained permission to raise a company

"A Friendly Scout Signaling the Main Column"—*Century Magazine*, March, 1891

of fifty scouts. On their first expedition they followed an Indian trail that revealed an overwhelming number of Cheyenne, something like ten to one. The Indians charged repeatedly, but were held off by the scouts' Spencer repeating rifles. However, General Forsyth was severely wounded and his second in command, Lieutenant Frederick Beecher, killed. The fight, which took place on the Arikaree Fork of the Republican River is sometimes called the Battle of Beecher Island. One of the scouts in this command was nineteen-year-old Jack Stillwell. He and Pierre Trudeau were selected on the first night to go for help. Their expert plainscraft took them through the surrounding Indians. They traveled by night and hid by day, and on one occasion took refuge in a buffalo wallow to elude a wandering band of Indians. It was here that Trudeau became a part of Western lore by spitting in the rattlesnake's eye.

Apache Indians made able scouts. The warfare that went on between subtribes and bands of Apaches made them readily available. One civilian scout who was very successful in handling Apache scouts was Al Sieber. Several young officers also made reputations in this warfare of the deserts. Lieutenant Britton Davis led a band of scouts and served as Indian agent. Captain Emmett Crawford, trailing Geronimo across the Mexican border, was killed when his Apache scouts were mistaken for hostiles by a unit of Mexican troops.

One of the most heroic exploits of the Apache wars was that of Lieutenant Charles B. Gatewood in entering Geronimo's camp to persuade that Chiricahua leader to surrender. One of the three or four who accompanied Gatewood on that perilous mission was a courageous scout named Tom Horn. A few years later Tom Horn was hanged in Cheyenne for dry-gulching (i.e., killing from ambush) a thirteen-year-old boy in the cattle wars.

Then there was Lieutenant George O. Eaton, who stopped a battle between two Apache bands while moving them to a new reservation. This recalls that John Burwell Omohundro, Jr., "Texas Jack," a scout at Fort McPherson, was once hired by the Indian Bureau to accompany a band of Pawnees on a buffalo hunt to keep them from fighting white or Sioux buffalo hunters. Texas Jack was with Buffalo Bill on the stage. He married the show's leading lady, Mlle. Morlacchi, *première danseuse* credited with introducing the can-can to America.

So there you have the Scout—actor, showman, trapper, poet, man of varied talents, capable of murdering a small boy or spitting in a rattlesnake's eye, dime-novel hero and prodigious liar, whose deeds often were more astonishing than he dared boast about. The scout's reputation may be exaggerated in comparison with others who contributed to the opening of the West, yet the frontier line would never have vanished so soon without him.

We're marching off for Sitting Bull
And this is the way we go;
Forty miles a day on beans and hay
In the Regular Army, Oh.

U.S. Army Marching Song
of Sioux Campaigns

STANLEY VESTAL

The Soldiers

THE REGULAR ARMY of the Indian campaigns following the Civil War contained so many men from foreign nations that it has been compared with the French Foreign Legion. Irish and Germans, British and French, were most numerous, but there were also Italians, Spaniards, Russians, Scandinavians, and others. Some had fled from Europe to avoid conscription, only to volunteer when they reached the States. Some were soldiers of fortune. Others were Union veterans of the Civil War, or ex-Confederates who had fled the impoverished South, or who as prisoners of war volunteered to fight Indians under the Stars and Stripes, and so gained their freedom. Such men were called "galvanized Yankees," because they were brought to life, as it were, by the shock of freedom.

Many of the non-coms had been officers in the Civil War, demoted when our forces were reduced after 1865. For some years after, ex-Confederates could not hold a commission in our Regular Army. There were efficient Negro troops, serving under white officers, and known to the Indians as "buffalo soldiers" because of the wool on their heads. Many of the older officers had served in the Union Army or in armies abroad. Some lacked an arm or an eye, or were otherwise handicapped by old wounds.

American recruits were veterans who "loved the damn Army," or men who in the long depression of the '70's were out of jobs. Then too, there were always the "Snow Birds" who enlisted in early winter for shelter and rations, only to desert when spring brought warm weather. There was then no adequate penalty for desertion. The West was wide. General Custer once remarked that, if all the men who had enlisted that year in the Seventh

66

Cavalry had remained in service, he would have had a brigade instead of a regiment.

As auxiliaries, the regulars had civilian scouts temporarily employed, such men as Kit Carson, Ben Clark, Frank Grouard, Mitch Bouyer, Jim Bridger, and Buffalo Bill. More numerous, and generally quite as effective, were the government Indian scouts of friendly tribes. Such Indians, loyal to the whites, were natural-born fighters, trailers, and marksmen, who never deserted, never touched liquor, and took good care of their ponies. They made their living shooting running buffalo from the bare back of a racing pony and (when not in service) had to buy their ammunition.

In addition to these fighting men were the medical officers, or contract surgeons, and the teamsters and packers who wrangled the army mules.

As time passed, the U.S. Army veterans developed high respect for the military efficiency of the Indians they fought. Custer praised their tactics and their "individual daring" highly, and rated their horsemanship "the best in the world." Captain John G. Bourke declared them "the finest light cavalry in the world." General Charles King called them "foemen far more to be dreaded than any European cavalry." An officer of the Canadian Mounties rated the Sioux as "superior to the best English regiments." Colonel Ford called the Plains Indians "the finest skirmishers I ever saw." General Anson Mills wrote that they were "then the best cavalry in the world; their like will never be seen again." And General Frederick W. Benteen accounted for Custer's destruction with these words: "Too many Indians, good shots, good riders, and the best fighters the sun ever shone on."

These Indians had had daily practice in horsemanship, scouting, and the use of deadly weapons since their early teens. By contrast, enlisted men often came from sedentary occupations, and on the post were kept so busy with work details that they had little time to devote to military training. Many frontier forts were actually built by the soldiers sent to man them.

Moreover, the Army had enemies at home. It was continually criticized and hampered by the prejudice and hostility of pacifists and reluctant tax-payers safe in the East. These combined with the Indian Bureau to blame the Army for all trouble in Indian country, professing to believe the soldiers a base lot of butchers, sots, and lechers whose presence was sure to corrupt the soul of the Noble Redman. Meanwhile, certain officials of this bureau and the corrupt Indian Ring in Washington connived to rob the Indians and so foment Indian wars which the Army had to fight.

Even the settlers in the West, scattered on lonely farms and ranches, continually berated the little Army for not protecting them, which a force ten times as great could not have done. Congress was so stingy with Army appropriations that soldiers went unpaid for months, and often had scarcely enough ammunition to protect themselves, much less to attack or use in target practice. Custer tells how the insolent warriors would ride at a gallop along a line of soldiers "within easy carbine range" time after time and never lose a man, though occasionally a pony went down.

There was no official briefing of officers, and all too often, as General Sully reports, they "knew nothing of Indian character or manners except what they may have learned from reading novels." Such officers, unable to distinguish Indians of one tribe from those of another, would retaliate for hostile forays by shooting the first redskin they saw, or by clapping some friendly visitor into the guardhouse. Two Sioux chiefs who brought in a white woman, Mrs. Eubanks, whom they had bought from her captors, were hanged in chains at Fort Laramie. "Every officer," Sully reports, "had notions peculiar to himself for managing Indians." Such success as the troops had in these campaigns was due oftener than not to the fact that their commander acted on the advice of his civilian scouts.

Moreover, officers who had distinguished themselves in the Civil War and knew nothing of Indian strategy and tactics, were rash and contemptuous and underestimated their enemies, sometimes to their own destruction. Some young officers had romantic notions about war, considering it an opportunity to perform individual exploits and engage in knight errantry. Occasionally they left their commands, without orders, to chase Indians over the hill, as did Lieutenant George W. Grummond and Lieutenant Horatio S. Bingham near Fort Phil Kearney on December 6, 1866. Whether Major Joel H. Elliott, at the Battle of the Washita, left the battalion he commanded with a few volunteers to chase Indians under orders from General Custer, or on his own initiative, is disputed. He shouted when he rode off, "Here goes for a brevet or a coffin." Three times such eager-beavers with all their men were wiped out by the Sioux: Lieutenant J. L. Grattan at Fort Laramie, 1853; Colonel W. J. Fetterman at Fort Phil Kearney, 1866; General George Armstrong Custer at the Little Bighorn, 1876.

Under the Peace Policy of President Grant, various commissioners, and even generals, handed out arms and ammunition to the Indians, some of them rifles outranging the carbines of the cavalrymen. This policy of trying to buy peace with presents resulted in what its bitter critics called "feed 'em in the winter, fight 'em in the summer."

The defense of the rolling frontier fell to General William Tecumseh Sherman. Sherman's problem was that he had to fight Indians when the nation was technically at peace. Congress was reducing taxes, appropriations, and the Army. Settlers and miners demanded absolute protection. The railroads had to be built and defended. The vast distances over which transportation had to be provided, the mice and rats which devoured so much grain in the stables and made cavalry so terribly expensive, and the continual westward rush of population into Indian country, which year by year pushed

"Forsythe's Fight on the Republican River, 1868—the Charge of Roman Nose"—from *Drawings by Frederick Remington, 1897*

the frontier—and the frontier posts—before it, made his problem complex and enormous. He tried to keep the white men and the Indians from contact with each other, but it was an impossible task.

When Fetterman and his command marched into the trap at Fort Phil Kearney, Sherman declared, "We must act with intensive earnestness against the Sioux, even to their extermination, men, women, and children. Nothing else will reach the root of this case." With Sheridan, who declared, "The only good Indian is a dead Indian," to direct operations in the field, and such field commanders as Custer, MacKenzie, Crook, and Miles to harry the Indians, it was evident that the Army was in for a lively time. From 1865 to 1883 Sherman was successively in command of the Military Division of the Missouri and the entire U.S. Army. Though his subordinates have received most of the military glory of that time, Sherman's was the master mind. His hatred of war, his love of discipline, his understanding of the frontier settlers, and his passion for results made him a great contributor to the conquest and settlement of our last frontier.

War with the Sioux might have been avoided, or postponed, had the President enforced the treaties which reserved the buffalo country to the Indians. Sitting Bull went as far from the white men as he could get, and only fought them when they invaded his hunting grounds. He and Crazy Horse agreed, "If they come shooting, shoot back."

Of all our Indian fighting commanders, Custer was the most colorful. Tall and slender, he was a man of tremendous vitality and vigor, an excellent horseman and a good shot. He used neither liquor nor tobacco, and needed very little sleep. Utterly devoted to his wife, Elizabeth, he would, after a hard day in the saddle, scribble long letters to her.

To his last day, Custer was recognized as the most dashing, aggressive, and intrepid cavalry officer in the Army. Through the spring of 1865, his command led Grant's Army in the pursuit of General Lee's Confederates. It was to him that they brought their white flag. General Sheridan declared, "I know of no one whose efforts have contributed more to this happy result than those of Custer." The public knew him as "the boy general who had never lost a gun or a color," and "Custer's luck" was a proverb. When President Grant refused to let him accompany the expedition against Sitting Bull's Sioux, Sheridan persuaded Grant that Custer's services were indispensable.

"Long Hair, the Last of the Cavaliers," played the popular hero well, wearing a vivid red necktie outside his blouse, and a shirt with a wide sailor collar on which to display his stars of a Major General of Volunteers. In the field, he affected fringed buckskin jackets and wore his hair long as a challenge to Indian scalping knives. He and the Indians found a common passion in glory.

As Lieutenant Colonel of the Seventh Cavalry, he was a skillful organizer, raised the regiment to a high pitch of efficiency and *esprit de corps.* They even had their own battle march, the rollicking "Garry Owen." Though a strict disciplinarian, he himself was often insubordinate, and was court-martialed more than once. His requests for leave were frequent, and he once left his command without leave to visit his wife. He did not hesitate to use whatever political pull he had, and antagonized a number of his officers by his favoritism in allowing his relatives to serve in the Seventh. His greatest achievement in the West was to force the Southern Cheyenne to settle on their reservation in 1869, and so make a peace which lasted for nearly five years.

Impetuous, self-confident, he remained the boy general, loving a fight as he did a practical joke, neglecting reconnaissance, preferring the Indians' own technique of surprise attack. For this he was unfairly blamed. His plan had worked well on the wintry Washita where Indian ponies were half-starved. It failed in summer on the Little Bighorn. Both times, Custer's fear was that the Indians would run away. If they *had* escaped him, leaving only their camp in his hands, he might have been court-martialed, as was Colonel J. J. Reynolds for his failure to corral Two Moon's Cheyenne on Powder River only about three months before.

He was a man well loved or well hated by those who knew him best.

In death, as in life, "Long Hair" was the figure who inspired the little Army of the West to greater efficiencies, to dogged determinations, and finally to victory. Perhaps his ghost stood a little haughtily on the Montana knoll that day in the 1880's when Lord Wolsey, Commander-in-Chief of the British Army, declared that, man for man, the U.S. Army was the best in the world.

That army had been whipped into shape by nearly forty years of fighting Plains Indians. They had to be good, for they were matched with and outnumbered by foes who could outshoot, outride and outfight all but the best, and who inflicted far heavier casualties (including civilian) than they suffered in wars which, for numbers engaged, were bloodier even than the Civil War, the bloodiest in our history.

"Fort Laramie in 1849"—from the *Century Magazine*, November, 1890

Powder River, let'r buck ... she's a mile wide ... an inch deep ... full o' dust and flatfish ... swimmin' holes for grasshoppers ... cross'r anywhere ... yeou ... uhh ... yippee ... she rolls uphill from Texas.

Author Unknown

CHARLES W. TOWNE

Cowboys and Herdsmen

THE SLENDER YOUNGSTER poked the buffalo-chip fire until it blazed, pulled the wolfskin jacket around his neck and hunkered back against the dugout wall. The norther swirling across Kansas hummed like steel guitar strings. Instinctively, he leaned closer to the fire, brown eyes dreamy for the soft winds of the Gulf Coast and his sweetheart at Matagorda. Her face was just beginning to smile back at him from the shadows when the dugout roof caved in and a red steer fell onto the fire, bawling like four banshees, horns and hooves slashing. Charlie Siringo dove between the steer's hind legs for the dugout door, scuttled up the riverbank on all fours, unhitched his horse Whiskeypeat and set out after the spooked herd. A week later, he blew three months' pay in a spree in Kiowa, Kansas, and rode south to join Pat Garrett's posse for the shoot-out with Billy the Kid in the New Mexico mountains. . . .

That was 1875, a high-tide year for an American epic. The longhorn herds bawled from Old Mexico to Montana, clear up the 1,500 miles of the Great Plains. Dodge City, Abilene, and other Kansas towns boomed in a welter of grog shops, loading chutes and pineboard shanties at the railroad crossovers of the Texas trails. "Remuda," "chuck wagon," "lariat," were new words in Yankeedom.

But, greater than all, loomed the shadow of a nimble man on horseback, rigged in a slouch hat, sheepskin or fur vest, floppy breeches whipped from an old cowhide, and high-heeled boots, a man slow-spoken but as proud as an eagle and as ready for a fight as a bobcat. For the first time in history, the cowherd was being endowed with the glamour, wit and noble spirit of a knight-errant. It could happen only in this New-World democracy. Even

72

so, it had taken more than two hundred years to develop him. So the cowboy zoomed to his American firmament.

The epic years ran from 1866, when the first big longhorn drives crossed the Red River into the Indian Territory. They lasted until 1897 when "Scandlous John" McCanless pushed a small herd north to write "exit" for the Texas trails. In those thirty years, there were probably never more than 25,000 "working cowboys" on the plains in any one year. Yet they constituted one of the most motley collections of dare-devils ever assembled: veterans who had starved through to the last days at Appomattox with Lee, second sons of English nobility, Negroes new to freedom, steamboat gamblers "on the lam," overland freighters, farm boys running away from home, Mexican vaqueros and half-breed *comancheros*. Facing unknown hazards ahead—dust, mud, stampedes, Indians, outlaws, nesters, quarantines and high-jackers—they hit the long trails in the spirit of joyous adventure.

Behind them stretched two hundred years of tradition in the New World. And, beyond the Atlantic, their professional forebears trailed back to the drovers who pioneered the ox-trails between Norseland and Rome, conquered the mountains of Spain and France, and hiyoodled Hannibal's elephants across the Alps.

The word "cowboy" first appeared in the English language on the big cattle ranches of Ireland about 1000 A.D. Some historians contend it was introduced to New England about 1640 by Irish prisoners of war shipped west by Cromwell and the Roundheads during the Puritan Revolution. At any rate, the cloaked, leather-jerkined herdsmen who drove John Pynchon's first herd of stall-fattened beeves from Springfield to Boston, Massachusetts, in the spring of 1655 were called "cowboys." And cowboys, so-called, tended the cattle herds of back-country Virginia, Carolina and Georgia from 1750 on—skilled in horsemanship, lassoing, roundups and branding, using the long rifle with the same studied nonchalance that was to become the pattern for the Western cowboy and his six-shooter.

During the American Revolution, the cattle thieves and raiders of New York's Hudson Valley who favored the British cause were called "cowboys," as opposed to the "skinners" who sided with Washington and Congress. The first cowboys of the Southwest—as against the more dignified term of "cattlemen"—were raiders, too. In the troubled days that led to the founding of the Texas Republic, gangs of young Americans roved the ranchlands between the Nueces and Rio Grande rivers for the cattle, horses and sheep owned by Mexican landlords.

"Generally timing their forays with moonlight," J. Frank Dobie reported in *The Longhorns*, "a band of ten or fifteen 'cowboys' would rush from two to six hundred cattle together and head them northeast in a long run, which they would keep up for twenty-four hours, after that merely walking or trotting. . . . Some of the cattle thus lifted were driven to the New Orleans market. The majority were used to stock the coastal ranges. . . . For forty years the Bloody Border knew no peace."

So the cowboy, like the cow, is a blend of East and West. The term "cowpuncher" came along much later, when ranch hands used metal-tipped poles to chouse cattle into railroad stock cars.

Whatever the title, the livestock of the West required herdsmen. The first one was the Aztec slave, branded on the cheek with the letter "G" (for *guerra*—war) by Hernando Cortes, conqueror of Mexico and, by royal decree, "Marquis of the Valley of Oaxaca."

Before 1700, the Indian vaquero was keeping watch at far-flung water holes in the Southwest. His only shelter was a lean-to, open on three sides, with a rear wall and roof made of hides and in front a feeble fire fueled with cow chips. Wearing a big hat, serape, shirt and sandals, he rode his mustang barelegged, with roweled Spanish spurs strapped to his heels. His only food and drink were water, *atole* made from corn meal, and what game he could bring down with bow and arrow. (His Spanish masters didn't trust him with firearms.) Hovering over his smoldering fire, half-starved, he hesitated to butcher a steer, for that was the property of his *rico* employer, to whom he was fanatically loyal.

As skilled and daring a horseman as the Comanche, this peaceful cowherd boasted that he could ride any outlaw in the *remuda*, and, like his predecessors in Crete, Carthage and Spain, could perform wonders with his rope. Not only could he snare an unruly steer, but his *reata* often brought to earth a fighting stallion or, with some help from his *compadres*, a marauding grizzly. For sport, he would sometimes mount and ride a plunging longhorn, preceding by two hundred and fifty years the Brahma-bull riding of the modern rodeo. His solitude was interrupted by cruel raids. Apache, Comanche, Navajo, once they acquired horses, stampeded and stole his cattle, and often killed the courageous vaqueros.

Next, the *cibolero* became an omnipotent figure on the lower Great Plains. The Buffalo Bill Cody of his day, he was the New Mexican half-breed who provided dried meat for the villagers. He rode a wiry mustang, dressed in leather trousers and jacket, a flat hat and spurs, and was armed with bow and arrows plus a long-handled spear. The hunt over, he skinned his kill and sliced the buffalo hump and loin meat into thin slices. These he kneaded with his feet, claiming that it helped flavor and preservation in some way. Then he sun-dried the strips or, if he was in a hurry, smoked them over a buffalo-chip fire. (Bison-dung smoke gave meat a peppery flavor.) The result was *carne seco*, jerked beef.

Pretty soon, the *cibolero* branched out as an Indian-trader and became a *comanchero*. He loaded his ox-cart with trinkets, headed into the Staked

Plains, and bartered for the horses, mules and cattle the Comanches and Apaches had stolen from ranches in Old Mexico. In time, and often backed by American merchants, he enlarged his trading stock and volume of business. The Indians usually got the worst of the dicker. A good mule traded for a barrel of bad whisky, a pack horse for ten pounds of coffee, a buffalo robe for two-bits or less, and cattle for anything left in the cart. As a trader, the wily *comanchero* had it all over David Harum. So successful were these transactions that, at the end of the Civil War, a New Mexican confessed to Charles Goodnight that the loot from Texas stockmen had amounted to 300,000 cattle and 100,000 horses and mules.

The *comanchero*, in turn, led to the horseherders from the States who ventured on the plains from the 1790's on. Traders or outright thieves, they were almost equally esteemed. As far back as Colonial days well-known Easterners liked horseflesh of Western origin. Patrick Henry described in detail the kind of personal mount he wished a friend to bring from Indian tribes across the Mississippi. Legend has it that Daniel Boone was not above snitching Spanish horseflesh from the same source.

One notable character was Philip Nolan (not Edward Everett Hale's "Man Without a Country"), an ex-army officer who in 1795 raided the Indian country and appropriated 250 horses which he drove to Natchez. Later he obtained 1,000 head from San Antonio which he wintered at his Mississippi ranch. Again, in 1800, Nolan and twenty-five companions crossed the Mississippi, and at the Washita encountered half a hundred mounted Spaniards who were out looking for him. But when they saw the long rifles of the gringos they changed their minds and swore they were looking for Choctaw Indians.

Proceeding unmolested, Nolan's party found a lot of wild horses near the Brazos, which they impounded in a corral. But to Nolan's chagrin, a group of Comanches summoned him to a parley on the south fork of the Red River. Fearing treachery and not daring to go alone, Nolan took along his armed followers. By the time the gabfest was over, all the corralled horses had died of thirst. And not long after, when the party was attacked by Spaniards, Nolan took a musketball in the head and fell dead.

The superior quality of California horses made them attractive to Utah and New Mexico buyers, and there was a brisk market for them regardless of the source of supply. Among animals honestly gathered were those of Ewing Young who was in California in 1830 intending to trap beaver and to buy horses and mules. The mule project didn't pan out, but Young did drive 1,500 horses to Santa Fe.

In the fall of 1831 David Jackson and eleven men, each hired at $25 a month, headed west with seven mules loaded with Mexican silver dollars to pay for stock. The party reached San Diego in November. But Jackson's

"Jerked Down," by Charles Russell.

Courtesy of the Thomas Gilcrease Institute and Brown & Bigelow

advance agent had failed to collect any animals, although he had been ordered to pay up to eight pesos each for 1,000 broken mules three to eight years old. Jackson headed for San Francisco. Here he could obtain only 600 mules, not enough to pay for a long drive to Louisiana. They were driven east and sold in Santa Fe, along with 100 horses picked up on the trip.

The prize horse thief of early days was the notorious Peg-leg Smith, who got his nickname when, in a scrap with Indians, a bullet lodged in one of his knees. With no surgical instruments but a knife, a thong, and a hot iron, Peg-leg amputated his own limb. Thereafter, he stomped about on wood.

Once a traveler stopped at his horse camp. Asked where he got all the hundreds of well-bred Spanish horses, Smith replied that he had gotten them from California "at great personal expense." Because several of his Indian pals had been killed on the raid, he felt he had paid for all he had driven away. When asked how many head this foray had yielded, Peg-leg replied, "Only about 3,000, and the damned Spaniards got back almost half of them."

Smith's partners on this raid were Chief Walkara of the Yampa Utes, a big-headed, bandy-legged savage; half a dozen white men, and 150 other Indians. The famous mulatto guide Jim Beckworth had been sent ahead to spy out the land. When Smith and Walkara appeared at the Cajon Pass, the raiders were thoroughly briefed. As a result, every ranch from the Santa Ana River to San Juan Capistrano was looted. At San Luis Obispo 1,000 mares and half as many horses were stolen. In this operation, under cover of night, the thieves cut an opening into the corral. Under the noses of sleeping guards, the finest saddle horses were released and driven away. Completely stripped of horses, the red-faced *padres* were reduced to sending an Indian on foot for help. To avenge this wholesale thievery, posses were organized. The Los Angeles jail was emptied to form a cohort of prisoners.

The wily Peg-leg was equal to the occasion. He divided his band, one group hurrying ahead with the stolen animals, the smaller group hiding themselves and their mounts in the willows bordering a favorite watering place. When the thirsty sheriff and his men dismounted and threw themselves to the ground for a drink, the thieves quietly slipped out of the willows, mounted and drove off all the horses. The stranded party wasn't picked up until the next day, when the pursuit was continued. The job of getting away with 3,000 animals was slow going. Eventually the Californians, after a lively scuffle, succeeded in recovering 1,200 of the slower animals.

On May 7, 1853, three enterprising "State-of-Mainers"—Benjamin and Thomas Flint, and Llewellyn Bixby—headed a sheep drive from Keokuk, Iowa, with a Noah's ark assortment of 1,880 sheep, eleven yokes of oxen, four horses, two cows, two wagons, four helpers, and three dogs. On their way they were joined by a Mr. and Mrs. Johnson, newlyweds; the "Missus," a splendid cook, was especially welcome. Eight months later they arrived in

California, where the Flint-Bixby team sold 900 wethers for mutton at $16 each and went ranching with the rest.

Thomas Flint, a doctor, kept a diary in which he made daily entries summarizing expenses, distances, and hazardous incidents of the trail, which can be conveniently classified as: crossing streams, stampeding and straying, dry drives, poisonous weeds and water, footsore stock, and Indian hazards.

Rivers had to be crossed either by ferry, ford, or swimming. About a month after leaving Keokuk, a flat-boat propelled by oars took two days to carry the band across the Missouri at the rate of 150 sheep to a load. This cost $57. A previous crossing at the Mississippi had cost $62. As the party traveled west, toll charges mounted. At the Loup River in Nebraska they were $100. At the Green River in Wyoming Dr. Flint, protesting an intolerable charge, found a 200-foot crossing where by raising his wagon beds, he drove into the river, followed by a white wake of swimming woollies. At a crossing of the Virgin River in Utah, the men packed the sheep one at a time on their backs and spent an entire afternoon wading the 100-foot ford.

Early in the journey, the horses took fright and stampeded, bowling over several sheep and breaking a leg of one, which had to be killed for mutton. Three months later Flint reported the band "in a contrary mood and hard to guard." Just before Christmas, many wandered off and got mixed up with a nearby band being driven to California by Colonel W. W. Hollister. It took half a day's hard work to get 87 of the Hollister sheep and 175 of Flint's disentangled and restored to their proper bands. Incidentally, Hollister's arrival in California from Ohio coincided "neck and neck" with Flint's.

On December 3, both parties began to negotiate a 100-mile drive without water except halfway, at the meager Bitter Water Springs bordering the Nevada-California boundary. It took eleven days to cross this waterless stretch, where Flint, who had gone ahead, wrote: "I packed my horse with . . . provisions and started back to meet Ben and Llewell with the sheep. Met them some six miles out. They had used up all their water and food . . . some of the men . . . were beside themselves, imagining they would perish from thirst."

Poisonous plants were repeatedly mentioned during July, August and September: In the Black Hills, ten poisoned, four saved "by giving them lard"; between Independence Rock and the Sweetwater, seven killed by poison. On August 21, the band found itself surrounded by weeds which had already killed three sheep, and as many cows owned by fellow travelers. Here Flint notes: "Had a rattle with Indian dogs that were hungry for a feed of mutton." The July 1 entry read: "A great deal of alkali water in pools, injurious to sheep, lost three head on account of their drinking it."

In common with other drovers the Flint-Bixby party were solicited near Scottsbluff, Nebraska, by a half-blood Sioux who made money by pay-

ing $4 to $10 a head for footsore cattle and $1 for a sheep "if it is fat." At
American Fork, Mormons offered groceries and other supplies in exchange
for worn-out sheep.

A month out from Council Bluffs, in resisting an attempt by Omaha
Indians to steal the doctor's horse, James Force, a guard, was shot and
killed. At another time half a dozen Indians "bounced out of the brush and
commenced to pillage the wagons. The three teamsters were scared out of
their wits and offered no resistance; but Mrs. Johnson went after their hands
with a hatchet when they tried to help themselves to things in her wagon."

The rig of the cowboy as he began the saga-drives up from Texas at
the end of the Civil War was a cosmopolitan blend of New England, Georgia,
Tennessee and Ohio traditions plus the work tools of the vaquero and *comanchero* and a few Indian colors added for the cow-town swaggers. The trail
boss, the point, flank, swing and drag riders, chuck wagon and cook, the
horse wrangler and *remuda*—all were part of the routine, as carefully planned
and "engineered" as a modern streamliner schedule or DC-7 flight. Then, as
now, the inventors and their salesmen flocked to this new "consumer market"

"Cowboy Fun"—from the *Century Magazine*, February, 1888

as it developed. Hence the Stetson hat out of Philadelphia; the Colt out of Connecticut; the Yacht Brand lariat from Plymouth, Massachusetts, the Levis from San Francisco, the Fish Brand yellow slicker from Gloucester, Massachusetts, all, in time, became "standard cowboy equipment." Sheepherders and even turkey-drovers took up the costume.

When young Jimmy Cook hired out to Charlie Slaughter in the 1870's, this was his briefing from Joe Roberts, the trail boss: "They tell us you can catch a cow and can shoot a rabbit's eye out at every pop. Now, if you can ride for the next four months without a whole night's sleep, and turn your gun loose on any damned Injun that tries to get our horses, well, get ready. We roll out tomorrow."

Jimmy found that lack of sleep was almost as bad as the Comanche raiders or the summer thunderstorms that stampeded the cattle and often set the prairies afire. The cowboy's day would end about nine o'clock, when he grazed the herd to the bedground. Then every man in the outfit, except the boss, horse wrangler and cook, would have to stand two hours' night guard. If a man's guard was from midnight to 2 A.M., he would stake his night horse, pull off his boots and sleep from nine to midnight. Coming off guard, he would get another 90 minutes' sleep, until Cookie yelled "Roll out" at 3:30. Some cowmen rubbed tobacco juice in their eyes to keep awake.

The bed, when you did get the chance to "hit it," was the bare ground. "A Tucson-bed," Jimmy Cook explained, "is made by lying on your stomach and covering that with your back. It was allowable to put your saddle and saddle blanket over your head, as protection from any hailstones larger than hen's eggs."

This was the environment—the impact of land and animals and savagery —that reacted over a thirty-year period of an aggregation of carefree, gutty men from every walk of life and of every color, background and creed to produce the most appealing "hero" yet to emerge on the American scene. This was "the makings" of Will Rogers, Charles Russell, Andy Adams, Charlie Siringo, Colonel Goodnight and that whole array of Western immortals ... the companies of the big sky ... the source-stuff for thousands of movies, TV shows and books. No writer or statesman has ever given them a worthy epitaph. Colonel Henry C. Hooker, the Arizona cattleman, came close when he said:

"We take a man here and ask no questions. We know when he throws his saddle on a horse whether he understands his business or not. He may be a minister backslidin' or a banker savin' his last lung or a train robber on his vacation—we don't care. A good many of our most useful men have made their mistakes. All we care about now is, will they stand the gaff? Will they sit sixty hours in the saddle, holdin' a herd that's tryin' to stampede all the time."

You know the rules in a cowcamp when they have no regular cook? When anybody complains about the chuck, they have to do the cooking. One cowboy broke open a biscuit and he says "They are burnt on the bottom and top and raw in the middle and salty as hell, but shore fine. Just the way I like'm."

JOE M. EVANS– "A Corral Full of Stories"

RAMON F. ADAMS

Cookie

WITHOUT QUESTION he is the most important man in any ranch outfit. Men must be well fed to work efficiently, and this means that the food must be well prepared and cleanly cooked. No matter how plentiful the quantity, if poorly prepared by a dirty cook, it is reflected in the work and morale of the men. The old-time cowhand did not require fancy foods. He knew nothing of the highfalutin dishes seen upon Eastern menus. The "five pillars" of the cowman's food were: coffee, beans, meat, sourdoughs and his famous stew.

The wagon cook had to be self-reliant. He had to do things with the material at hand. There were no handy shopping centers such as the modern housewife depends upon. Accidents might happen to some item of food, giving the cook an opportunity to show his ingeniousness with substitutes. The city cook will wonder how it was possible to carry two months' provisions for a crew of men through the heat without refrigeration. Most of the wagon cook's supplies were of the dry variety, such as coffee, beans, baking powder, flour, rice, dried fruit, salt pork and canned foods. Such perishables as fresh vegetables and eggs were unknown at the chuck wagon.

The old-time range cook became a unique character, too, because he developed a universal reputation for crankiness. Perhaps this emanated from the fact that he worked under such adverse conditions. Battling wind, sand and rains with limited supplies and equipment, trying to prepare a meal within a limited time for a crowd of savage appetites, doubtless contributed to his ill temper.

Half the time he was short of fuel. Often it was wet. Some animal was perhaps kicking dust into the food. Everything seemingly contrived to test his temper. Eventually he just took pride in his reputation for crankiness, and did his best to live up to it. Not only did he enjoy the power which he had arrogated; now he had a reputation to uphold.

The supply of good cooks was always low, and the demand keen. Even in the early days his profession was sufficiently recognized to demand a standard wage scale. By reason of this higher pay and the fact that they were essential to the operation of the whole outfit, some cooks felt that they were above the common rider. The cowhand held the opposite view, though few of them had the courage to express such an opinion within the cook's hearing.

The range cook made his own rules of deportment and saw that they were obeyed. He was lord over the chuck wagon and its immediate surroundings. Woe be to him who invaded this royal realm without permission.

A good roundup cook could not follow strict rules such as laid down by modern cookbooks. Neither did he carry around measuring cups nor kitchen scales, and even at the ranch he had no benefit of electric timers, or oven thermostats. Experience taught him what dash of this to throw into a pot of that.

Neither were there any fancy garnishes for the cowman's food. He needed no such to tickle a jaded appetite. No one could accuse the cowboy of having an appetite which could be called dainty. A little dirt was to be expected from open-air cooking. At the ranch, if the cook was in a good humor, he might serve flapjacks for breakfast, and make a pie or pudding for the other meals. Most good cooks would make these latter at the wagon, too, in good weather.

How did the cowboy survive on such starchy foods as beans, bread, corn, potatoes, rice and occasional cake or pie? In spite of them, one rarely saw a fat cowboy. His work and hours in the saddle burned up a lot of energy. He needed these foods to furnish more. Most cowmen lived to a ripe old age and in years when life expectancy was much shorter than it is now. Whoever heard of a cowman with ulcers? Or with indigestion? Most of his troubles came from stiff joints and rheumatism from exposure to wet and cold, and from sleeping upon the damp ground. Life in the open and his simple foods were what kept him healthy.

One of the first requirements of a good outdoor cook was to learn to build a proper fire. This might be either of the open-pit or closed-pit variety. He used the open-pit fire to boil his coffee and broil, boil or fry his meat. When he baked or roasted he used the closed-pit fire. If he used a Dutch oven, he could do both these latter on an open-pit fire. This heavy iron skillet with deep-dished lid could accomplish wonders when properly preheated, then placed on hot embers with more embers placed on top of the lid. Control of an open fire in cooking came only with practice and long experience.

Most cooks prepared a shallow trench for the fire. The sides protected the fire from wind, keeping it from blowing embers over the camp site and ashes in the food. It made it possible, too, to build a deep bed of hot coals. The deeper the bed the longer it lasted. The fire had to be small. A large fire was hard to control, created too much heat for the cook to work near, and, of course, used too much wood where wood was often scarce. A small fire furnished heat in the proper place.

Most cooks would use nothing but hardwood, if it was possible to procure it. Hardwood burned longer, gave more heat and made better embers. Cookie was also somewhat careful to choose limbs of uniform size because these would reach the ember stage at nearly the same time. Large sticks mixed with the smaller ones would still be blazing after the smaller ones became embers suitable for cooking. Some cooks built a second fire close by and used it as an additional ember supply when needed.

On the trail between camps the cook kept his eyes open for limbs and dry sticks just in case his next camp happened to be devoid of wood. If enough of this material was close together, he halted his wagon and threw the wood into the possum-belly under the wagon bed. A cook working in a timberless country often had to resort to cow chips for fuel. He did not relish this, not because they produced an unpleasant odor, but because they burned out so fast that it kept him busy replenishing his fire.

Present-day suburbanites like hickory-smoked barbecue. It is stylish to build a barbecue pit in the back yard. The degree of smoke flavor depends upon the amount of smoke from the fire and how it is controlled, done sometimes with dampened chips of wood. Occasionally the cowman might like a bit of wood-smoked meat, though his was mostly mesquite and not hickory flavored. But on the whole he liked the taste of meat, not the taste of smoke. Therefore his meat was cooked over hot embers, not over flame.

One of the essentials in the cowman's bill-of-fare was coffee. It could be made in most anything from a tin bucket to a granite coffeepot. He wanted it every meal. The cook who kept the coffeepot on a bed of hot coals all during the day was held in high regard. It was almost essential when riding out, or coming in, before and after night guard.

Most range cooks prided themselves on their coffee. Cookie knew his charges wanted it strong and black. He used lots of coffee in proportion to the water, let it boil hard for a time and served it fresh. Just before it was ready, he added a pinch of salt and a dash of cold water to settle the grounds. He had no percolators. His recipe for making coffee suitable to drink was "take one pound of coffee, wet it good with water, boil it over a fire for thirty minutes, pitch in a horseshoe. If it sinks, put in more coffee." The cowman liked his coffee straight. He wanted no sugar, or cream-weakened concoction.

In spite of the fact that the cowhand drank quarts of this strong brew daily, no one ever heard of him spending a sleepless night.

One of the most famous foods of the range cook was perhaps his sour-doughs. If properly made one will never sink a tooth into better bread. Every cook strove to turn out the best. The cowboy preferred them to any other kind of bread.

In starting on the roundup, the cook got hold of the proper jar or keg for his sourdough starter. Into this keg he poured three or four quarts of flour, added a dash of salt and enough warm water to make a medium thick batter. Some cooks added sugar or molasses, or a quantity of boiled and mashed Irish potatoes, to hasten fermentation. The keg was then covered and placed in a warm place and allowed to ferment a day or two. The range cook had no yeast cakes.

This starter was a delicate mixture. If it got too hot or too cold it would die. The cook watched it closely and nursed it as a brood-hen would her chick. On cold nights he even took it to bed with him. The fermentation must never stop.

When he got ready to bake his bread, he poured into a large dishpan enough flour to fill the pan about two-thirds, scooped out the center, and into this poured the amount of moist starter he thought he'd need. He added a little salt and soda, dissolved in a little warm water. A small amount of lard or bacon grease was next. Some cooks added a little sugar to make a browner crust.

The dry flour was worked into this mixture from the edges, being careful that the soda and shortening blended thoroughly, until all became a soft pliable dough, firm enough to handle easily. The cook then drenched his work table with flour and kneaded the dough until mixed to the right texture.

During the time he had been doing this, he had a hot fire going to have plenty of red-hot coals burned down for the baking. Raking these into a compact bed, he put a generous amount of grease into his Dutch ovens and placed them on the beds of coals, the lids also receiving coals on top so that they, too, would be thoroughly heated.

With a roller, or beer bottle, some rolled their dough out about half an inch thick and cut their biscuit with a lid or can into which had been punched a hole for air. But more commonly the wagon cook simply pinched off pieces, rolled them in his hands and placed them in the greased Dutch oven. He turned this pinched-off dough so that each side received a coating of grease to prevent sticking. After performing this with each biscuit, he jammed each tightly against the other so that they would rise higher and be lighter.

When the ovens were full, they were set near the fire for about thirty minutes to allow the bread to rise. During this time the cook usually took the opportunity to add enough flour, salt and lukewarm water to replace the starter he had used from his keg. Let him forget this chore and he would soon be without bread. Sourdoughs should be served hot, therefore the cook learned just when to start his breadmaking. Sourdoughs are better when fewer coals are used at the bottom and plenty above so that the top crust will be brown and the center soft and tender.

No cook would start his wagon without a goodly supply of beans. Beans have always been the staple food of the West. The cowman was rather choosy, too, in the kind of bean he used. He did not care for the kidney bean, nor the navy. The pinto, or frijole, was the one high in his favor. The cowman knew nothing of proteins, minerals, and vitamins, but he did know the pinto had a flavor he liked, and that it furnished a food which satisfied his hunger and stuck to his ribs. The man higher up, too, knew that they were easy to carry, easy to keep without spoilage, easy to cook, took few cooking vessels, and were cheap to buy.

When the cook planned to cook beans, the first thing he did was to pour out the desired quantity from the sack and pick the gravel out of them. Then he washed them and put them to soak overnight. Next morning he drained off the water, covered them with more cold water and placed them on a slow fire. He then dropped in a quantity of dry salt pork cut into chunks or strips for seasoning. Water was never added. Salt was withheld until the beans were done since the early addition of minerals hardened beans. They were cooked at least five hours. A full day's cooking was better where the fire could be kept slow enough to cook them without mushing.

Living in the cattle country, it was natural that the cowman be a meat eater. It was about the only fresh food he saw. When he killed a beef, none was wasted. He had meat for breakfast, dinner and supper. He never tired of it. About the only meat he refused was mutton. The city man demands that his meat be "hung"—seasoned and refrigerated before using. The cowman liked his beef freshly killed.

The city man, too, can choose his cuts of beef at the butcher shop and get the choice cuts which suit him most. But when the cowman killed a beef all of it had to be eaten. He had to like it fried, boiled, broiled, stewed, or any other way. He had to eat meat from tongue to tail, from shoulder to hoof, from inside and out, any that is edible.

Broiled steaks were not considered good by the cowboy, because the juices and flavor were lost. He liked his steaks fried and never tired of them. If steaks were to be served, the cook sliced off a sufficient number of medium thick ones and cut them into generous slabs. After pounding with a cleaver or heavy butcher knife to tenderize them, he cut a quantity of the suet trimmings into small pieces, and put a handful into the Dutch ovens he had heating on the coals. Steaks were much better fried in the fat suet of the beef itself. When this suet had melted and the oven was covered to a depth of an inch or so in grease, the cracklins were fished out. The steaks were then salted, rolled in flour, dropped into sizzling fat and the lid placed on.

Because there was no refrigeration on the range, the killing was done in the late afternoon and the meat hung up to be chilled by the cool night air characteristic of the high plains. Early the next morning it was wrapped in tarps, or slickers, and placed in the wagon bed. There it was covered with bedrolls so that it would hold its temperature and be kept from the day's heat. The nightly cooling would be repeated as long as the carcass lasted.

About the most famous, as well as the most unusual, dish of the range cook was his "son-of-a-bitch stew." No one seems to know who originated this widely known yet mysterious concoction. The origin of the name is as mysterious and uncertain as the genesis of the stew itself.

There are as many ways of cooking this stew as there are cooks. Many arguments have developed as to its preparation. Though perhaps no two cooks make it exactly alike, each doubtless thinks his way the best.

The one ingredient which gave this stew its bad name among the uninitiated was the word "marrow gut." This is not "gut" at all, but a long tube connecting the two stomachs of young cud-chewing animals. It is good only when the calf is still nursing, being then tender and full of a substance which resembles marrow. Hence the name. Through this, the partially digested milk passes. This is why calves not completely weaned are selected for this stew. The marrowlike substance is left in when cooking the stew and is what gives it its delightful flavor.

I could give you at least a dozen recipes for this dish, if I had the space. Each would be a little different. Where one would use kidneys, another would not. One liked using the spleen, another preferred leaving it out. Some liked onions, others a dash of chili pepper. Here is a sample recipe:

½ the heart
½ the spleen
¼ the liver
All the tongue
All the sweetbreads
Marrow gut (about 3 feet)

All the butcher's steak (the strips of lean meat on the inner side of the ribs), or an equal amount of tenderloin,
2 cups of melted leaf fat
One set of brains

After the calf was killed and while the meat was still warm, the heart, liver, tongue, marrow gut, some pieces of tenderloin, or butcher's steak, sweetbreads and the brains were taken to be prepared. The cook cut the fat into small chunks, put them into the pot. While this fat was being melted he cut the heart into small cubes, adding it first because it was tougher. The tongue was also skinned and cubed, then added, thus giving the two toughest ingredients longer cooking time. While these were cooking, the cook cut the tenderloin, sweetbreads and liver into similar pieces, using the liver sparingly so as not to make the stew bitter. To all this was added the marrow gut after being cut into rings, or inch long pieces. Cover all this with lukewarm water, adding more from time to time.

The ingredients were added slowly, a handful at a time, the whole being slowly stirred after each addition. During this time the brains were cleaned of blood and membranes, then cooked separately, some cooks adding a little flour to make them thicker. When they became beady they were added to the stew, this being the last ingredient added except salt and pepper to taste, or a little onion if desired.

Thus coffee, sourdoughs, beans, meat and this famous stew formed the "five pillars" of the cowman's food. Cookie might serve such canned foods as corn and tomatoes, cook rice for his "spotted pup," i.e., rice cooked with raisins, or, if he was in a good humor and had the time, he might bake a pie of the dried peach or apple variety. A good boss saw to it that the food was of sufficient quantity, no matter how scant the variety, and did his best to find a good cook, who was clean and efficient enough to keep his hands happy and working. It was a good investment.

From Owen Wister's *The Virginian*, Macmillan Company, 1911

For some must push and some must pull,
As we go marching up the hill,
So merrily on our way we go,
Until we reach the Valley, O.

"The Handcart Song"

RICHARD L. EVANS and KENNETH S. BENNION

The Mormons

JUNE 30, 1847, WAS JUST ANOTHER DAY on the long trek from the Missouri River to "somewhere in the Rocky Mountains." The wagon train bumped through the sagebrush, stirring up a long line of choking white dust. Scouts galloped back to the lead wagon to report a large river ahead. There was a good crossing but wagons would have to be floated. More delay!

Still, those first Mormon pioneers had made many such crossings. They had learned by costly experience just how much timber to tie alongside, and just where to place it so the wagons would not roll over. So the vanguard of many thousands of Mormon pioneers rolled down the Green River's slope in western Wyoming.

If Brigham Young had felt less sure about his destination—and his destiny—he might have been more troubled in his heart. Not about the river ahead. That meant only a few hours' delay. But only a day or so ago he had met and talked with Jim Bridger, famous mountain man. Bridger had shaken his head when he learned that President Young planned to lead 3,000 people this summer—and more next year and the next—to settle in the vicinity of the Great Salt Lake. The land there, Bridger thought, wouldn't support so many people. The seasons were short. Crops wouldn't mature. Tradition has it that Bridger offered $1,000 for the first ear of corn that ripened there.

The trail from the Missouri River had been long—months long, with hardship every mile of the way. How would his people live, in the hard valleys ahead? Still, his file leader, Joseph Smith, had prophesied that persecutions would continue and that his people would be driven to the Far West, where they would make settlements, build cities, and "become a mighty people in the midst of the Rocky Mountains."

89

Besides, Brigham Young had, himself, seen in vision the valley where he and his followers were to settle. Surely the Lord God who led ancient Israel safely through the Red Sea and the wilderness of Sinai would also guide these believers, like a modern Israel, to "the place which God prepared, far away in the West."

As the wagon train rocked down to the river, three riders hullooed from the west shore. They swam their horses across, and were conducted to Brigham Young's wagon. One of them was Sam Brannan. The history of the West hung on the interview that followed.

Sam Brannan, a colorful, fabulous character, had, the year before, in 1846, taken a shipload of 235 Mormon colonists from New York City southward around Cape Horn and up the west coast to California, to the harbor of Yerba Buena, now San Francisco. He had established the first English newspaper, the *California Star*, and had brought several copies with him, telling of the opportunities in that area. It was a glowing picture of rich, lush country. The Rocky Mountain valleys and deserts would call for hardship, sacrifice, and long years of labor. California seemed to offer everything.

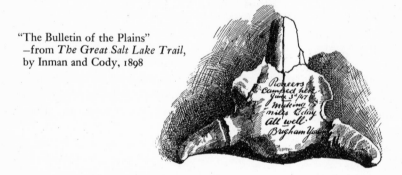

"The Bulletin of the Plains"
—from *The Great Salt Lake Trail*,
by Inman and Cody, 1898

But there stood Joseph Smith's prophecy—"a mighty people in the midst of the Rocky Mountains"—as well as Brigham Young's own vision of a wide valley somewhere in the mountains. Perhaps in the rapidly growing population of California the people would lose their identity. They might even forget the very principles for which they had sacrificed so much. Perhaps, facing the stern struggle for existence in the wilderness valleys ahead, they would be led astray. Quickly but firmly the decision was made. The Mormons would stay in the mountains.

Sam Brannan rode back to California. Most of those who remained with him were swallowed up in the rapidly expanding population, especially in the gold-hunting madness that swept the land a year or so later. Brannan himself had a meteoric—and erratic—career which took him to great heights of wealth and power, and then down through poverty to drunkenness and death. He once owned about one-fourth of Sacramento, one-fifth of San Francisco, and a hundred twenty thousand acres in Los Angeles County—but he forgot the things that mattered most, and died a broken man.

Not many days later, on July 24, 1847, after struggling over "Big Mountain," and "Little Mountain" and down "Emigration" canyon, the wagons came at last to the foothills of a wide valley. Ill with "mountain fever," Brigham Young asked the driver to turn his wagon aside on a rise of ground, so that he could see. Long and carefully he studied the wilderness before him—a wide, open valley, marked here and there by lines of trees, indicating water courses; another range of mountains to the west and southwest; and the shining waters of the Great Salt Lake to the west and northwest. Then he lay back on his bed, saying: "This is the place; drive on."

Down in the valley, some three miles farther, quite undramatically, wheels jolted to a stop, and the long journey was over. Horses were unhitched, plows were pulled out of the wagon. Several acres were plowed and planted to potatoes—though it was already midsummer. The ground was so hard and dry that two or three plows were broken. So a dam was built in the stream nearby, and the water turned out on the land. Such was the beginning of community irrigation in modern western America. The potatoes did not fully mature but they produced a bounteous seed crop for planting the following spring.

Teams went to the mountains for logs and firewood. Winter was coming, more wagon trains were on their way. People must have shelter from the cold and protection from roving bands of Indians. A ten-acre square was laid out and a fort built of logs and mud with room enough for a wagon train to drive in. Inside, with roofs sloping inward, a series of rooms was built for families. Cattle, horses and sheep were herded out on the hills, away from the growing city. The first winter was mild and open, and stock wintered well. Teams continued to plow and clear the land; by snowfall 5,000 acres were ready for spring planting.

Having made their first settlement in the valley of the Great Salt Lake, from here, in the years to follow, the pioneers moved out to make settlements in what is now Utah, Arizona, Idaho, New Mexico, Nevada, western Colorado, western Wyoming, Oregon, and southern California (and even into old Mexico). Over this whole vast inland empire, many first community beginnings were made by the Mormons. (Los Angeles, today, is perhaps the second largest Mormon city, with a six-million-dollar Mormon temple completed there in 1956.)

Who were these people, and why were they here? For answer we must go back to the "beginning."

The "Mormon" Church—officially known as the Church of Jesus Christ of Latter-day Saints—was organized on April 6, 1830, in Fayette, Seneca

County, New York, by Joseph Smith, a Vermonter, and five associates who believed and testified that it was "a restoration" of the original church of Jesus Christ established "in the Meridian of Time by the Saviour Himself," but that the authority and form and function of His Church had been lost through the centuries by practices of apostasy.

At about this time also, in 1829, Joseph Smith translated the writings on certain ancient gold plates which, he declared, had been deposited in the Hill Cumorah near Palmyra, New York. On them was engraved a record of some of the ancestors of the American Indians, who had come to the Western Hemisphere centuries before the birth of Christ, and were of Israelitish origin. The part of this record that was published was called the *Book of Mormon*. (It was to the inhabitants of ancient America what the Bible was to the people of ancient Israel—a sacred and secular history of prophets and peoples.)

Joseph Smith's declaration that the heavens had been opened again, that the Lord God still spoke to his children, and that He had actually made men "in his own image" proved to be very unpopular with established religions of the day. Much persecution was directed against him and his followers. This persecution became so bitter that the "Mormons," or "Saints," as they were commonly called, moved from New York westward to Kirtland, Ohio, where they built their first temple. Persecution continued, however. They moved southwestward into Missouri. But here, on the rough-and-ready frontier, where the law was loose, and where there was conflict of political and other interests, they met even more violent opposition, with whippings, burnings and loss of property, and some brutal loss of life.

Then they moved eastward into Illinois, where for a time, they found a degree of peace. Having acquired title to the townsite of Commerce, on the east bank of the Mississippi River, they drained the swamps and built Nauvoo, the "City Beautiful." (It had a population of some 20,000 and was then said to be the largest city in Illinois.) A new temple was begun, and the industrious people were beginning to prosper and grow strong.

Then persecution again—and the situation grew swiftly worse, reaching its climax when Joseph Smith and his brother Hyrum, under the promised protection of the governor of the State, were murdered by an armed mob, at Carthage Jail, June 27, 1844.

Many thought that would be the end of the Mormons. But it was not a movement founded on a man. The "mantle of Joseph" rested upon a young man already high in the councils of the church, Brigham Young, senior member of the Quorum of the Twelve Apostles. His qualities of leadership rallied the scattered, driven, and perplexed people. Under his leadership, the Nauvoo Temple was completed, and used for a time.

But as persecution continued, it became evident that going to the Far

West was the only answer, as the Prophet Joseph had predicted.

Even so, they had hoped to stay in Nauvoo, the beautiful city they had built, until a favorable time for travel. But the mob forced them to flee, many of them in winter weather. So cold was it that one wagon train crossed the Mississippi River on the ice, in February, 1846. And the night the first company camped on the Iowa shore, nine babies were born—within sight of the warm, comfortable homes they had left across the river. Of these events Eliza R. Snow wrote:

"As we journeyed onward, mothers gave birth to offspring under almost every variety of circumstances imaginable except those to which they had been accustomed; some in tents, others in wagons—in rainstorms and in snowstorms. . . . Let it be remembered that the mothers of these wilderness-born babies were not savages, accustomed to roam the forest and brave the storm and tempest—those who had never known the comforts and delicacies of civilization and refinement . . . most of them were born and educated in the Eastern States—had there embraced the Gospel as taught by Jesus and his apostles, and, for the sake of their religion, had gathered with the Saints and under trying circumstances had assisted . . . in making Nauvoo what its name indicates: "the beautiful." They had lovely homes, decorated with flowers

Mormon immigrants, too poor to buy oxen and wagons, crossed the plains in 1856 with hand carts. Picture from *Marvels of the New West*, by W. M. Thayer, 1887

and enriched with choice fruit trees, just beginning to yield plentifully. To these homes, without lease or sale, they had just bade a final adieu, and with what little of their substance could be packed . . . had started out, desertward, for—where? To this question the only response at that time was: God knows."

The epic journey across Iowa, as winter turned to spring and the frost went out of the ground, leaving boggy waterways instead of roads, is a story for another book. But what those Mormon pioneers did to safeguard the welfare of the thousands who were to follow, was a foreshadowing of what they would do when they reached the "Valleys of the Mountains." They plowed, planted, and fenced choice spots along the way, and left men and teams to care for the crops. They built log and sod cabins, corrals, and repair shops. Thus, when others followed, relief stations were ready.

At Winter Quarters, across the Missouri River from Omaha, a semi-permanent settlement was made. Another winter was approaching. Persecution was left behind, but problems of stark necessity and survival were upon them. Sickness and death visited the camp during the winter of 1846. Many hundreds were buried on the eastern bank of the Missouri. But schools were established, and religious services held. A large council house was built where the leaders held meetings and perfected plans for the journey to the mountains. And despite sickness and privation, there was music and dancing. One of the pioneers, William Clayton, a British convert of a distinguished family, wrote the words of a new song and set his words to an old English tune. It became the marching song of the Mormon pioneers. Here is a verse they especially loved:

> "We'll find the place which God for us prepared,
>   Far away in the West,
>   Where none shall come to hurt or make afraid;
>   There the Saints will be blessed.
>   We'll make the air with music ring,
>   Shout praises to our God and King;
>   Above the rest each tongue will tell,
>   All is well! All is well!"

In the early summer of 1846, there came into the Mormon camps in Iowa Captain James Allen, bringing "greetings" from Colonel S. W. Kearny of the United States Army. The United States was at war with Mexico. Five hundred men were wanted, to form a Mormon Battalion, and to march southwestward to Santa Fe, into what was then Mexican territory, then westward to the Pacific.

The Mormons were fleeing as refugees from mobs against which the government did not protect them. Besides, every able-bodied man was urgently needed for the long trek ahead. Yet there was no hesitation. Brigham Young promised the men; 500 recruits were almost immediately sworn in. On the long march through the deserts of the Southwest, they won for themselves and their people much honor. Their wages, $7 a month plus equipment, proved to be a great blessing to the pioneers. On the day of the arrival of the Mormon Battalion at the mission of San Diego, January 30, 1847, Lieutenant Colonel P. St. George Cooke wrote of them: "History may be searched in vain for an equal march of infantry."

Some of the returning battalion men reached Salt Lake Valley from California only five days after Brigham Young's wagon train, in July, 1847. Other members of the battalion participated in the gold discovery at Sutter's Mill, near Sacramento, January 24, 1848.

During the remaining months of the summer of 1847, more than three thousand people entered the valley; thousands more were camped at Winter Quarters; others were leaving the eastern states and Europe for the long overland trip to the Great Basin. As Jim Bridger had warned, the valleys around the Great Salt Lake could not support so great a company.

Here came into full play the qualities of Brigham Young, the colonizer. Scouting parties went south, north, east and west to look for three essentials: land for farming, water for irrigation, and timber for building. Wherever they found these, they reported back to their headquarters.

And Brigham Young knew his people! He traveled over the valley, noting the men who were making good homes and successful farms. He observed where there was a good blacksmith, or a man who could build sawmills or gristmills, or one who could handle livestock successfully. Then, when word came of a new site for settlement, he would call ten or twenty or more families to go on a "mission" to settle it.

Sometimes there was trouble with the Indians—serious trouble. Some new settlements had to be abandoned for a time. In general, however, Indians and the Mormons got along fairly well. Since the *Book of Mormon* designates the Indians as a branch of the House of Israel, the Mormons looked upon them with considerable sympathy and forbearance. Furthermore, Brigham Young's own philosophy was, "It is better to feed them than to fight them."

Colonists had been called to help settle Eagleville, in the Muddy River country in southern Nevada, where there was sufficient water rising in an old river bed to make farms and gardens. For a few months this new community flourished, until a band of Paiutes made camp directly across the wash from the settlement. It was known that some in this band had taken active part in the massacre of an immigrant train bound for California. Word came from the presiding officer of the pioneers, farther down the river, that the new settlers must get out at once—leaving livestock, tents, everything.

But the settlers did not like the idea of giving up their horses and cattle, now grazing in the nearby hills. So their leader walked across to the Indian camp, and told the Indian chief that the settlers had to leave and go back to their other town. He asked the Indians to send twenty men in the morning to help round up the cattle and horses.

The chief looked very dark and stern. But next morning, twenty braves were at the Mormon tents. The pioneer women had prepared lunches. The Indians were paired with twenty white men and boys. By three o'clock the forty men and boys and Indians were back in camp with all the livestock.

In the meantime, other men had loaded the wagons. Not everything could be taken. One settler who had built a rock cabin, with a strong lock on the door, piled his excess baggage in it and locked the door. The leader, who had only a tent, called the Indian chief to him and said, "I leave my stuff here. Someday I come back for it. This is my garden. You take everything you want. You water and take care of it. It is yours."

Months later he returned, and found that the locked door of the rock cabin had been broken down and everything taken. But his own tent was in good order, and even the garden stuff had been harvested and placed in it. The Indians urged him to live with them and be their leader.

Some 80,000 Mormon pioneers crossed the plains and mountains into the valleys of the Great Basin before the railroads came. Over 6,000 of them lost their lives and lie buried along the way. Today more than 1,500,000 of their descendants live in the communities laid out by Brigham Young and his lieutenants, brave builders of the West. Their belief that "the Glory of God is Intelligence" has produced some of the most fertile farms of the Far West, built huge livestock, fruit, sugar and mining industries and created a self-help welfare system that enables them to provide for their needy members wherever they live.

Temple Square in Salt Lake City is one of the most visited ten acres in the world. Here recitals are given each day on the world-famed Tabernacle Organ and from here the Tabernacle Choir has been heard each week with "Music and the Spoken Word" for more than twenty-five years on nationwide radio networks. This is Mormon Country . . . land of the vision. Anyone who hasn't seen it and felt its pulse has missed a significant part of what makes America.

"Mormon Gold Coin"—from *Harper's New Monthly*, April, 1853

WALTER HAVIGHURST

The Sodbusters

THE RAILROAD BOOK SAID: "The traveler beholds, stretching away to the distant horizon, a flowering meadow of great fertility, clothed in grasses and watered by numerous streams, the margins of which are skirted by timber." But when the wagon halted on that March day in 1871 the plain lay bleak and somber under a darkening sky. It looked like the end of the world.

After their place had burned in Spencer County, Indiana, Matt Hawkinson put his family on the train and headed for homestead country. On the way the kids picked up a song, "Uncle Sam is rich enough to give us all a farm," and sometimes Matt heard his wife humming it above the rumble of the rails. At Grand Island, halfway across Nebraska, he bought a bull team and a wagon. They loaded in their gear and started for the claim on Willow Creek, sixty miles across the snow-patched prairie. Nobody sang the night they got there. When the supper fire winked out, the wind brought the quavering of coyotes.

Morning sunlight showed the land dipping and swelling to the wind-streaked sky, pale with old snow in the draws and washed with a new green on the ridges. The oxen grazed on the creek bank. Mary was kindling a breakfast fire while young Tom and Hildy ran over the prairie gathering buffalo chips. The wind came fresh, smelling of grass and distance. Not a barrier anywhere—not a road, not a fence, not a house; nothing but space, freedom, wilderness. It was like the beginning of the world.

From the surveyors' mound, Matt paced off the 160 acres that would be his farm. The ground was alive and yielding under foot. For ten thousand years the grass had grown there—gray bunchy buffalo grass, pale jointed grama grass, tawny bluestem, knee-high under the creek bank, horse-high

97

in the hollows. Matt knelt at his far corner and dug in with a knife blade. Under the grass the soil lay black and fine as gunpowder.

Why, he told his wife over the breakfast porridge, it took his grand-father thirty years to clear forty acres in Indiana. And here was a whole county, a whole country, ready for the plow.

The oxen leaned into their harness, the trace chains tightened. Matt tilted the plow and bit in. With a tearing sound the first furrow curled over. In the hollows where wiry switch grass tangled with rank bluestem it would take three teams to open the stubborn sod. Now he stayed on the ridge, running his furrows regular and true. He wanted an even sod, three inches thick, eighteen across. He was plowing up a house as well as a farm.

"Yeah," said the loan agents, "the government bets a hundred and sixty acres they can't live on it six months." Over the prairie, restless as tumble-weeds, had moved the buffalo, the Indians, the hide hunters, the cattlemen. But the sodbuster was different. He took the bet and dug in. He came to stay.

The easiest shelter was a dugout in a side hill, a cave with a sod-walled entrance and a sod front roof. A hole in the ground, Matt's wife said. All homestead women disliked dugouts, though hundreds of bachelors were holed up on the prairies. On the way from Grand Island the Hawkinsons had stopped for fresh water at a dugout on Blue Creek. A sleepy Swede came out, blinking, with grass stems in his hair.

Ya, he told them in singsong broken English, he had water, he had running water in his house. He had dug himself a deep room and he didn't know there was a spring until it bubbled through his back wall. Now the water ran in a ditch across his floor. He might have to move though he liked it here, snug and cozy under the wind.

When they rocked away, Mary Hawkinson said a dugout would darken a child's life and deaden a man's ambition. (In that year, 1871, Silas Garber was living in a dugout across the Platte River; three years later he was Governor of Nebraska.) Besides it was bound to be muddy in wet weather, and wandering cattle might step through the roof.

So Matt built a sod house, four thick walls rising on the prairie. With a spade he cut the sod furrows into three-foot lengths. Then it was like laying bricks—pile up the sod, chink the joints with earth, leave openings for a door and a window. Roof poles came from the willows a few miles up the creek. A layer of grass on the crisscrossed poles, a layer of sod on top, and it was done. Later he would get a door and window and his wife would cover the shaggy walls with sheets of newspaper.

This was the little old sod shanty on the claim, cool in summer, warm in winter, windproof, fireproof, but pervious to water. The homesteader's song described it—

"My house is constructed of natural soil,
The walls are erected according to Hoyle;
The roof has no pitch but is level and plain,
And I never get wet till it happens to rain."

Under a sod roof you got wet long after the rain was over. Saturated soil would drip for days. Sometimes a sodbuster's wife held an umbrella over the stove while she turned the pancakes.

Outside on the radiant spring prairie, Matt turned more furrows and chopped into them with an ax. Young Tom followed, dropping corn into each cut and stepping it into the damp earth. A year of wind and weather would soften the field for cultivation. But the first crop was sod corn, growing in the matted grass roots.

In that wide, wild, windswept prairie every feature was precious and significant, like a personal possession. A boulder jutting from the blowing grass was noted for miles around. A prairie-dog town where the gophers crouched at their burrows was worth a long walk on a Sunday afternoon. There were golden hollows scattered over the prairie, grassy bowls where the buffalo had wallowed, now covered with a bright tangle of pea vines and coreopsis.

Where the hide hunters had camped, piles of buffalo bones lay white in the sun. They were the sodbuster's first crop. With the children helping, Matt loaded his wagon; then he creaked off, alone, on the long trip to town. He traded that load of bones for a door, a window, a barrel of provisions and three joints of stovepipe. The bones went on to the fertilizer plant at Omaha.

Before the summer was over, neighbors came to the Willow Creek prairie. Straddle-bugs stood in the rank grass—three boards nailed in a flimsy pyramid to mark another claim. New soddies grew up on the ridge, with new breakings beside them. Those little fields, lost in the blowing grassland, were the beginning of a changed country. Soon roads would mark the long section lines, settlements would grow at the township corners, wheat and corn would ripple in the wind. Matt pictured the grain carpeting that high prairie. Wheatridge, he called it in his mind, seeing the fields of the future.

The first white men to see the homestead country were explorers—Lieutenant Zebulon Pike crossing the plains of Kansas, and Major Stephen Long leading his party to the headwaters of the Platte. Both men left their names on the front range of the Rockies, and they left another name, GREAT AMERICAN DESERT, on the treeless plains. Reported Major Long: "It is a region destined . . . to be the abode of perpetual desolation." For thirty years that gaunt name filled the map between the Missouri and the mountains. But when Texas cattle were driven north to the Kansas railroad they flourished, even in winter, on the short gray buffalo grass. The Kansas-Nebraska Act opened the territory in 1854, and settlers edged in. Claiming government land at $1.25 an acre, they pre-empted the wooded river valleys beyond the Missouri.

In 1862 President Lincoln signed the Homestead Act, and the dream of free land became reality. In December of 1862 Daniel Freeman, a Union soldier on leave from his regiment, took a look at the public lands and went into Nebraska City. The town swarmed with land-seekers, but they allowed Freeman first filing. On New Year's midnight the land office was opened, the first homestead was claimed. That quarter section was made a national monument in 1936, long after the Great American Desert had become the nation's breadbasket.

The old prairie trails ran north and south—the buffalo trails, the hunting trails, the long trails of the cattlemen. East and west ran the new trails of the emigrants. In the 1850's the great bend of the Missouri was lined with outfitting towns—acres of tents and wagons spread along the river and caravans creaking off for Oregon, California, Utah, Colorado. After the Civil War came the iron trail under its thin line of telegraph poles. The Union Pacific reached across the plains in 1867. For twenty years it brought the sodbusters, from half the states of the Union and half the countries of Europe, lured by the promise of free land.

"The winters," the railroad book said, "are short, dry and invigorating." Easter morning, 1873, the thirteenth of April, dawned mild and clear, over a prairie green with spring. But at noon the sky darkened. The wind came, cold and loud, and the green earth was lost in a blinding whiteness. That blizzard raged for three days and nights. One homesteader blundered into a neighbor's dugout, nine feet by ten, where he found a family of four and also a calf, a cow, and a team of horses; they all stayed there while the wind howled and snow drifted over.

From a sod house a woman struggled out to feed her hens; five days later she was found, frozen rigid, a hundred feet from her door. All over the prairie people huddled around their stoves, feeding the fire with twists of hay and sticks broken from their scanty furniture. When the snow melted, the draws were strewn with dead horses and cattle.

That summer, while the fields grew lush in the sun, the first barbed wire came to the plains. Now a farmer could fence out the range cattle. He could drill a well and raise a windmill, harnessing the everlasting wind. Sodbusters!—the cattlemen hated them more than ever.

"Bob-wire" was a boon to the Western farmer, but it could not fence out calamity. On a cloudless July day in 1874 the Hawkinson family sat down to dinner. When the sunlight dimmed, Matt went to the door. A vague cloud was thickening in the west—no, not a cloud, it spread too far and moved too fast. Then came the whirring of billions of tiny wings.

Grasshoppers. In a minute the wheat was black with them. The corn-field, the garden, every green and growing thing was covered by that creeping curtain. With sticks and staves the family beat at the living ground. Then breathless and tormented, scraping the insects from their arms and faces, they ran into the house. The dinner table was crawling with grass-hoppers.

There had been other invasions, but this, in 1874, was the worst. From the Arkansas to Canada, grasshoppers covered the farms in a devouring carpet. Roads were blocked and rivers were black with them. At Kearney, Nebraska, a train on the Union Pacific was stalled by a three-foot drift of grasshoppers. They ate curtains from farm windows, canvas off covered wagons, harness on the stable walls. In their Agency lands, the Indians made a grasshopper mash and stolidly ate it, while the whites were eaten out.

After two breathless, disastrous weeks, a wind came up. The whole pestilence rose in the summer air, leaving a ravaged prairie. Slowly Matt Hawkinson walked over his land. The garden lay bare as winter, the wheat was chewed to a ragged stubble, a ruin of bare and broken stalks was his cornfield. Silently he began a late planting of potatoes and corn.

Luckily it was a late fall that year, a long hazed fall with the prairies burning under the high October sky. In all the sloughs and swales settlers set fire to the rank grass where grasshoppers had left their eggs.

That winter many sod huts stood empty. Hundreds of homesteaders had lost the bet, packed the wagon, and gone back to a kinder country. Matt Hawkinson drove to Grand Island, borrowed money at the land bank and bought lumber for a new house. When the lumber was loaded he went to the land office and filed on the quarter section beyond his wheat field. By plant-ing ten acres of box elder trees he could claim 160 acres under the Timber Culture Act.

Back at home, he had news for his neighbors. The railroad men were talking about a branch line to Willow Creek.

Where the old maps read "Great American Desert," new names spattered the prairie country of the 1890's. Ohiowa was settled by homesteaders from Ohio and Iowa; Viborg, Volga, Gothenburg, by Old World immigrants. Broken Bow, Loup City, Red Cloud, Weeping Water, kept the Indian names after the Indians were forgotten. In a western Nebraska settlement people prayed for the end of drought; the preacher, who was also the post-master, named their village—Rain.

Wheatridge on the rise beyond Willow Creek kept the name Matt Hawkinson gave his first ten-acre breaking. By 1895 it was a settled, ordered town, with wagons creaking in to the elevator and ponies, showing the old range brands, tied to the Main Street hitching racks.

Like a thousand other prairie towns Wheatridge could be seen a long way off. Across the long plain rose a square dark tower, the Farmers' Mutual elevator. From its cupola the town lay like a handful of blocks dropped on the checkered farm land.

On a cold and windy morning in December, 1895, Tom Hawkinson sat in the office of the Wheatridge elevator. Another dry year, half a wheat crop in the county and less than half a crop of corn. Tom had gone to work in the elevator because there wasn't enough corn to keep him busy during husking time. But elevator business was slow too. He damped off the stove, pulled on his coat and mittens, and went for the mail.

He was a man of thirty, and the town was half as old. He remembered when Enoch Strong had opened a store at the crossroads, and Emil Dutcher unloaded a forge and anvil above Willow Creek. When the railroad came across the prairie the first station was a plank laid down in the mud. The first circuit preacher held services in a shed that was a dance hall on Saturday nights. Now Wheatridge had a red railway depot, two churches, a school, a two-story hotel, a lumberyard, a cattle pen and a livery stable. It had the biggest elevator in the county—too big for this dry season.

Back from the post office, he found a wagon on the weighing platform and his father and old Sven Carlson rubbing their hands above the stove. Wind-burned men with shrewd eyes and stubborn faces, they wore the mark of the wild country they had changed.

They were talking, as usual, about old times—before the railroad, before the town, when wild grass rippled in the wind and the road ran like a lariat over the empty prairie. While Tom opened his mail they went on talking—about the good fat years of the eighties and the lean years now. The rain would come again, it had to. Next year, or the next.

Tom had pulled a book out of a wrapper, a railroad book describing homestead lands in the far Northwest. "Sheltered by mountains and richly watered by their streams . . . regular rainfall and a long growing season . . . will yield abundantly, as soon as the sod is broken."

He was on his feet then, pacing the narrow room. Old Matt looked at the open book with its picture of a far green valley under the Idaho mountains, and he looked up at his son. What he saw was a wagon halting in a wild land, a land that was like the end, or the beginning, of the world.

From the *Century Magazine*, volume v

Old cowboys claim they knew for shore
If a nester was married or not,
By the way he hung the cabin door
On his little ol' homestead plot.

If the doors swung in, without a doubt,
He was free from wedded worry.
But a married man swung his door out,
So he always could leave in a hurry!

S. OMAR BARKER

ALICE MARRIOTT

The Ladies

LANTERN-JAWED THEY MIGHT BE, strong-jawed they were sure to be. Some of them, like Susan Magoffin and Elizabeth Custer, went with officer husbands posted to frontier forts. Others rode and walked west because husbands or fathers had decided to shift the base of family operations, and take up land in the new country. Still others were impelled by the missionary spirit. They were wives of preachers or teachers who traveled westward to lighten the heathen darkness of Indians and whites. And there were, inevitably, the drifters and camp followers along the rivers, railroads, and cattle trails.

Some were women of taste, education and background. Others were illiterates, who found life in a dugout on the plains no worse than life in a shanty in the Georgia pine woods. There were all shades and variations of womankind ranged between these two extremes. Some fought to maintain their accustomed standards of living; some abandoned all conventional standards; some discovered standards of life and behavior for the first time. But each one brought and kept some treasures.

One of the great lost statistics of history is the number of pianos that were taken from east to west between 1846 and 1896. It would be significant to know how many pianos went west in that half-century, how far they traveled, and how they were transported. Not the oaken "dressers" that sank into western quicksands, not the sets of Haviland china abandoned beside the trails, or the silver services buried, and never dug up, when the going got too heavy across Nebraska, not even the rocking chairs or cast-iron pots or shoots of bushes from home dooryards that reached journeys' endings. Just the pianos.

Because, somehow, by main strength and awkwardness, pianos were delivered to the most unlikely places. Four Dakota sisters, in the seventies, had a rosewood concert grand in the parlor of their home. Their father, a pioneer merchant of the town, saw to it that the girls got lessons—and practiced, too.

He was a Frenchman, that father. He got himself from Paris to Dakota, without one word of comprehensible English, right after the Civil War. Since he cooked his way across the country, I suspect that he attached himself to an army colonel or brigadier general, and got to Dakota—there was only one Dakota then—in a military wagon train.

Later he opened a general store, and throve and prospered. He acquired an Alsatian wife, too. His daughters are a little hazy, at this late date, about how Mama got west. But she spoke French of a sort; she was biddable and a good cook. So the father married her.

Papa was a man of standards. His daughters should not run wild; they should be educated like ladies at a convent of French-born nuns in St. Louis. They should never, never ride horseback; ladies didn't. But he did allow them to drive, and bought spirited horses for their rigs. When the girls drove into town to shop, all other traffic took to the prairies. The charioteers had the roads to themselves.

Four times a year Papa's store received shipments of dress goods. The girls could select a dress length apiece from each shipment. Wonderful fabrics! Chinese silks, India mulls, Lyons velvets. Papa knew cloth and color, and had a Frenchman's interest in clothes.

The girls hurtled into town when the shipments arrived, and made their selections with much debate and mind-changing. As soon as they headed for home, Papa called in his most favored customer, and displayed the new merchandise to her.

This lady had a house—a "five-dollar house" even in those days—and she liked her girls to look like the luxuries they were. Sometimes alone and sometimes with one or two employees, always dressed in duplicate costumes, the Madame went to the store and made her selection of fabrics. Only then, to the intense annoyance of the rest of the feminine community did the new merchandise go on the counters for sale.

Those pianos! There was one, and a harmonium, at Fort Abe Lincoln in 1876. Elizabeth Custer has written how the wives of the officers of the Seventh Cavalry played the instruments and sang hymns while they waited for news of their husbands, out on campaign against the Sioux. We can guess how that piano got where it was: by river steamboat, as did Custer's field

"The First Woman in Camp"—*Frank Leslie's Illustrated Newspaper*, April 19, 1884

cannon. But nobody has bothered to tell us that detail. It was just natural to have a piano around the fort. If ladies were there—so were the piano and the harmonium. Who tuned the pianos? How did they keep them that way? Women could have done the job. Did they?

They were not all so busy as the wives and daughters in one company of David Payne's Sooners, who came into the no man's land west of the Cross Timbers in 1880.

Payne, a land clerk in the Washington office of the Department of the Interior, had found that there was a stretch of open land in the heart of present Oklahoma—land that belonged to nobody. No Indian tribe officially claimed it; no treaties with tribes or European nations secured it to the United States. At a time when land everywhere was running out and land in the

West coming to be highly prized, here was a free expanse, without claimants. Payne decided it should belong to him, and to other landless men willing to help him hold it. He returned to his home town in Kansas, and organized a land company. As soon as the word got around, volunteers joined Payne.

"If David Payne hadn't been a handsome man," said the daughter of a Sooner, "Oklahoma would never have been settled. He was exciting to look at, he was so handsome. He had the kind of voice that got you all stirred up, just listening to it. It wasn't just women who were willing to follow him anywhere. It was men, too. You had to trust him, because of his looks and his voice."

Payne divided his group. One section moved into the area west of Council Grove, about where Oklahoma City stands now. They began working to break the soil on the north bank of the Canadian River. Soon a detachment of cavalry arrived from Fort Reno, with a polite request that the settlers move on; they might be occupying Indian lands; it would be better not to establish themselves until the matter was settled.

A girl in the Sooner group covered her brown curls with a sunbonnet, and, so protected from dust and freckles, for ninety days drove the four-horse team of the family wagon. "Oh, sugar, it wasn't nothing, driving that team," the girl said in her old age. "It was a sight easier than washing clothes on a fire in the yard, back home in Kansas. It was fun. And clean! My lands, you never saw a country was so clean. Until you've walked on land that's never been broken, and smell air that's never been breathed, you don't know what clean is. If you cut your finger in those days, you didn't get blood poisoning. There weren't any germs. It would just heal right over."

She went on, "We got to know the soldiers real well. The ones from Fort Reno would move us south of the river, and keep us drifting southwest till we

"The Coming of Winter"—from the *Century Magazine*, December, 1888

got into the Fort Sill area. Then they'd go on back and the soldiers from Fort Sill would come out and start shifting us north and east till we were back around Fort Reno again. That way we kept the soldiers too busy all summer to notice what was going on east of us, in the Sauk and Fox country. Payne and his bunch managed to get some crops in, and even harvested. Yes, you might say we got to know some of the soldiers *real* well. I married one myself."

And what did they do on Sundays, the day when soldiers and colonists alike rested? Why, they all gathered in a single group around the preacher's wagon, and sang hymns to the accompaniment of a portable piano.

There were pianos in the crib-houses and saloons of the West, of course. A piano there was more than a means of entertainment. It was a mark of prestige. A piano-player might be lacking among the girls and the customers. But the piano itself seldom failed to grace the main room. Some, like the girls, had seen their best days. They were acquired second- to twenty-second-hand from respectable households that were moving on, and had steeled themselves to sacrifice. Other pianos were new and fine, like the mahogany grand that adorned the parlor of a famous resort in Las Cruces, New Mexico.

The story—possibly apocryphal—is that that piano was made in Germany. It was shipped by steam packet from Hamburg to New Orleans. From New Orleans it went up-river by boat to "Shreesport," and thence overland by wagon to San Antonio, El Paso and Las Cruces. With the piano came a man sent by the manufacturer to tune it. For once we have information on this important point. One wonders what finally became of him. Did the Señora Patrona turn her tuner loose and let him tune other peoples' pianos? Did he stay in the West, or return, homesick, to Germany?

A piano beyond the Missouri was more than a piano. It was a symbol; a symbol of the East, of home, of civilization, of religion and good manners and three meals a day, and of almost-forgotten comforts. A woman would go West with her man. She would abandon many things that had made her life worth living. It's a notable fact that the "ladies"—the respectable white women with standards—were the first females to go West. The gals of the dance halls and "houses," who came more or less under their own steam, trailed along later.

Because pianos were symbols, they were important and treasured. You can cook over a campfire without yearning to the bottom of your soul for a kitchen range. You can wash clothes in rivers, particularly if you're not used to stationary tubs and running water. Homemade soap is homemade soap in Massachusetts or Idaho; making it equally odorous wherever it takes place. But a piano, or an oak dresser, or a set of Haviland china, or a silver service, is a sign of permanence, of stability, respectability, of dignity and a place in the world. Its importance is beyond value; it is not lightly surrendered.

Sure, the things were nuisances to haul around. Sure, they were of no earthly use, compared to plows and saddles. More than one husband must have reached the end of his string the fourth or fifth time his wife ordered him to load the piano back into the wagon before she would go "another foot" herself. But the piano and the wife and moving both from one outpost to another were all part of this life in the West.

Oh, yes, the West was a man's world. But men are incurable dreamers. Divest them of women, and what did they do? They either invaded some Indian village and begged, borrowed, or eloped with a woman, or they spent their spare time sitting around and mooning about the ones back home. Even the most hardened character might finally make the trip "back to the States," to return with "the little woman" beside him on the wagon seat. And her piano loomed above all the other household goods.

Most women in the early West were respectable. If they didn't start out that way, they could become so by the simple process of a wedding ceremony. One good woman remarked, "Shucks, honey, even if it had been good manners to ask where people came from and what their names were when they lived there, most of us was too busy to bother. I know I never cared. It was whether they was good neighbors *now* that counted. My next-door neighbor worked in a girl-house beside the railroad when she first come out. Her husband met her there and married her and brought her here. Come right down to it, what business did he have in a place like that, any more than she did? What I'll always remember about that woman is she baked the whitest, sweetest bread I ever put in my mouth. Then she sat up all night for three nights running when my youngest took diphtheria. Pulled him through, as well as a doctor could have. They're the things worth remembering."

Over the Old West, and the men and women who inhabited it, a cloud of misty romance has hung for a long time. As the years increase the distance, the men grow increasingly heroic in stature and behavior; the women more doll-placid and doll-pretty. Where do writers and producers get such ideas? Men and women of the Old West live among us even today, indistinguishable from ordinary people.

Take a look at a file of old Western photographs some time. A pretty woman then was a treat for the eyes—few women had time or energy to do the work necessary to grooming themselves as well as the horses. People stopped and turned to stare on the streets of Laramie when Elizabeth Custer, who was pretty but no raving beauty, went by. And Elizabeth had her husband's "striker," a Negro maid, and a groom to help her with her childless household. Still, she mourned the sacrifice of her "looks" to hard water and alkali. What most Western women had in their faces was character. It took strength of body and mind, as well as a mighty supply of will power, to survive. Survival was more important than prettiness.

It smells like gangrene starting in a mildewed silo, it tastes like the wrath to come, and when you absorb a deep swig of it you have all the sensations of having swallowed a lighted kerosene lamp. A sudden, violent jolt of it has been known to stop the victim's watch, snap his suspenders and crack his glass eye right across.

IRWIN S. COBB– Definition of
"Corn Licker" given to
Distiller's Code Authority, N.R.A.

OREN ARNOLD

The Honkytonkers

AMONG THE FASCINATING FALLACIES cherished by us idealists is that which says the West was opened by Christians whose chief recreations were singing hymns and pitching horseshoes. Some of these saints did arrive. But the majority were people who somehow or other just didn't fit in back East; neurotics, outlaws, malcontents, rebellious spirits in general, fleeing from sheriffs or from something even worse that seethed deep in their souls.

As all individualists do, they carried a great reservoir of strength and capability, a priceless fact to us who are their posterity. On arrival they sought the Good Life by grabbing whatever promised mental escape and/or physical pleasure at any given moment. From them, and for them, arose some of the most lurid recreation centers man has ever known.

These were operated by professionals possessed of sure and ageless skills. Many undoubtedly had been gifted children, mentally superior, who somewhere along the line got off the beam of decency and developed shrewdness in the alluring back alleys of sin. They were the saloonkeepers, gamblers, thieves, pimps and whores. Spontaneously they acquired a name which had generic origin among the Negroes of the old South. They were called Honkytonkers. Their business establishments were Honkytonks. Obviously, the word means "a place to hang around."

We cannot dismiss them with a shrug of revulsion or contempt. It is of academic interest that they usually dominated any new Western community, sans Health Departments, Dr. Wassermann or the heritage of Charles

109

Goodyear. "The first establishment," one pioneer diary records, very typically, "was a saloon set up in a tent by Gage Walters. Soon he had ten girls from we know not where. They began selling their bodies to the miners and trappers. Then a pianoforte instrument was brought over [the mountains] on muleback at great trouble and expense." Twelve other such establishments—honkytonks—were flourishing before the preacher got his little church going.

If you have never been in a honkytonk—and I hope you haven't, because it is no place for a refined person—you can have little real idea of what one was like. There was no set architectural pattern. Gage Walters' tent served until he could get a log structure built. Some of the best—or worst—were sod houses. Others even more notorious were made of adobe bricks. In short, they operated in whatever was available or could be contrived. They seldom had exterior eye appeal, or needed it. Reputation was enough. Somewhere along the years the swinging doors came into use. But the lowest honkytonks often reached such depths that not even a discreet screening was sufficient. These had to be approached up or down "secret" stairways, through darkened halls, behind falsely respectable fronts. These were the grandaddies of the speakeasy and the blind pig.

Dominant inside, always, was the heart of the enterprise, the bar. From about 1840 to 1880 bar making became one of the finer crafts, with many a woodsmith reaching his peak designing the fixtures in a honkytonk. Chairs and tables for gambling could be crude, and often were. But the bar and back bar had to show a richness that suggested quality to men hungering for it. Some of those old handmade, hand-rubbed bars, priceless now, are still in use in the posh resorts of California, Arizona, Colorado and New Mexico.

Decorations grew elaborate as the place prospered and acquired "tone." Red plush curtains, thick rugs replacing original sawdust, fancy chandeliers, sprayed perfume, all were routine. But in almost every place the *pièce de résistance* was the nude and nubile girl painted life-size on canvas just above eye level of men at the bar.

The proprietor would bet any pal a pinch of dust (gold, that is) that no patron would enter his place in any given twenty-four-hour period without casting at least a surreptitious glance at the bar painting. He never lost. Bigger places might have a dozen or so such works of art.

Even so, the property was seldom as impressive as the personnel. In the raw beginnings of a community, the honkytonk host was sure to be an individual so grim-visaged and dirty as to frighten all except his own kind. Out of a barrel he ladled diluted whisky at fantastic prices, thereby netting enough profit to tone up the place and import the girls. As they arrived, some latent gallantry—call it that—stirred in him so that he shaved part of his face, cut his hair, washed all over in the nearby creek, put on a new suit with a heavy gold chain across the vest, and opened his mouth in a gold-

"The Hurdy-Gurdy House"—from *Beyond the Mississippi*, by A. D. Richardson, 1867

toothed smile. This often gave him enough respectability to be elected mayor, marshal, judge, or other dignitary. He was affability itself now, a glad-handing hypocrite with a derringer up one sleeve and another in his right boot.

And the girls he brought in? Decent folk, housewives especially, have always nursed an abiding curiosity about whores. Could it be they actually enjoy their work, as they seem to? Could be, ma'am. Have they no hint of conscience, no feeling for monogamy, or loyalty?

Do not shudder, ma'am. Then as now, most were mentally retarded creatures more to be pitied than scorned. Few honkytonk pros were truly face-pretty or shapely. But in a community three hundred or even thirty miles from the nearest civilized town and inhabited only by males, any female of the species—repeat, any—is beautiful. Their scarcity made them valuable merchandise. Importing them was held to be a vital necessity.

In some cases the importation was respectable. For instance in Seattle in 1864-66 Mr. Asa Mercer imported more than three hundred girls of ages fifteen to twenty-five, bringing them all the way around the Horn from New York. In gratitude, the men elected Asa to the Territorial Legislature, then made him first president of the University of Washington. Quite incidentally he himself married one of the prettiest—Annie Stephens.

In the real honkytonks there was little subtlety about the wenches or their patrons. The direct approach was standard—"Hello sweetheart!" a five-minute dalliance at the bar, hearty laughter, then an arm-in-arm promenade to her personal crib. The genial proprietor provided cribs, so-called because they were usually too small to be dignified as rooms. He also usually collected the fee—five to fifty dollars and up, depending on the scarcity and skill of the girls and on the lust and drunkenness of the men.

For the younger men and shy ones, dancing might precede cribbing. But it was not the stately cotillion of a Waldorf ballroom. It was a quick-tempo'd, chest-to-bust dance plus the bumps and grinds still favored in our modern (and, of course, refined) burlesques. Many a lusty man fresh in from the hills couldn't weather such preliminaries. The girl was usually prepared for this and well coached. So, while the gambling stopped—the other girls giggled— the boys at the bar whooped, he and "Sweetheart" stripped naked as they danced. No cover charge.

Glaring back from mid-twentieth century, we ask who in the holy horrors would enter such a depraved place?

The answer is—everybody. Even the preachers used the honkytonks. You must remember that the West was adorned by the five most picturesque actors ever to perform on the great American stage. These were, in the order of their appearance, the Indian, the Mexican, the trapper, the prospector, and the cowboy. Each was, still is, a romanticist of derring-do, an individualist with active gland-power. Whenever three whites built shacks within hollering distance they had a town; when ten built, they attracted a honkytonk proprietor. They were his customers.

The red man ran his own sex business at first, selling his daughters and squaws to lusty whites. Later he too patronized the "civilized" honkytonk in town.

Most of these folk, as well as the woodsmen, farmers and artisans who quickly followed into the new communities, could not read. Those who could, didn't have anything *to* read. Few games were available, especially for night use. There was no lodge or club, no corner drugstore to which the men might amble, not even a schoolhouse, playground or church.

Conceivably the church missed a bet by not providing facilities for wholesome recreation in the West—I have often thought we church people have been sadly slow to grab opportunity by the forelock. So, our five actors and their associates, gregarious by nature, basically honest in attitudes and appetites, surged through the only doors available, those of the honkytonks.

In almost every major Western village, the leading bar and brothel was also the "stage stop." Up to the Golden Nugget or the Bucket of Blood or Mamie's Place pulled the stagecoach with a flourish of dust and hearty hilarity —for the excellent reason that there was no other public place to pull up. Good drinking water was a scarcity, hence it became natural to quench thirst here with fiery alcohol. Likely enough, too, the air was biting cold or

"The Faro Players"—from the *Century Magazine*, volume xx

insufferably hot outside, but relatively mild inside. So even the timid entered and sat at the tables, waiting while stage horses were changed and people could go to the outhouses.

In time we sensitive ones got used to the naked painting over the bar, to the stench of rotgut whisky and the worse stench of unbathed bodies. All these details were a part of our Wild-Western civilization anyway, accepted just like the inescapable litter on the streets. We didn't necessarily approve of honkytonks. But we lived with 'em.

Because the leaders hung out there, we went there to get them. A miner was shot? His wife rushed to the saloon to get Sheriff Earp or Dr. Harrison, or, if need be, Mortician Jones. A bull gored Sebastian Tucker? We rammed a dirty cloth in his wound, threw him across a horse and galloped him to town and to—where?—the hospital? What hospital? To the only public place of any kind, the Golden Nugget, or the Bucket of Blood. Roughly tender hands carried poor Sebe inside, laid him on the sawdust or the rug and doctored him with whisky and sympathy.

In such emergencies one of "the girls" frequently stepped into higher character. She became Florence Nightingale. She bathed Sebe's wound, stroked his fevered brow, held his hand while he died or while he recovered. And likely as not, Sebe married her when he got back on his feet again, knowing she had been a whore, daring any man henceforth and hereafter to mention that fact again.

Strangely enough, nobody ever did—at least in Sebe's hearing. Strangely enough, too, she and Sebe begat a family and reared it in respectability, complete with Sunday School and a family pew. We modern sophisticates would be dismayed to learn how many of us had a grandmother or great-grandmother out of a Western honkytonk.

Death itself sometimes became a game in the tonks. There was Ezra Williams, who got himself shot down in California. The records slip a few cogs about Ezra, but we do know he was toted inside the local tonk and stretched out on a table under the hanging lamps while Dr. Thomas D. Hodges operated. Ezra groaned.

"He's mighty bad off," a gambler said, peering over a "girl's" bare shoulder at him. "I bet he dies before sunup."

"Fifty dollars says he don't!" snapped Doc, his pride touched.

"Done!" the gambler grinned. "Anybody else want to ante?"

In a moment $14,600 had been wagered on Ezra's dying or not dying. Then a honkytonker named Dutch Kate—later she became the first known stagecoach robber in the West—ambled in and bet a cool $10,000 that Ezra would die before the sun shone again. For hours everybody crowded around to watch him. Finally Ezra obliged; he checked out at 5:50 A.M.

If and when the preacher arrived in Newtown, Colorado—or Arizona or Nevada or wherever—he, too, had nowhere to turn at first but to Goldtooth Harry Brockett, proprietor of the Bucket of Blood. "Welcome, Rev'rund," Harry—no fool, and not all bad, mind you—would say. "A lot of folks around here want to get married. Some buryin' to be done. Lot of room for preaching. Light and take root, man. Here's a hundred dollars to git you started."

You can't combat that kind of cordiality. The preacher eyed the bar painting with tolerance, knowing masculine appetites. He shook Harry's hand.

Next Sunday morning, the Reverend rearranged the gambling hall chairs, covered the nude with gunnysacks, made the faro table into an altar . . . and conducted services.

You could have entered a frontier dive for no other purpose than to pass the time of day, to swap a few jokes, maybe, or just talk some about this new upstart politician, Abe Lincoln.

You could have met your friends there to plan a new business venture.

You could have gone there simply to tell somebody about the harassments of home.

The honkytonk became for our frontiersmen what the pub is to English-men, what the cocktail lounge—and I pause to spit—is to modern Westerners; except that the tonk had a greater monopoly, a more elemental honesty. Good· or bad, it was an important part of the West's adolescence. Merrily and accu-rately, the boys at San Francisco's Press Club still declaim:

> "The miners came in '49,
>   The whores in '51.
>   They rolled upon the barroom floor.
>   Then came the Native Son."

"Home for the Boys"—from *Harper's New Monthly*, June, 1865

The killer had his day, then came to a swift and violent end. There were exceptions, but so few as to emphasize the rule. If the law did not get them, another bad man did.

WILLIAM MAC LEOD RAINE– "Guns of the Frontier"

JAMES D. HORAN

The Gunmen

THEY'RE ALL GONE. Nothing remains but their hideouts, their legends and the names that sound like bells—the Sundance Kid, the Tall Texan, Poker John, the Fiddleback Kid, Calico Bob, Butch Cassidy. And, most dangerous of all, Kid Curry.

Puzzling back on the loneliness of their melodramatic lives, one wonders why the violence boiled in them. The official records are fragmentary. The rest is hearsay. We can only guess. They were born in an era of violent change, the like of which the human race may never see again—not, at least, on this planet. So they shone like angry comets above the mesa, the shabby towns and bleak mountains in the closing years of the Wild West. Even a man's occupation was dangerous. Raw courage, fierce pride, a sense of incredible partisanship—all were important. Skill with a gun, skill in killing, gave each one tremendous power.

But it made him lonely, too. And, deep, deep inside, fear fought with the desperate hope for peace and honor in the community.

That's him at the end of the bar, the man with the neatly trimmed mustache, wearing the blue pin-stripe suit and derby. You wouldn't notice him in a crowd except, perhaps, for the pointed, high-heeled puncher's shoes he wears. His Indian-dark face is impassive. He doesn't talk much. There's an almost melancholy air about him, as though he is staring at something far beyond the horizon. He was born Harvey Logan but, to the West, he will always be Kid Curry, outlaw and killer.

The creaking of an oxcart in the Cumberland Gap in the 1870's opens his story. His mother, widow of a farmer turned private in the Army of Northern Virginia, is taking her four sons, Harvey, Lonny, Johnny and Harry, to the home of her uncle and aunt, the Robert Lees of Dodson,

116

Missouri. The Logans are as poor as Jeb's calf. They have a few ragged clothes, a plow, an old cow, the wagon and the ancient horse. Mrs. Logan either died on the way or deserted her children. It is Harvey, the oldest, who brings the wagon into Dodson. He is about ten years old.

The Lees' farmhouse was typical of the period, situated on a small hill, sitting back from the northeast corner of Dodson Avenue (now 86th Street), Kansas City. It was a rough frontier settlement, described in 1900 as "sixteen miles out in the country." Robert Lee, a helpless invalid who had fought in the war, settled in Dodson about 1868. He was a weak, sickly man, who sat on the porch endlessly rocking when the weather was nice. When it rained, snowed, or was too cold, he sat by the front window, bundled in a shawl, scarcely moving.

Harvey quickly became the man of the house. He possessed the elusive ingredients of leadership. His brothers never questioned him. Nor did Mrs. Lee, whom the boys called "Aunt Lee" all their lives. She was a kindly, religious woman who years later would stand over Lonny's body in the snow outside her house and whimper, "I could never believe they did anything to break the law. . . ."

Harvey stole a six-shooter from a town drunk when he was about twelve years old. He let his brothers in on the secret. They went to the woods to fire at small game and marks. Harvey was soon the best shot with Lonny and Johnny coming up in the rear. Harry joined them, but reluctantly. He hated to see the rabbits kick and didn't see much sense in spending his money for shells. Mostly, while his brothers made the woods ring with gunfire, he worked in the general store in Dodson.

They were a handsome lot, the mark of the Cherokee grandfather showing up in their swarthy skin, flashing black eyes and rather high cheekbones. Harvey had strong, even teeth and they lighted up his dark face when he laughed. Lonny was handsomest. With the exception of Harry, they possessed a wild streak and were in trouble on several occasions with the town constable. Once Harvey backed the law against a shed and in that cold, low voice—he never shouted or became excitable—told him he would kill him if he visited the little farmhouse of his aunt with another complaint. There is no doubt that he meant it.

In the fall of 1880—this is an approximate date—the brothers left Dodson, riding double on two stolen horses. Harvey and Lonny truly loved the old aunt and probably did say good-bye. Fired by the pulps, they had decided to seek their fortunes in the West; in the best American tradition they were going to become cowboys.

At noon Harry turned back. Harvey shrugged his shoulders. He didn't care. Harry was the weak one. The trail fades. Then in 1885 Nathan Champion and his riders thundered across into Wyoming's history. Riding stirrup to stirrup with Champion were the Logans and George "Flat Nose" Curry, described by a secret operative of the Pinkertons as "king of the rustlers." Somewhere on the trail the three Logans had met up with Curry and became his protégés. He taught them all the tricks of the running iron, the secret canyons where stolen herds were kept, and the way stations on the outlaw trail that ran into New Mexico.

In 1892 Champion and Nick Rae fell under the gunfire of the stockmen's invasion at the K.C. Ranch in Powder Springs. George Curry took over, with Harvey second in command. He was no longer the farmboy from Dodson; he was a slim, dark-eyed man, known to be fast on the draw and a killer. Two dead men were at his back now; a Mexican and a breed.

The gang used the Hole in the Wall, that vast and lonely land, peopled today by the ghosts of Tom Horn, the stockmen's hired gun; Elza Lay, the educated rustler; Butch Cassidy, the merry outlaw; Big Nose George Parrott, whose skin was made into a wallet by his lynchers; Bob Lee, who shot sheriffs "to see them kick"; and Harry Tracy, the killer who is a folklore figure in the Northwest.

About the fall of 1888 the Logans rustled a herd and a posse took out after them. There was a gun battle in which Harvey received the first of the two gunshot wounds in his violent career. He was hit on the left wrist; the wound left a livid scar. Thus the "Wanted" posters said. Cattle were gold in the lean years following the great plains blizzard of 1886-87. The stockmen let it be known there would be a noose, and no fancy trial, for them if they returned. The Logans took the hint. With John Thornhill, a rustler from the Star Valley country, they rode to Montana.

They stayed in Chouteau County, about twenty miles from Chinook, where they built an L-shaped loghouse and corral, raised some cattle—all stolen—and a horse herd—also stolen. It was a peculiar custom, but many of the American outlaws adopted the names of their mentors when they went on their own. The Logans took the name of Curry, Harvey assuming the title of "Kid" Curry. George Leroy Parker took the name of Mike Cassidy, who had helped him to steal his first herd in Utah.

Two years in one place was too much for this lawless trio. In the early '90's, Harvey announced they were pulling stakes. They drove the cattle and horses to town, sold them and set out for Landusky, a wide-open frontier town ruled by its founder, Pike Landusky, an ex-miner, whose scarred face witnessed it is terribly difficult for any man to kill a bear with bare hands.

The Logans and Thornhill temporarily settled on a small ranch a few miles from Landusky. Lonny discovered Pike's daughter, Elfie. The inevitable happened. In the fall of 1893 Elfie went to Pike and told him he was about to become a grandfather. Pike picked up his shotgun and went looking for Lonny.

The tragedy would be quick enough for Pike, but this time he missed the Logans. They had gone back to the Hole, for what reason we don't know. Christmas week 1894, they returned—with a large roll of bills. The saloon in Landusky was typical—a wooden counter on one side, a dry-goods and general store on the other. The owner-bartender was a peg-leg who used a Winchester as a crutch. He had blown a hole in at least one unruly customer.

Christmas Day, Kid Curry walked into the crowded bar and told the cowboys, miners, rustlers and outlaws to belly up. As the day wore on, he lapsed into one of his dark moods.

It was dusk when he suddenly ran from the saloon-store, mounted a horse and rode up and down the rutted street, shrieking like a Comanche. Lonny and Thornhill joined him. As one eyewitness said, "You couldn't put a tin cup out of doors 'fore it would be full of holes." Gradually the wild desire for violence died down. Kid pulled up in front of the store, went in and bought everybody a drink.

Then Pike Landusky appeared. The rough loud voices died down. Everybody at the bar turned as Pike walked into the low room. He wore a

"A Fight in the Street"—from the *Century Magazine*, October, 1888

long overcoat, and his twisted face was almost hidden by a fur cap.

"What'll you have, Pike?" the one-legged owner said.

"Whisky," Pike grunted and moved to the bar. It appeared he had forgotten his daughter's condition, or else thought it wise not to cross guns with the Kid.

But the Kid's blood lust was up. As Pike passed him, he lashed out and knocked the old miner down.

The simmering hate spilled over. Landusky bounced back at Harvey, flung him to the floor, like an old buffalo bull, and started to stomp him. Lonny smashed him in the face. Pike slammed the Kid across the room. Bolts of goods, hams, barrels, crashed. The Kid rolled clear of Pike's mine boots, stood up, banged at the scarred face with his fists, then danced clear of the clutching arms. Finally one of the Kid's blows knocked Pike down to one knee. Then he kicked the old man in the chest and rolled him down.

Pike saw the Kid go for his gun, then. Frantically he tried to paw open his heavy coat. It was too late. The Kid blew the top of his head off.

"Get the wagon. We're moving out," the Kid snarled. Lonny and Thornhill ran outside and stole the first buckboard they saw. The Kid backed to the door. The one-legged bartender kept his hands on the counter. The others didn't say a word.

They rode out of town with Thornhill working the whip. The Kid had his six-shooter cocked waiting for a posse to show its head. When no one followed he fired several shots at the houses they passed. Even firing at inanimate objects stirred him.

Weeks later they appeared at the Hole to be welcomed by this hostel of outlawry. They found a new name on everyone's lips—Butch Cassidy of Circle Valley, Utah, who had ridden with the McCarthy gang. The Logans rode over to Powder Springs where Butch, a tow-haired young outlaw with a friendly grin, was holding court. They decided they liked Cassidy and joined forces. Thus the Wild Bunch was born, to spawn countless legends of weird signs on rocks that were supposedly messages in code.

Actually the Bunch was a loosely organized group made up of several small bands: Black Jack Ketchum's train robbers, Kid Curry's gang, Bob Lee's rustlers, and others. At times they acted independently of each other. Again, they rode together under Cassidy's leadership as one of the largest outlaw bands in the history of the West. The Reno brothers in Indiana invented train robbery in America. Jesse James, that evil son of the middle border, elaborated on the Renos' technique. Cassidy and Kid Curry perfected it. They not only stopped the trains, hurrahed them with gunfire, but used dynamite to blow apart the express car carrying the Adams Express Company's bonds.

Rustling was not overlooked. The Wild Bunch riders were expert with a running iron. They made extensive use of their knowledge. Their head-quarters was Hole in the Wall, Star Valley, which lies in Wyoming and Utah.

Tom Horn entered the Hole in the 1890's, wearing a Pinkerton badge, to kill a few minor rustlers from ambush—his favorite method. He never crossed guns with any of the Bunch. Kid Curry would have cut down this inflated bushwacker in short order. But despite the violence and bloodshed a sort of grim humor existed in the outlaw communities. They opened a saloon in Star Valley. The back of the bar was plastered with Adams Express Company bonds which they couldn't negotiate. When Kid Curry or Cassidy or their riders became bored, they would practice marksmanship on the bonds.

Kid Curry, operating independently of the Bunch, staged a few success-ful train robberies. Apparently he proved to Butch Cassidy that train robbery was more lucrative than rustling. Soon the gangs joined forces to plague the Union Pacific and Great Northern. The Train Robbers' Syndicate organized by Curry and Cassidy is no fantasy. Reports of the Union Pacific and Pinker-ton Superintendent J. P. McParland, the hardheaded nemesis of the Molly Maguires, recognized this. Charlie Siringo, the cowboy-detective, as he tells it, posed as a killer from Texas on a white horse, to join the gang and leak secrets back to the Denver office. Once he got close to Elfie—now calling herself Elfie Curry—in an attempt to find out where the Kid and his gang were hiding.

Despite Siringo's infiltration, the Wild Bunch continued their strikes.

As the months passed, Cassidy and Kid Curry led the Bunch across the West in a pounding of hoofs and rattle of gunfire. More dead men were added to Curry's score. Following the Wilcox, Wyoming, Union Pacific robbery the Kid killed Sheriff Joseph Hazen, and so savagely brought the battle to the posse in a wild canyon near Teapot Creek, outside Casper, that the lawmen were forced to retreat.

Sheriff John Hyler of Grand County, Utah, and his deputy, Sam Jenkins, flushed one of the gang from his hideout after Hazen's death, to kill him in a gunfight. When the Kid heard of his rider's death, he rode out of the Hole to Moab, Utah, called out Hyler and Jenkins, and killed them both in the street. Then he stepped over the bodies of the dead officers, mounted and galloped out of town. Posses numbering a hundred outraged citizens searched the land. The Kid escaped back to the Hole.

In the Belle Fourche, South Dakota, bank robbery, Curry's gun cowed the town. On April 13, 1897, the Kid cold-bloodedly killed William Deane, a brave but foolhardy Johnson County deputy. In the chase following the Tipton, Wyoming, train robbery on August 29, 1900, the Kid killed another deputy and winged a posse rider.

Between raids, the Kid ranged far and wide across the West. In 1899, the Sheriff of Dodson, Missouri, reported he had been seen doing chores back at the Lee farmhouse. One can visualize this strange man with the blood of many men on his hands, calmly chopping wood for the white-haired old lady who still believed he was the boy who "went to services." This reckless return to Dodson underscores the frightening loneliness in all of them, the strong craving for companionship and perhaps love. Annie Rogers, a young "soiled dove," as they said in those days, met the Kid in Fannie Porter's sporting house in Fort Worth. She told how the Kid would talk for hours about Missouri, and how nice it would be to own his own ranch and hang up his guns. But he knew in his heart it was only a dream. He had traveled beyond the point of no return.

As the years passed, Curry's violent moods flared up more frequently. In at least one holdup he earned Cassidy's wrath by cold-bloodedly shooting down an Adams Express Company guard. In one Montana robbery staged by the Wild Bunch, Cassidy knocked up the Kid's gun when he aimed at an amiable old conductor who twice before had been a victim of the gang. Instead of obeying Curry's demands to stop, he had kept walking toward the last car.

"Just setting the brakes, Butch," he explained after he came back.

"I ought to blow your damned head off," Curry snarled.

"Let him alone, Kid," Cassidy said quietly. The Kid, through genuine affection or fear, never turned on Cassidy.

Just before the century turned, the Kid heard that a cattleman named James Winters had told the authorities about some of his activities. The Kid and his brothers, Lonny and Johnny, rode four hundred miles to kill Winters. But some cowboys who had heard Curry's plans for murder, informed Winters. When the Logan-Currys rode up to his ranch, Winters was ready. The Kid shouted for Winters to come out and be killed. The answer was a shotgun blast that tore off Johnny's head. After he had buried his brother, the Kid sent Lonny away. He waited patiently. At last he got his chance. "Winters," he shouted one wintry day as the cattleman was about to saddle up. Winters turned. He saw Kid Curry and went for his gun. The Kid outdrew him and cut him down. Then he rode over to the dying man and emptied his revolver into his twitching body.

Killing followed killing. In San Antonio he killed a cowboy who had threatened Deaf Charley Hanks, the comic relief for the gang. Charley, with his shaven head, shrewd eyes and deafness, provided many a laugh for the gang. But the Kid didn't think it was funny when a cowhand slapped Charley and told him to draw, for some fancied drunken insult. Hanks just stood there, his head cocked to one side, struggling to hear a sound in his world of silence.

The Kid said quietly that he would take over. The space around him widened.

The young cowhand protested, "I ain't got no trouble with you, mister."

"You made the play—now draw."

The cowboy went for his gun, only to die on his feet. Someone shouted out in the streets to the rest of the cowboy's outfit, and they came on the run.

The Kid was a killer but not a coward. He waited until they crowded through the swinging doors, full of bluster and threats. Then he slid his six-shooter back into his holster.

"Anybody want to slap leather, let's go," he said in his cold, even voice.

This swarthy-faced man with the smoldering black eyes, who thought so little of his life, and that of others, was in dead earnest. The cowhands, who used their guns to kill rattlers or loco steers, had no appetite to test him. When they failed his challenge he pushed through them and mounted, with Charley Hanks coming up behind. As a last gesture he flipped a coin at the crowd. "Bury him," he said and rode off.

The shiny back of his vest offered a fine target. But no guns were drawn. Yet all a man had to do to collect the $40,000 of aggregated rewards for Curry was to pull the trigger.

The century turned. The old Wild West was ended. To some men it seemed to vanish overnight. Sheriffs' posses now entered the Hole in the Wall country without fear. Violent death took some of the riders, including Lonny Logan. The handsomest of the outlaw brotherhood had fled to Montana with W. O. Sayles, the Pinkerton man, on his trail. Lonny at last returned to the only refuge left in his bleak world—the farmhouse in Dodson, Missouri.

Robert Lee was dead, and "Aunt Lee" struggled to maintain the farm with a young hired hand. Lonny cashed one of the banknotes he had taken in a train robbery—perhaps to help the old lady. The note turned up in a bank in Kansas City; the conclusion was obvious. One of the Curry-Logans was back in Dodson. Sayles hurried to Dodson and began a cautious questioning of the townspeople. The owner of the country store was so terrified when he heard of it that he closed his business and went to Kansas City for a week.

Sayles obtained enough information to wire William Pinkerton in Chicago that it *was* Lonny who was in Missouri. Pinkerton ordered him to get in touch with the local authorities and arrest the outlaw. Sayles paid a visit to Police Chief John Hayes, who assigned detectives Joseph Keshlear and Thomas McAnany, along with his own secretary, Edward Hickman, all crack shots. Captain Mahady, superintendent of the Kansas City Pinkerton office, and operative B. F. Kimble joined them. They set out in four buggies on a bitter winter morning.

As they started to surround the farmhouse, Lonny sprinted out the back door, gun in hand, headed for the timber across Dodson Road. He ignored the shouted commands to halt. Shots rang out. He spun around, started firing, then fell. From behind a mound of snow he continued to fire. One shot traveled up Sales' sleeve to come out the elbow without drawing blood. The cold morning rang with gunfire. Then abruptly it broke off. The officers slowly advanced across the snow. They found Lonny dead, the gun still in his hand.

Mrs. Lee, white-haired, shivering in the cold, tears running down her cheeks, could only whisper that she couldn't believe it. . . .

The body was removed to Stewart's Undertaking Parlor on Walnut Street. Later Coroner Lester and Justice Alvin Douglas of Dodson City accompanied the corpse to Kansas City, "to protect the reputation of the Lees, who had settled in Dodson shortly after the war."

In the West, the Wild Bunch riders were traveling fast. Sometimes the law caught up with them to put them in prisons in Utah, Wyoming, Montana, or New Mexico. Other times, men who had waited long now settled their grudges. Deaf Charley Hanks died in a gun duel in San Antonio. At a rendezvous, probably at Lost Soldier's Pass, Butch Cassidy told Kid Curry he was moving out—the frontier was gone. But there was the wild and unbroken land of South America. He and Harry Longbaugh, the Sundance Kid, intended to introduce outlawry, American style, to the pampas. He asked the Kid to come along.

The Kid refused. Instead he urged Cassidy to make one more strike. Cassidy, probably because he needed money, agreed. On August 24, 1901, the gang held up the Great Northern and blew an express car to bits near Wagner, Montana. They got $41,500, of which $6,500 would be deposited by Cassidy in the River Platte Bank in Buenos Aires six months later.

Cassidy, Kid Curry, Ben Carver, the Sundance Kid and Ben Kilpatrick, the Tall Texan, rode from Montana to Texas, using relays of horses their horse holders had been tending a week before the robbery. The Kid had planned the robbery; its organizational details were perfect.

In Fort Worth they had their famous photograph taken. It shows the Bunch, the most wanted men in the American West, wearing derbies and neat dark suits, staring into the camera. The Kid, solemn as a bishop, looked the paragon of respectability. Annie Rogers tells of the last days. They all drank champagne, ate the best foods and staged riotous parties at Fannie Porter's Sporting House. After a last good-bye to the Kid, Cassidy, Longbaugh and Etta Place, the pretty young schoolteacher who was to ride on their South America raids, left for South America via New York.

"Robbery of the Montana Coach"—from *Beyond the Mississippi*, by A. D. Richardson, 1867

The Kid began roaming. Twice the Pinkertons and Union Pacific detectives almost caught up with him. Once he shot his way out of a rooming house to escape in a hail of bullets. His luck gave out in Knoxville, Tennessee, where he shot down two police officers. They had been summoned by the owner of a poolroom to arrest the Kid after he broke the heads of some young toughs who had jumped him in a game of pool. The lawmen came in to see the Kid standing over the toughs, holding a shattered pool cue. Officers and outlaw went for their guns. Curry outdrew them and shot them down. One fired from the floor to nick the Kid as he plunged through a rear door, only to fall twenty-five feet down an embankment, badly spraining one leg. Coatless, limping and bleeding badly, he eluded posses for five days in sub-zero weather, until he was discovered, frozen and weak, thirty miles from Knoxville.

The first man to see him in the Knoxville jail was Lowell Spence, the famous Pinkerton detective, who had chased Kid Curry for several years. The Kid had sworn to kill Spence after the detective had announced he'd take him alive. As Spence re-created the scene for me, several years ago just before he died, Kid Curry grinned at him through the bars.

"Hello, Spence," he said.

"Hello, Kid," replied the detective.

"I won't be here long," Curry said casually. "When I get out of here I'll look you up."

"I'll be waiting, Kid," Spence said.

William Pinkerton, warned by Spence that Kid Curry was probably planning a break, notified the United States Attorney's office to be on the alert. After a two-week trial Curry was sentenced to life in prison. A day before he was to be transferred to the "escape-proof" Federal jail at Columbus, Ohio, he escaped. His classic breakout has been included in at least one anthology of famous escapes. The Kid used a noose fashioned from broom wire, lassoed the keeper, took his keys and locked him in his own cell. Then, adding insult to injury, he stole the sheriff's horse and rode leisurely out of town.

An eight-year-old girl, standing on her lawn, waved to the Kid. That little girl, now a grandmother, wrote me several years ago: "I can still see him, a rather good-looking man with a mustache, a cigar tilted in one corner of his mouth, riding past our house at a leisurely pace. He seemed like a man out for a morning ride. 'Good-bye honey,' he called when I waved. I watched him until he was out of sight."

One of the country's biggest man hunts swung into action. Pinkerton men, Union Pacific agents, joined forces with local and Federal police. Roadblocks were set up; mounted posses covered Tennessee. Lowell Spence was summoned from Chicago, under orders from William Pinkerton to "Get Kid Curry." He bought two horses and a complete outfit. For more than a year, he followed the Kid's rambling trail from Knoxville to New Orleans, from California to the Canadian border. There the clues petered out. The Kid seemed to have vanished. Reading Spence's reports half a century later, one catches a glimpse of this weary man hunter after a day in the saddle, holed up in some backwoods boardinghouse or hotel, writing by the weak light of the lamp: "The man named Jenkins who wrote to the sheriff at Denver is wrong. I found the man he said was Curry. He is a rancher near here who bears a remarkable physical resemblance to Kid Curry. I will resume my investigation tomorrow. . . ." It was endless plodding, endless questioning of ranchers, sheepherders, bartenders, small town marshals, eager for the rewards.

Meanwhile in South America the police of Peru, Bolivia and Chile protested to our State Department that a band of American outlaws—Cassidy, Kid Curry, Longbaugh, and the woman, Etta Place—was terrorizing their countries with train and bank robberies. Paymasters for the construction companies building the Bolivian Railroad had to ride in express cars guarded by a company of soldiers.

The State Department contacted the Pinkertons, requesting dossiers on all the outlaws. Included in the names was Kid Curry. Frank Dimaio, the Pinkerton man who had chased Cassidy and Longbaugh for a year in South America, was summoned. Dimaio shook his head when Pinkerton showed him the roster received from the State Department. "Kid Curry's not there," he said. "The Tall Texan, in prison, said he got a letter from him in Bolivia. We checked with the postal authorities. That letter had been sent from Texas. It was a plan to make us believe he was in South America. He's not—he's somewhere in the West." Lowell Spence, still doggedly hunting the Kid between other assignments, agreed with Dimaio. Kid Curry had never left the States.

In 1902 Pinkerton sent a letter to every sheriff and United States marshal in the Police Chiefs Association, alerting them to the possibility that Curry was still in the West. He urged all law enforcement agencies to send pictures of captured or killed desperadoes to Chicago to be compared with his rogues gallery.

In the Spring of 1903, a cowhand rode into Parachute, Colorado. He looked tired and sick and said he was Tap Duncan from Texas wanting to tie up with a local spread for the winter. He joined a small outfit several miles from Parachute and got to be known in the town as a quiet, morose man, who made few friends. There was little talk about him until the day some of the hands were firing at a whisky bottle, with poor results. Tap Duncan, his face impassive as stone, slapped leather. The gun flew into his hand and crashed. The bottle disappeared into fragments. The dark-faced man put the gun back into his holster and walked away.

The railroad ran nearby. Later, some of the folks in town recalled how Duncan seemed to hang about the depot when the trains came in. In the last week of June, 1903, four rough-looking men dressed as cowhands rode into town. They stayed a few days, then rode on. Somewhere out of town, they met Tap Duncan. He laid the plans to rob the train on the late afternoon of July 3. The technique was the standard one; the red lantern, the harassment by gunfire to cow the passengers, the dynamiting of the express car.

After the door was blown open, they managed to get the safe outside to blow off its door. Then, they pulled out a few empty bags. By a strange twist, the company had changed their gold shipment schedule. By a day, the gunman had missed a fortune in bullion.

When the train finally pulled into town, a posse was gathered. The chase went on for two days and nights. Finally the gang was trapped in a canyon a few miles from Glendale Springs, Colorado. The night echoed with the crash of gunfire and the shouted orders of the sheriffs to their deputies.

In a brisk exchange toward morning, a man's voice in the canyon cried out. There was a silence, then another man's voice called out: "Are you hit?"

The first voice replied weakly: "Yes—I'll end it here. Take the boys and go. . . ."

There was a sound of galloping horses. Some of the posse took out after them, others rested their rifles and six-shooters on the rocks to wait impatiently for the dawn.

The high keening wind of the Western dawn rose, then the summer's sun, first a seed of gold, a half golden pie, a fiery ball.

A revolver shot shattered the quiet. The sheriff waved his hand. The possemen crawled on their bellies into the canyon. They found Tap Duncan dead, a hole in his right forehead, his old Colt clutched in his stiffening hand.

Tap Duncan was buried in the tiny churchyard at Glendale Springs. Luckily the sheriff notified the Denver office of the Pinkerton Agency of Tap Duncan's physical description. J. P. McParland, the famous Western Pinkerton man hunter, wired William Pinkerton in Chicago that the description tallied with Kid Curry's. Pinkerton summoned Spence, who hurried to Glendale Springs. Spence had the body exhumed and took one look. "That's Kid Curry," he said. He had several pictures taken of the Kid's body, tied to an upright board, before returning to Chicago.

When Pinkerton announced to the State Department that Kid Curry was dead, Special Agent Canada of the Union Pacific scoffed publicly. So did many Western sheriffs and marshals. In the midst of the controversy the Cody, Wyoming, bank was held up. The headlines said: "Kid Curry Robs Cody Bank!" The sheriff gathered a posse and set out for Kid Curry. A stumbling old man, a ghost of the past, took up his rifle and said that he, Buffalo Bill Cody, would capture Logan. But somewhere between loading his rifle and saddling up, he changed his mind and went hunting.

The controversy made headlines for a year. At last Robert Pinkerton wired to his brother William, suggesting that Spence take all the pictures of Logan in life and in death along with his Bertillon charts to Knoxville to show the sheriff who had jailed Logan, the keeper whom he had lassoed, the United States Attorney who had prosecuted Curry, and the jury which had convicted him.

Spence made the rounds. Each man positively identified the corpse of Tap Duncan as that of Logan. His physical description in the Federal records in Knoxville also tallied with that of the body in the tiny churchyard in Colorado.

"The cowboy, Tap Duncan, is Kid Curry," William Pinkerton said. "The case is closed."

Sitting in his apartment in Chicago in 1949, Lowell Spence, now feeble and white-haired, reread his personal report which he had written nearly half a century before.

"All I can repeat," he said quietly, "is this last line: 'and thus I must conclude on this impressive evidence, that the dead man known as Tap Duncan and now buried in the churchyard in Glendale Springs, Colorado, is Harvey Logan, alias Kid Curry, the rustler, killer, train robber and member of the gang known as the Wild Bunch'!"

They are all gone now, even the white-haired old men who knew them. The cold wind of the Andes shakes the weather-beaten board headstone over the graves of Cassidy and the Sundance Kid, shot down in a night-long siege in a barrio near La Paz, Bolivia.

The ghost of Kid Curry still roams restlessly about the West; as late as three years ago men were insisting he was last seen on Green River, or in the Powder Springs country, or in Chinook, Montana.

The sun is hot on the big rocks near Lost Soldier's Pass where the Kid's horse relays used to wait, while Brown's Hole, Star Valley, Robbers' Roost and Hole in the Wall have settled back into their ancient quiet, still vast, still mysterious. And lonely.

"Highwayman Waiting for His Prey"—from *Fifteen Thousand Miles by Stage*,
by C. A. Strahorn, G. P. Putnam's Sons, 1911

*"Hear ye! Hear ye! This honorable court's now in session;
and if any galoot wants a snort afore we start, let him step
up to the bar and name his pizen. . . ."*

JUDGE ROY BEAN

WAYNE GARD

The Lawmakers

IN THE CHAPARRAL COUNTRY of western Texas, one elderly justice of the peace was called Old Necessity because he knew no law. On his bench was a mail-order catalogue bound in sheepskin. Before announcing a penalty, he always consulted this book. Once, when a man was brought before him for a misdemeanor, he put on his spectacles, opened the volume at random, looked at it a moment, and announced, "I fine you $4.88."

When the man jumped up to protest, his lawyer yanked him back. "Sit down," he said. "Be thankful that he opened it at 'pants' instead of at 'pianos.' "

Long before legislatures were set up in the new territories, the West had its own laws. Many, brought in the memories of early settlers, stemmed from the statutes and common law of Back East or—in parts of the Southwest—Spain. Others evolved on the frontier to meet special needs.

Even Indian customs provided some of the unwritten laws of the West. To the bronze tribesmen, early white trappers and hunters owed the ban on firing guns within a camp. From them, too, the frontiersmen adopted the death penalty for horse thieves, the rule that the first man to touch a stray horse became its owner, and the "law" for division of meat in which the man who killed a buffalo took the hide and tongue, leaving the other parts for his helpers.

Other unwritten rules arose from the kind of life followed by the pioneers. The frontiersman dismounted at the gate of a home and waved his arm to show that he held no gun. And a man who left another unhorsed in the wilderness, subject to blizzards and scalpers, was branded as the worst of criminals.

Anyone who became involved in a violent quarrel was considered

130

justified in defending himself. If his opponent drew first, or even began to
reach for a gun, he was privileged to shoot to kill. But he must not shoot
an unarmed man or fire at anyone in the back.

In parts of the West the development of order and law ran almost the
whole gamut of evolution from primitive society. In the relations between
settlers and Indians, often the only law was that of vengeance—a scalp for
a scalp. Colonists on the Atlantic Coast and Spaniards in the Southwest had
offered bounties for Indian scalps. So the practice of lifting Indian hair
became common in the West. Most frontiersmen needed no money incen-
tive to kill Indians, though sometimes rewards were offered locally. In 1867
a Denver resident promised $10 for every scalp of a hostile warrior. Citizens
of Central City, at a mass meeting, raised $5,000 to buy Indian scalps at $25
each. In Dakota Territory in 1876, miners at Deadwood, resentful of sniping
in the hills, offered $200 each for Indian scalps. Indian heads carried into
town brought high prices at auction.

This tomahawk justice, based on vengeance, was carried over into some
of the relations of whites with whites, via personal duels and feuds. The war
of the Regulators and Moderators in eastern Texas and the Pleasant Valley or
Tonto Basin War in Arizona were two of many bloody frontier feuds in
which opposing groups sought justice by ambushing and killing their
enemies.

Little above the level of feuds were some of the range wars that at
times spread terror over parts of the frontier. In the Texas Fence-Cutters'
War of 1883, small ranchers sought economic justice against the powerful
ones who had fenced the "free" ranges. Deprived of grass and water in a
drought year, they went out at night and cut mile after mile of the new
barbed-wire fences. Many snipped not only unlawful fences on public land
but those with which ranchmen enclosed their own property. A special
session of the Texas Legislature had to be called to cope with the situation.

An even more dramatic clash between the big and little cowmen came
in the Johnson County War in Wyoming in 1892. The big operators, who
had fraudulently grabbed most of the best land, resented the coming in of
small stockmen and grangers, among whom were some rustlers. The lesser
cowmen and farmers, for their part, bitterly resented some of the actions of
the monopolists. They accused the latter of destroying crops, poisoning
water holes, and branding as their own the calves from small ranch herds.
The armed invasion of Johnson County by the cattle barons and their hired
Texas gunmen, intended to wipe out the intruders, ended by establishing
the rights of the small operators.

Longer and bloodier was the struggle between sheepmen and cowmen.
The frontier cattle raiser viewed the sheepman as the pariah of the plains,
an interloper who deserved no quarter. In many cases he had no compunc-

tion against poisoning sheep or, with several of his fellows, riding into a sheep camp at night and shooting the woollies or cutting their throats. It mattered not that the sheep were grazing on public land and, in some instances, had been there before the cattle.

More easily recognized as steps toward order and law were the California miners' courts, which settled disputes over claims, and the Committees of Vigilance. Those who went to California in the early part of the gold rush found almost a vacuum in government. The loose *alcalde* system of the Mexicans was falling apart. Nothing had taken its place. Miners had to set up their own camp courts to make rules and to punish thieves, claim-jumpers, and other wrongdoers. In San Francisco in the 1850's, the failure of statutory courts to end waves of crime by the "Sidney Coves" and other newcomers left vigilante action as the only means to restore order.

Western frontiersmen hanged hundreds of killers and horse thieves without formal trial under statutory law. Yet they were not trying to superimpose their will above that of the courts. They acted not in violation of laws and courts but (1) in the absence of formal institutions or (2) the inability of those institutions to maintain order and punish crime.

The Committees of Vigilance were not mobs but were informal agencies that acted to stamp out lawlessness and rid their communities of desperadoes. They acted in the period before more orthodox means of law enforcement caught up with the frontier. Often as not, they did their unpleasant work by daylight and without masks. The members were not riffraff out for excitement but responsible community leaders determined to make their neighborhoods safe. Many vigilantes later held important posts as law officers.

In only a few instances did the vigilante activities degenerate into mob action or become involved in frontier feuds. Some of the groups were purely temporary—called into action when occasion arose, disbanded as soon as work was done. Others were formed on a more lasting basis, and elected officers. Usually the groups acted only after conditions became intolerable. They took into custody only those whose guilt was virtually beyond question.

In nearly all cases, the vigilantes gave the men they arrested an opportunity to prove their innocence. Occasionally they released one whose guilt seemed in doubt. As a rule, trials were brief and informal. Yet in some instances defense lawyers were allowed, witnesses called, and hearings extended over several days. Except in their freedom from delays and technicalities, trials held by San Francisco's noted Committee of Vigilance in 1856 lacked little of the formality of a statutory court.

One condition that tended to make vigilante action inevitable on the Western frontier was the lack of jails. Often a man awaiting trial had to be placed in a dry cistern or chained to a tree or a telegraph pole. In 1862 a Colorado sheriff, for want of a local hoosegow, handcuffed two husky horse thieves to the posts of a bed in which his wife was confined with a new baby. The earliest jails often were flimsy frame buildings, left unguarded at night. They were easily broken out of by prisoners or broken into by their confederates.

Most of the local enforcement officers on the frontier were honest and able. Others were weak and ineffective. Some collaborated with outlaws. A few were leaders of desperado bands, who used their public offices as shields for banditry. At Bannack, Montana, in 1863, Henry Plummer, who by night secretly led a notorious band of highwaymen, was elected sheriff; the following January, vigilantes hanged him. In the spring of 1866, Idaho vigilantes strung up David Updyke, head of a band of horse thieves and highwaymen, whose political influence had gained him the post of sheriff. In 1878, Texas vigilantes put to death as a cow thief a man who had recently been a sheriff.

Many of the early courts were far from dependable. Scores of courthouses were burned to destroy the records of pending criminal cases. Often it was impossible to find witnesses who would testify or jurors who would indict or convict. Whether the motive was sympathy with the defendant or fear of vengeance, the effect was the same in weakening law enforcement. In such instances, only action by the vigilance committees saved the communities from anarchy.

In the two decades following the Civil War, outlawry was rampant in many parts of the West. Bands of desperadoes stole cattle and horses, robbed stagecoaches and trains and banks, and committed murder on slight provocation. Favorite scenes of operation, since they afforded easy access to refuge, were areas bordering on the Indian Territory and on the Rio Grande. Some bandits were former soldiers who turned to outlawry to prolong the sectional conflict or to offset unpopular reconstruction measures. More were local bushwhackers or guerrillas who had used the war as an excuse for terrorism and dared not return to their old homes. Against such lawbreakers, Texas vigilantes were especially active in the 1870's.

Any administration of justice as informal and as speedy as that of most of the vigilance committees of the frontier West was bound to be mistaken and unjust in some instances. Cases in which "the wrong man" was hanged were extremely few, though. In those it probably was safe to assume that the one strung up was guilty of other serious crimes. Most of the vigilance committees took out their ropes only after guilt was clear. They disbanded as soon as formal courts and elected officials became able to preserve order and to protect lives and property.

A force especially adapted to bringing law to the long, thinly populated frontier of the Southwest was that of the Texas Rangers. Started in 1823, when Texas still was a part of Mexico, this outfit was recruited to protect

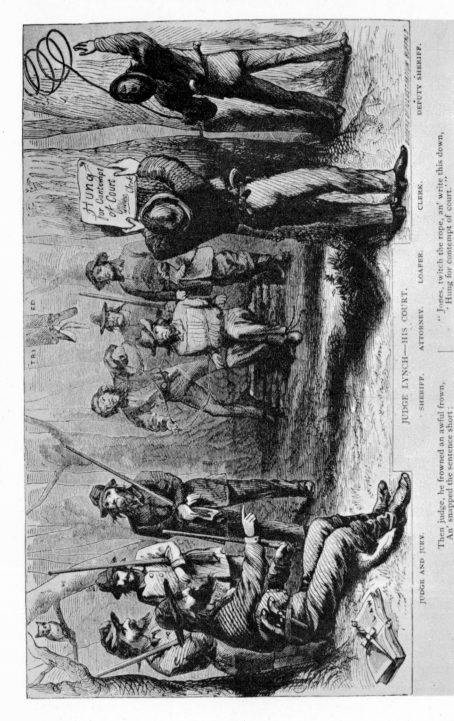

JUDGE LYNCH—HIS COURT.

JUDGE AND JURY.   SHERIFF.   ATTORNEY.   LOAFER.   CLERK.   DEPUTY SHERIFF.

Then judge, he frowned an awful frown,
    An' snapped the sentence short:

"Jones, twitch the rope, an' write this down,
    Hung for contempt of court."

From *Eoff* to *Land* by W. E. Webb, 1872

scattered colonists against Indian raids. Later it proved equally useful against Mexican border bandits, white horse thieves, cattle rustlers, and other outlaws. The Ranger, as John S. Ford put it, could "ride like a Mexican, trail like an Indian, shoot like a Tennessean, and fight like a devil."

In the Texas Republic period, the gallant Captain John C. Hays led his small band of Rangers against large bodies of Comanche marauders. In 1875 Captain L. H. McNelly led his tiny force across the Rio Grande in pursuit of Mexican cattle thieves. Facing a hostile force of soldiers many times more numerous than his men, he refused to budge until after the stolen cattle had been returned. In another exploit of the 1870's, Captain Lee Hall broke up a wedding dance of armed feudists to take the men he wanted. In still another, Lieutenant John B. Armstrong went to Florida and, singlehanded, captured the notorious Wes Hardin.

Across all Texas, the Rangers were feared by lawbreakers and respected by honest citizens. Texans came to have so much confidence in them that usually only a single Ranger was needed to quell a disturbance or a threatened riot.

Throughout the West, courageous sheriffs and marshals also made names for themselves by facing gunmen of the most dangerous types. One of the greatest was the first marshal of the Kansas cow town of Abilene, Tom Smith. Seldom needing a six-shooter, Smith used his fists to put respect for the law into the minds of boisterous cow hands. His successor, James B. (Wild Bill) Hickok, kept many in awe with his amazing ability as a marksman.

A roster of such officers would include many names. One would be an Arizona sheriff, Commodore P. Owens, who made every bullet count against Apache County rustlers. Another would be Pat Garrett of New Mexico, who arrested Billy the Kid. Not the least would be Bill Tilghman, who, singlehanded, captured the notorious Oklahoma bank and train robber, Bill Doolin.

Some of the frontier peace officers, without the aid of fingerprints and crime laboratories, made admirable records as sleuths. In California, where Black Bart, with a flour sack over his head, had robbed twenty-eight stagecoaches, J. B. Hume took this highwayman's trail. Hume, a Wells-Fargo detective, found a handkerchief that Bart had dropped at one of his robberies. On one corner was a small mark, "FX07." Hume started through the records of San Francisco's ninety-one laundries. In a week he linked the mark with a man living quietly under another name between his visits to his "mines." Soon Black Bart was in San Quentin.

In the Big Horn Basin of Wyoming, masked cowmen attacked a sheep camp near Tensleep. They killed three herders, several dogs, and twenty-five sheep. Then they burned the wagons and cut telegraph wires. Sheriff Felix

Alston hurried to the scene. He noticed that one man's tracks showed a boot heel run over on one side. This led him to arrest Herbert Brink, who came the next day to view the bodies. Brink went to prison.

Some of the early statutory courts on the frontier showed no advance over those of the vigilance committees. Like Roy Bean, who tried to bring law "west of the Pecos," Jim Burnett on the San Pedro in Arizona kept a double-barreled shotgun to enforce his edicts. Once, when the body of a shooting victim was brought before him, he ruled that "it served the Mexican right for getting in front of a gun."

Yet the clowns and incompetents on frontier benches were the exception rather than the rule. Most of the judges were upright and well-informed men with the courage to make unpopular rulings. More than a few kept a six-shooter on or under the bench to make their verdicts stick. In the wake of the vigilance committees, they brought formal law to the West.

Outstanding among the early judges of the frontier was Isaac Charles Parker. He presided at the difficult Federal Court of Fort Smith, Arkansas, with jurisdiction over much of the Indian Territory. He was only thirty-six in 1875 when, after two terms as a Representative from Missouri, he was named to the Fort Smith post by President Ulysses S. Grant.

This Arkansas assignment was made one of the toughest in the country by the horde of renegades and cutthroats—white and black as well as bronze —who infested the Indian Territory. Bandits stole cattle from the Texas-Kansas trails. They ambushed, robbed, and often shot travelers. Their crimes led newspapers to refer to the territory as "Robbers' Roost" and "The Land of the Six-Shooter."

In his twenty-one years at Fort Smith, Judge Parker sent eighty-eight men to the gallows that stood within view of his first courtroom. Yet severity of sentences was not the only factor that made his court a landmark in the taming of the West. Of the more than 13,000 defendants brought before him, every one had a scrupulously fair trial. Often he told lawyers to speak more simply, or interrupted to explain something himself. His charges to juries were noted for their fairness. His sternness came from having to deal with unusually hardened criminals. He had little use for technicalities and delays. Often he showed sympathy for the defendants and their families. But his concern was not reserved for them alone. His task was to help make the West safe for law-abiding citizens.

Courts like Judge Parker's ended the need for vigilante action. As soon as legislatures, statutory courts, and elected officials were ready to take over, the volunteer lawmakers of the West put away their six-shooters and their hanging ropes. They were glad to have war whoops give way to school bells, and gun smoke to power lines.

BADGER CLARK

Preachers and Teachers

THREE ARIZONA COWMEN were working in a corral. One of them caught two fingertips between the rope and the snubbing post and got them severely pinched. An elderly minister came down the trail in his buckboard, driving his team of converted broncs. A Harvard man and an incurable quoter of Shakespeare, the Reverend sighted the bloody hand and, reminded of Lady Macbeth, shouted jovially: "Out, damned spot! Out, I say!"

The owner of the sore fingers, who had read books, grinned. The other two looked at each other strangely. "This is a day!" said one. "Did you ever hear a preacher cuss before? I never."

The above anecdote, which is true, has an element not usually present in tales of our lamented Westy West—the preacher. A considerable school of writers would have us believe that life in the early days consisted wholly of swearing, swilling and six-shooting. Since the clergy neglected those activities, they have been regarded as poor copy and left out. But they were there.

Missionaries to the Indians were among the first pioneers. Some of them were martyrs, like Marcus Whitman in Oregon and certain Catholic padres in the Southwest. All of them were up against a tough job in starting their work because so many of the pioneers—secular pioneers, so to speak—in dealing with the Indians, flatly contradicted the Christian precepts that the missionaries tried to inculcate. Yet the missionaries turned out to be workmen who need not be ashamed. Today there is a larger proportion of church members among the Indians than among the race that has a thousand years of Christian tradition behind it.

In the San Francisco of the Vigilance Committee, a preacher named William Taylor turned up, a lank man with a great beard, who in the evenings found a place for his box in the swarming streets and, mounting it, began to sing "Hear the Royal Proclamation" in a powerful voice that soon brought him an audience.

Preacher Smith walked into Deadwood Gulch in April, 1876, while the placer miners were still whipsawing boards to make sluices. He staked no claim, but maintained himself by manual labor during the week, and preached on Sunday wherever he could gather a group to listen. His only surviving "works" are an unfinished sermon, written in pencil, and a nostalgic little poem about his youth in the East. He was shot, apparently by raiding Indians, as he walked through the forest to a preaching appointment at another camp. His body was found beside the trail, unmutilated and decently laid out. It would seem that the Indians regretted their hasty shot when Smith's black coat and Bible told them what manner of man he was. They had learned that members of the clergy did not lie to them or try to cheat and debauch them. That seemed strange for "men of the pale shade," but the Indians liked it.

Such scouts of the Lord sowed their seed as best they might. The resulting crops were very thin until the good women, who are the *sine qua non* of church organizations, came West. Then the wheat sprang up and grew stoutly in spite of the tares. (Tares were pretty thick in mining camps and cow towns.)

The frontier minister I knew best during my impressionable years had his pulpit in a mining camp which contained five churches, twenty-six saloons and three or four other institutions of very doubtful repute, two of which masqueraded as "variety theaters." This preacher was my father, C.B. Clark.

He was a man above middle height. His Civil War service gave him a posture which made him seem taller. He had a full black beard, the somewhat piratical aspect of which was offset by the kindly crinkles around his eyes. Of course he wore the Prince Albert coat, badge of the professional man in those days. A sort of regional loyalty made him top his costume with a Stetson hat, always cocked slightly to the right.

At that time a minister was primarily a preacher, and C.B. could preach. His big, mellow bass needed no amplifying. Its tones had an effect on the nerves something like those of a well-played cello. The sermons were well thought out, with much walking of the floor and looking into books. The only record of them was a few lines of atrocious handwriting on the back of an old envelope. Once he had established sympathetic contact with the audience, he was likely to forget the envelope. His thoughts flowed easily and gracefully into ready phrases. He was enjoying himself. So was his congregation. "I had liberty this morning," he would say. And a parishioner said: "When he has finished, I feel lifted up and, at the same time, ashamed of myself."

C.B.'s war experiences had cost him much misery, and almost his life. Yet he loved the memory of them and was likely to get his religion tangled up with flaming patriotism. Pacifism was pretty much confined to the Quakers. Nobody had any trouble in reconciling his character as a man of peace with his evident love of the thunder of the captains and the shouting. When the Spanish-American War broke out, he arranged what he frankly called "a war meeting" in his church. Leading citizens made bellicose speeches, everyone sang the "Battle Hymn of the Republic" with ringing enthusiasm. The entire proceedings would make the average minister of today shy like a spooky horse.

Belonging to a generation which carried its politics to the point of bloodshed, C.B. was naturally a red-hot partisan, too. But there he had to be careful. In his position, he could not plunge into politics—only hover. Once when he was to give the invocation at the state convention of his party, the chairman, well versed in the idiom of the back room, announced: "The Reverend Clark will now entertain us with a devotional prayer." For once, the Reverend's sonorous voice seemed about to fail him; handkerchief to face, he choked and cleared his throat before he could begin.

At another state convention, C.B. was asked to speak for the nomination of his Sunday School superintendent for Congress. It gave him a legitimate excuse to make a political speech, and made him happy. The superintendent was nominated and elected.

He was the most sociable of men, and without class consciousness. He was seldom in a strange group—in a stagecoach or on a train—for ten minutes without dropping into conversation. He had many friends outside his church, and they were a mixed lot—a Chinese laundryman, a learned Jew with whom he discussed the Law and the Prophets, the motherly nun who headed the Catholic nursing sisters at the hospital, a one-eyed stage driver who was his principal source of tall stories ("I've been in holdups at night when there was so much shootin' goin' on that you could read a newspaper by it"), and an elderly shopkeeper of foreign birth whom C.B. spoke of, at home, as "old Brother Trichina" because he rarely could remember his real name.

Once he was stunned to learn that the well-dressed, gentlemanly stranger with whom he had enjoyed two hours of good talk on the train was a professional gambler. "Well," he said, recovering himself, "he was a royal good fellow, anyway." His random acquaintances were not always so happy. One night he walked the floor at home, saying: "A dirty man in a dirty sickbed in the back room of a saloon! How shall I get him out of there?"

Once, in a stagecoach on the plains, he had two men for fellow passengers. One of them was a militant atheist who lost no time in announcing that he had no soul, that he was "just an infinitesimal speck in the cosmos," and that his highest destiny after death was the enrichment of a very small patch of soil. Seeing it was the man's intention to start an argument as profitless as it would be endless, C.B. answered jokingly, and matched the man's zealous godlessness with trivialities.

Darkness and a blizzard overtook the stage in a particularly lonesome stretch of country. The trail was soon lost. There was nothing to do but go blindly on, trusting to the horses. After anxious hours, they came to a stop at what proved to be a claim shack occupied by a Norwegian and his wife. There they spent the roaring night, nodding in chairs beside the fire. At breakfast, C.B., with a significant glance at "Speck-in-the-Cosmos," said: "Gentlemen, last night we were saved seemingly by the instinct of our horses, but I firmly believe that God had hold of the bridle bits. Otherwise, our bodies"—he repeated—"our bodies would be lying out on the prairie, each with its own little snowdrift. Surely it is no more than decent that we return thanks for our lives." And he did, warmly and at length. Thereafter "Cosmic-Speck" talked politics.

C.B. was too compassionate to take funerals with quite the usual calm. Nor was he content merely to run through the ritual. He always tried to hunt up something good to say about the deceased. For these reasons he was asked to preach a good many funerals, especially the non-church funerals held in the city hall. Sometimes these were respected and respectable people; again they would be the sort whose records needed to be cloaked by what the newspapers used to call "the broad mantle of charity." But there was one non-church funeral which was held in C.B.'s church by his order. And so, though C.B. won his share of honors in life, though he lived many years, made many friends and did many good deeds, he is now remembered for just one thing— he preached Calamity Jane's funeral sermon.

Like the churches, the schools came West with the good women. It was the combined efforts of the preacher and the teacher—along with those of the women—which made the roaring camps cease their roaring and subside into innocuous rumbling. The teaching methods of those times are now pedagogic fossils. Each schoolroom had in its entry a bucket of water and a tin dipper from which all the kids drank, exchanging measles and whooping cough with democratic cordiality. Teacher training was primitive, by our reckoning. But even then that very useful human being, the "born" teacher, existed.

A very adventurous one of these was Annie Donna Tallent, of Sioux City, Iowa. In the fall of 1874, with her ten-year-old son, her husband, and twenty-five other men, she set out by wagon train for the Black Hills, in the van of the gold rush. The party was more than two months crossing the snowy plains, constantly alert for either Indians or United States troops, for they were in forbidden territory and feared the soldiers almost as much as they did the Indians.

Mrs. Tallent walked all the way, partly out of sympathy for the footsore oxen and partly to set a good example to the "boys," as a teacher should. She wore out two pairs of shoes on the way, then made herself deerhide moccasins and wrapped her feet in gunnysacks against the snow.

One man died on the trail and was buried somewhere in the Bad Lands. The rest, on arrival in the mountain wilderness, immediately threw up a log stockade for protection against the Indians and built seven log shacks inside of it. Twenty-five men thus caged together for a whole winter might conceivably have committed several murders before spring. But the lone woman took upon herself the responsibility of maintaining the party's morale. She sewed on buttons, she patched and darned, she laughed, she sang songs, she told stories, and she never complained. If she cried, it was in secret. The surliest man in the outfit soon came to admire her spunk, and carried himself better because of it.

In April a troop of regular cavalry placed the party under arrest as trespassers on Indian land and took them to Fort Laramie. The men had to walk. The gallant lieutenant in command permitted Mrs. Tallent to ride a mule. The Tallents lived in Cheyenne until they could enter the Hills legally. Then they went to Deadwood Gulch, where she cheerfully took up housekeeping in another log shack with a dirt floor. But within a year, of course, she was teaching a group of miners' kids.

She continued the work in a larger school, later to become county superintendent, and serve in other educational capacities. All her days she was honored as a pioneer of pioneers, the first woman of her race to set foot in the Black Hills. She had a rewarding life, did Annie D. Tallent. And she earned it.

Yes, Billy the Kid, Sam Bass and the outlaws, Wild Bill, Wyatt Earp and what we might call the inlaws, were conspicuous, empty wagons who made a tremendous rattledybang in their course. They still have a high entertainment value and are endlessly discussed in print. But it was the preachers, the teachers and their like who built a civilization in the West—the old story of the roaring tempest and the still, small voice.

RICHARD DUNLOP

Saddlebag Docs

IN THE KITS OF MILITARY SURGEONS and the saddlebags of frontier doctors the art of healing acquired in Eastern and European medical schools came to the Old West. But it was the irregulars, the self-taught practitioners and the folk healers who were first on the scene. Men like Kit Carson, Peg-leg Smith and William Clark never saw the inside of a medical school, but they weren't without practical medical knowledge.

At the age of eighteen the redoubtable Kit found himself alone in the wilderness with a companion who had a shattered arm. Using only a razor and a handsaw, he amputated the arm. Then he seared the blood vessels with a heated iron bar. Peg-leg Smith did Kit one better. When an Indian bullet mangled his leg, he sat down beneath a tree, ligated his limb with a buckskin thong and amputated with his hunting knife.

On the famed Lewis and Clark Expedition it was Captain William Clark who recorded in his journal dispensing "doses of nitre" or "thirty drops of laudanum" to the sick. All his patients asked of him in the way of a medical diploma was his ability to cure them, and during the next eighty years or so in the West that was the important question put to any physician.

Irregular doctors prescribing calomel, quinine, gentian or jalap practiced from Kentucky to California. Most of these became practitioners through happenstance. Alfred Robinson arrived in Mexican Santa Barbara in 1829 and found a woman in great pain. He suggested a few drops of laudanum, which so relieved her suffering that he found himself fairly launched on a medical career. In a neighboring town the esteemed "physician" was actually an American sailor who had deserted a whaling ship.

Everywhere the frontier went, men such as these did their best to fight disease and suffering. Few had formal training for their task. Beside them labored strange folk-doctors who drew upon the lore of Indian medicine men. The strangest of these were men like John Dunlap and Dr. B. Greenwood, who were white Indians. Each had been captured by the Indians when a small boy and raised to manhood in the tribes. Torn in their allegiance between white men and red, they spent part of their lives in the settlements and part with the tribes. They practiced medicine wherever they went.

Cut off from a supply of pharmaceuticals in the East, bona fide "sheepskin" doctors often fell back on the same cures used by the irregulars. Dr. J. E. Hodge of Slim Buttes, North Dakota, spent all his spare time crawling among the hills searching for raspberry leaves, spearmint, peppermint, barks and herbs. As many physicians did, he grew what medicines he could in his own back yard. But he didn't mind learning a thing or two from self-taught colleagues.

An M.D. would be happy to share the medical practice of a cow town or mining camp with a reputable irregular doctor. Yet there was a marvelous assortment of quacks in the Old West. These presented something of a problem to a sheepskin doctor as Dr. Edward Walters found out when he rode into Placerville, California, one day and hung out his shingle on a spanking new office made of planks and cotton sheeting.

It happened that a self-styled doctor, Dr. Hullings, considered Placerville his domain. He let it be known at once that he wasn't going to have any sawbones from the East jumping his claim. This was talk a miner could understand. Although Hullings was generally too drunk even to take the pulse of any man jack who fell ill, they listened sympathetically. Tall and bulky in a black coat, flaunting a Mexican sash about his waist, he strode into Dr. Walters' office with half the town at his heels. He demanded to see the newcomer's diploma and certificate. While the miners jeered at him, Walters got out the documents. Hullings seized the precious papers, ripped them in half and deluged their owner's face with a well-directed jet of tobacco juice.

Fortunately, Dr. Walters had had a liberal education as well as medical training. He called Dr. Hullings out of doors to fight a duel, then plugged him through the heart. His first triumphant act as Placerville's official physician was to sign his rival's death certificate.

In most of the Old West, a cowpoke rode a hundred miles with a bullet in his ribs in search of a doctor, and the infant son of a nester wasted away of the dread "summer fever" with only his sunken-eyed mother to look on. Yet in many mining camps there were actually more bona fide doctors per capita than in eastern cities. Some kept their diplomas secreted in their bags and spent all their hours panning for gold, like everybody else. Others treated the stab and gunshot wounds, shattered limbs and thighs and compound fractures, which were daily occurrences among the rough miners. Sometimes, they often had to do other work to stretch their income. Doctors drove ox-teams, served in barrooms and at monte tables, while, in the same town, quacks were draining the miners of their gold. Medical charlatans imposed fantastic and frequently cruel cures for the crippling rheumatism so common among prospectors, or for dysentery, typhoid fever and malaria, all endemic in the mining country. It got so that miners would nurse a sick companion for months rather than let him fall into the hands of these self-avowed doctors. And strangely enough, M.D.'s performed menial tasks at the very time.

Not all the hokum was among the quacks. A poem which ran rampant through the west is evidence of this. A popular newspaper editor, James King, was wounded by a gunman named Casey. While the Vigilance Committee stood by, ready to hang Casey, the top doctors in northern California prepared to remove the bullet, which they did in due course. Unhappily, one of the attending surgeons left a sponge inside the editor, who, consequently, expired. A bard put the story this way:

> "Who killed cock robin?
> I, says Dr. 'Scamon.'
> With my chloroform and gammon,
> I killed cock robin.
>
> Why was it given
> In a smothering dose, by heaven?
> I refuse to say,
> Replied Dr. Gray.
>
> Who put in the sponge?
> I, says Dr. 'Lunge.'
> They did me impunge
> So, 'bedad,' I left in my sponge.
>
> Who blabbed the whole?
> I, says Dr. Cole.
> It lay on my soul,
> And I blabbed the whole."

Miners and bandits, cattlemen and rustlers, all knew the poem, and none were anxious to play cock robin in a sequel. Yet if a doctor or an irregular once established a reputation for humanity, for curing the sick and saving the lives of the wounded, he became honored more than any other man. He alone could ride the trails confident that badmen would let him pass unscathed. In fact, miners in outlying spots would often give the doctor their ore to carry through the lawless countryside to the express office. No bandit could afford to offend the doctor, since at almost any moment he might need his medical services badly. Doc rode unmolested wherever he wished.

A call might take a doctor for a fifty-mile ride into the badlands to an isolated ranch where a horse had fallen on a cowpuncher, or, again, five miles out of town to the bedside of a child down with diphtheria. Except to the afflicted, the saddlebags he used were never a thing of beauty. Two leather pouches fitted with compartments for bottles were connected by a heavy broad leather strap which fitted across the saddle.

What could the doctor do for the cowboy? He might yank a board off the barn wall and employ it, together with part of a bedsheet, to make a splint for a broken leg. To relieve the child's diphtheria he carried a sharp pen-knife. Stabbing the small sufferer through the windpipe, he'd let life-giving air into the suffocating lungs. Sometimes when the patient still couldn't breathe through the puncture, Doc would place a handkerchief over the wound and, with his lips, suck the deadly secretions from the larynx.

Military surgeons, too, did their share to relieve suffering in the West. Usually they were the first trained doctors in a region. Such a surgeon, Colonel William B. Davis, wryly remarked that in most parts of the West you had to shoot a man to start a graveyard. At Fort Totten, where he was stationed, you froze them to death, too. With the temperature hovering around 50 below zero for weeks on end and howling blizzards sweeping down on this Dakota post, his first three deaths were freezings. Cases of frostbite were frequent and severe. So was photophobia, which accompanies snow blindness. One day a rancher was brought into the fort with a terrible case of photophobia. There seemed to be very little that could be done. Dr. Davis held a teaspoon of sulphuric acid in his hand so that the fumes rose against the useless eye. In this way, he succeeded in anesthetizing the organ and restoring vision.

Probably the chief medical problem of Army surgeons year in and year out was scurvy. On their diet of salt meat, white bread, soda biscuits, syrup, lard, black coffee and hard tack, the soldiers could not long remain healthy. They rarely obtained fruit or fresh meat and vegetables. Not until each post was required to have its own truck garden did the situation improve.

Army surgeons took to the field with the troopers when an Indian fight threatened. Dr. Thomas Maghee rode into battle at Bates Creek on July 4, 1874. While dressing a soldier's wound, Maghee had his forehead grazed by a Sioux bullet. Here is the official War Department version:

"While dressing the wound of Private Gable, he was the object of the direct fire of an Indian, partly hidden in a ravine, until, laying down his instruments for a moment, he took his carbine and, stepping out a few paces, killed the Indian and then returned quietly to his work."

Maghee then packed the wounded a hundred miles on horseback through heat, dust and flies to safety.

Later, Dr. Maghee went into private practice at Rawlins, Wyoming. In the dead of winter, with thermometers pushing forty below, he made regular trips to patients on the Snake River, sixty miles distant. The only way he could survive these long trips was to ride until he got thoroughly cold and then dismount. Holding onto the tail of his horse, he would run until he was warmed up again. Then he'd mount and ride until once again he was so stiff with cold that he had to get down and literally run for his life.

Neither Dr. Maghee nor any other saddlebag doctor had a nurse to help him. Only the shepherds, cowboys, miners or homesteaders were on hand to tend an injured friend. They weren't, though, the sort who faint at the sight of blood. Dr. Maghee recalled how tender and patient they were with the sick. With the aid of untutored men like these, he undertook plastic surgery on the face of a sheepherder who had discharged his shotgun in his face. After thirty-nine operations, the victim's face was restored in a fashion that modern doctors with the latest in facilities find remarkable.

All things considered, it seems in keeping that so many great medical discoveries came out of the Old West. Ephraim McDowell was already a great doctor when, in December, 1809, he made medical history in Kentucky. He was so tall that his legs almost touched the ground when he rode his horse into the snowy forest clearing where the Crawfords had built their cabin. Indoors he found Mrs. Crawford sick with a great tumor, which, if not dealt with, would soon cause her painful death. Nowhere had any doctor ever been able to prevent this fate. Dr. McDowell determined to remove the tumor. Such an operation had never been done before. But if death was inevitable, why not try? Mrs. Crawford agreed. The long-legged doctor and his grotesque patient rode over the frozen trails to Danville. Their progress was slow. Mrs. Crawford's tumor kept chafing on the saddle pommel. So news of what the doctor planned to do outran them. Before he got to town, the local clergy were denouncing the impending "butchery."

Dr. McDowell waited until Christmas Day because he felt that God's mercy would be greatest then. He dosed his patient with a few opium pills. There was no anesthesia. In the village church the preacher thundered against the butcher surgeon; in McDowell's house, Mrs. Crawford loudly sang hymns as the doctor cut her open. Her voice shaking with the terrible agony, she sang hymn after hymn. Dr. McDowell's face grew fiery red, but whispering tender and soothing words he continued the operation.

In the church, the preacher finished his indictment of the unheard-of operation. The congregation rushed to McDowell's house and shouted angrily for the butchery to stop. Mrs. Crawford only clenched the table harder and sang on. Readying a rope over a tree limb to hang McDowell in case his patient died, the crowd threw rocks at the house. Some of the men dashed at the door to break it in. The sheriff intervened, drove them back to the crowd. Within the house, the sobbing hymns grew weaker and weaker and finally stopped.

This elaborate operation within the body cavity was a success. Within five days Mrs. Crawford shocked her doctor by making her own bed. She soon threw herself back into frontier life. The crowd outside McDowell's door now cheered the surgeon. Medical men were astounded at the news from the American frontier. The abdominal cavity could safely be opened, and an ovarian tumor could be removed. No longer was it necessary to die of appendicitis and similar disorders, previously considered incurable.

Daniel Drake was another American frontier genius. A physician of eminence, who established medical schools and labored to spread medical knowledge, he determined to learn all he could about the medical geography of the interior of America. All the way to the Rocky Mountains he roamed, studying the topography, meteorology, plants, animals, rocks, water, men—everything he needed to know to understand the diseases of North America. He pursued his quest by canoe and on foot for ten years. Trappers in the lonely Northwest were astonished to see the tall, thin doctor stride out of the woods and sit at their campfires. There he learned of the diseases that troubled them, the animals, the weather. Doctors everywhere were flattered to have the celebrated physician look them up in their remote river towns. Indian medicine men found Dr. Drake interested in their cures. Finally Drake's incredible masterwork appeared. Titled *The Principal Diseases of the Interior Valley of North America*, it covered several thousand closely printed pages and has since become recognized as the greatest contribution to medical geography since Hippocrates.

While Dr. Drake pursued his amazing study, Dr. William Beaumont was a military surgeon on Mackinac Island, then headquarters of the American Fur Company. Trappers and voyageurs came back to the island in upper Lake Huron from all over the West. Beaumont was used to their wild revelry, the booming tom-toms and drunken war whoops of the Indians who accompanied them. He was used to mending bashed-in heads and gunshot wounds.

In the spring of 1820 he was confronted with one of the most baffling medical cases in history, and one of the greatest opportunities for medical research that a doctor ever had. One night of hard drinking and tall-story telling, Alexis St. Martin, a nineteen-year-old voyageur, stood close to a shotgun held in the hands of another man. The weapon was discharged accidentally. The full blast of the gun tore a big hole in the youth's stomach. Running to the desperately injured voyageur, Dr. Beaumont could see that with such a big puncture in his stomach it was almost impossible that even a tough young voyageur could live longer. The boy was conscious, and Dr.

Beaumont cleaned the wound. When in an hour St. Martin was still living, Beaumont dressed the wound with great caution. Tenderly he cared for the hopeless case as the days went by. Weeks passed. Dr. Beaumont watched fascinated while the boy's tissues expelled the shot and splintered bone. Still the hole in the stomach would not heal. Beaumont had to cover it with a linen compress to keep food from running out.

Months went by. The doctor tried everything he could think of to heal the hole. The youth lived, but his body could not accomplish this one last thing. However, a strange valve-like flap finally formed around the hole so that St. Martin could once more keep food in his stomach. Within the year he hobbled about and in time regained a voyageur's lusty good health.

Then started an amazing investigation. Through the hole in St. Martin's stomach, Dr. Beaumont was able to study the organ during digestion. He suspended raw and roasted meat through the opening and watched the effects of the gastric juices which nobody had seen before. He learned a great deal about the influence of the emotions on digestion. It isn't surprising, of course, that St. Martin grew tired of this guinea-pig life. One night he ran off to become a voyageur again. He married and started a family.

Dr. Beaumont, his experiments half completed, searched the West over for the voyageur with the rare hole in his stomach. Finally he was located. Beaumont rejoined St. Martin at Prairie du Chien on the Mississippi. He brought his wife and children with him. The two men, one a great medical scientist, the other an ignorant voyageur, resumed their odd collaboration which for the first time revealed the mysteries of digestion.

Not all the great doctors who practiced in the Old West confined their contributions to medicine. Dr. John Evans often wrapped himself in his shaggy buffalo robe and slumped down on the floor of a frontier cabin to get a few hours of rest. Lying there in the filth, he dreamed of great seats of learning in the West. His dreams became reality when he founded Northwestern University in Evanston, Illinois, a town which bears his name, and Denver University in Denver. Abraham Lincoln made him the second territorial governor of Colorado. As governor he proved a master at maintaining peace with the Indians during the Civil War, when the settlements were exposed to savage attack.

Certainly saddlebag doctors and military surgeons alike—and many irregular practitioners, too—met the same hardships, knew the same adventures, as other men, enjoyed the same triumphs in the winning of the West. But true to their calling, these were men who found the challenge of disease even more fascinating than the challenge of the western frontier.

The prospector is a man of imagination . . . the spirit of unrest burns in his blood. It matters nothing that he discovers a "good thing"—this is well enough but he wants something better, and after a day or two spent in "locating his claims" he is off again.

J. ROSS BROWNE– "Adventures in the Apache Country"

JOSEPH STOCKER

The Prospectors

SOMEWHERE IN THE WEST a treasure is tapped beneath the thirsty surface of the earth. The news seeps out, quickening men's hearts, stirring the juices of adventure and acquisitiveness. Off they swarm, across the prairies, through the desert and into the canyons and mountain passes, risking all—their resources and even their lives—on the search for subterranean riches.

These are the prospectors. In a hundred years and a little more, the West saw three waves of them—men very much alike in guts and temperament but seeking different kinds of wealth. Some found what they sought; most didn't. But they starred the map with imperishable names, like Comstock and Cripple Creek, Spindletop and Signal Hill, Moab and the Colorado Plateau. And each wave wrote a unique chapter in world history. Minerals! Oil! Uranium!

First there were the hunters of minerals—gold, silver and copper. Their saga began near Sutter's Fort, on a bright California day in January. . . .

John August Sutter was a Swiss, an adventurer and colonizer who drifted into California with the early pioneers. Near the conjunction of the American and Sacramento rivers he established a hacienda and built a fort to protect it from the Indians. New Helvetia, he called it. It grew into a little empire, sustained by ranching, farming and a trading post. Gold? Nobody gave any thought to the possibility of gold in California—until it happened.

The date was January 23, 1848. Sutter had sent his carpenter, Jim Marshall, to build a dam and sawmill on the American River. The mill was nearly finished when Marshall realized that the tailrace was not deep enough. He opened the water gate to let the river in, so that it would wash out the earth

149

and deepen the channel. The next morning, while the mill hands were at breakfast, he shut off the water and sauntered down for a look.

Suddenly, that was no longer of any consequence. For there, on the flat, wet stones at his feet, he saw glistening specks of yellow. He pounded them. He bit them. They were soft and malleable. He tucked them into the crown of his hat and ran off to show them to the mill hands.

"Boys!" he shouted. "By God, I believe I've found a gold mine!"

He had. And the rush was on.

Into California by the tens of thousands poured the Forty-niners. They swept onto and over Sutter's little empire, devastating his crops, slaughtering his cattle. His mill hands and ranch hands deserted, to head for the diggings. Sutter, embittered, left California, to die in poverty and obscurity. It was the first great irony of the century of prospecting. But it was by no means the last.

From the Sacramento Valley the treasure hunters fanned out all over the West. They placer-mined the rivers and creeks for the free gold washed down from the hillsides. When that played out, they dug into the mountains in search of "mother lodes." The gold camps sprang up—lusty, boisterous, lawless places that flamed so long as the gold lasted, then died out like spent skyrockets.

There was Nevada's Comstock, discovered by a Mormon named William Prouse. He paused to pan in a stream on the eastern slope of the Sierras, and found some bits of gold. But he didn't realize that he was standing at the threshold of the Comstock Lode. On he went to California, his chance at fortune forever gone.

The word slipped out, though. More prospectors worked into Nevada. Two of them were brothers—Hosea and Allen Grosh. They hacked some ore from a canyon ledge, had it assayed, found it to be almost pure silver, and staked a claim. But Hosea struck his ankle with a pick and died of blood poisoning; Allen, crossing the Sierras for supplies, perished in a blizzard.

A Canadian miner named Henry Comstock arrived a year later. He moved into the Grosh cabin, pre-empted the Grosh claim (there was no law and order to say that he couldn't) and gave his name to the most prodigious treasure trove the world had ever seen. Within five years, a hundred million dollars in gold and silver was plucked from the Comstock Lode. One of its claims—the Big Bonanza—proved to be the greatest body of rich ore in all of history, with two mines alone that yielded an average of $1,500,000 a month.

The Comstock gave rise to such boom towns as Gold Hill and Silver City. The liveliest of them all got its name from a tosspot known as "Old Virginia." Drunk one night, he stumbled with a bottle of whisky, and crashed the bottle on the stone step of his shack. Lurching over, he picked

"Placer Mining"—from *Marvels of the New West*, by W. M. Thayer, 1887

up a fragment of glass, let the last drop of whisky dribble on the ground and mumbled, "I christen thee Virginia Town." And so they called it Virginia City.

Then there was Pikes Peak, catapulted into immortality by two prospectors who gathered twenty-five cents' worth of gold in Cherry Creek with a bread pan and shovel. That started the rush to Colorado. Westward over the Kansas plains and into the foothills of the Rockies rolled Conestoga wagons with "Pikes Peak or Bust" splashed across their canvas hoods. (Those who failed to hit it rich came clattering dejectedly out of the hills with a new inscription on their wagons: "Busted, by Gosh!")

Gold and silver worth millions were taken out of the Pikes Peak country. The rush produced, among many other things, the city of Denver, the state of Colorado, the beginnings of the Guggenheim fortune, and a singular character known as Haw (for his initials, H.A.W.) Tabor. He made his pile out of California Gulch, near Leadville, and then, in Denver, built the

"Bust!"—by W. M. Cary

Tabor Grand Opera House, a monument not so much to grand opera as to Tabor. Strolling into the lobby one day as the place was being given its finishing touches, he noticed the picture of an odd-looking man painted on the wall.

"Who's that?" grunted the Bonanza King.

"Shakespeare," replied the architect.

"What the hell did he ever do for Colorado?" demanded Tabor. "Put my picture up there."

So Shakespeare was painted out and Tabor painted in.

Haw Tabor was only one of many singular characters to emerge from the gold and silver camps of the West. Another was Winfield Scott Stratton, an ex-carpenter with more mining money than he knew what to do with and a temper tenuous enough to make him spend it on pure whim. During a party at Denver's Brown Palace Hotel, he decided it would be fun to toss champagne bottles over an upper-floor railing, just to hear them pop on the lobby floor below. The manager tried to stop him.

"I'm Stratton," said Stratton, "and I'll do what I like."

"No, you won't!" said the manager. "Get out of my hotel!"

The next day Stratton went to the owners of the Brown Palace, bought it for $1,000,000 and handed over a check in full payment. Then he went back to the manager. "Now you get out of *my* hotel," he barked. He owned the Brown Palace until he died.

The shine was wearing off the Colorado boom when Cripple Creek was discovered. Then the rush was on all over again. A cowboy named Bob Womack, who went prospecting when he was supposed to be herding cattle, made the first big strike in the Cripple Creek district. He got drunk and sold out his interest in the El Paso Lode for $500. Two Colorado Springs druggists, ignorant of geology and mining, threw a hat into the air, dug where it landed—and hit pay dirt. They called their mine the Pharmacist. Two grocers accepted a half-interest in a claim in payment of a miner's grocery bill—$36.40. They sold the half-interest to a schoolteacher, who prospected the claim, struck a vein of gold, and made $13,000,000.

Thus, from mining camp to mining camp—tales of fantastic fortune and equally fantastic misfortune, of lucky strikes and luckless men. After Colorado came major gold discoveries in Idaho and Montana. Then, off to the east, a Sioux Indian chief gave a Jesuit priest a handful of nuggets, and the invasion of South Dakota's Black Hills was under way. It was an invasion that spawned Deadwood Gulch, Calamity Jane, Wild Bill Hickok, and a thousand Hollywood horse operas.

Down in Arizona, a frontiersman with the curious name of Pauline Weaver panned gold out of the Colorado River and started the rush to La Paz. An Austrian immigrant, Henry Wickenburg, watched a vulture sweep lazily over a distant ledge, found gold there and called his mine the Vulture. Farther south, Prospector Ed Schieffelin disregarded the Apache peril and the warnings of friends ("Instead of a mine, you'll find a tombstone"), and struck it rich in silver. "You're a lucky cuss," said his brother, Al. The mine was dubbed the Lucky Cuss; the town that grew up there was Tombstone.

The gold and silver began to peter out. Some prospectors drifted away. Others stayed and dug deeper, down through the strata where the gold and silver had been found, deeper than anyone ever had dug before. They hit a new kind of pay dirt—copper.

In Butte, Montana, a peripatetic trader, one W. A. Clark, spied some copper-stained outcrops on a wind-swept hill. He built a small furnace for smelting the copper and started Butte on its way to becoming the "Richest Hill on Earth."

In Arizona an army scout found copper at Jerome and staked out a claim which he called the Verde. A small metals firm in New York, Phelps Dodge & Company, heard about it and sent Dr. James Douglas to have a look. Douglas didn't think it very promising. But Clark came in from Montana and took $60,000,000 out of the United Verde. Douglas, meantime, ambled on down to the Mexican border, to the little town of Bisbee, where he bought a claim for Phelps Dodge. That was the Copper Queen. It disgorged two billion pounds of copper and netted PD $100,000,000.

To many prospectors, it must have seemed that the West's parched earth by now had surely yielded up just about all the treasure it was capable of yielding. But a new and even more wondrous era of Western prospecting was about to begin, and a new kind of prospector was about to make his entrance. He was the oil-driller—the wildcatter.

Anthony F. Lucas and Pattillo Higgins were among the first of this breed. Lucas was an engineer in the Louisiana sulphur mines but less interested in sulphur than in the possibilities of oil beneath the salt mounds where

"Millionaires Laying Plans"—from *Roughing It*, by Mark Twain, 1872

the sulphur lay. Higgins was a wildcatter, drilling a well on a salt mound known as Spindletop, just across the border in east Texas. But he was having tough luck. A storm blew over his wooden derrick; quicksand filled the hole and ruined it.

Then Higgins met Lucas. They decided to drill a second well at another point on the salt mound. They went down to 1,160 feet and found only sand and water. They drilled farther. On January 11, 1901, Spindletop blew in, hurtling its black spume 190 feet into the air. The Gulf Coast field had been tapped. The age of oil had dawned in the West.

Out of this boom grew the Mellon family's Gulf Oil Company, the Texas Company, and more boom towns. Beaumont exploded from 10,000 to 30,000 people in three months. Land values went the same way. A woman garbage collector sold her pig pasture for $35,000. Property worth $40 an acre before Spindletop brought $40,000 afterward.

Oil was an expensive and risky business, though—not at all like gold. You could hunt for gold with a pan and a shovel, or a burro and a cart and a few pieces of dynamite. It cost thousands of dollars to drill an oil well, and nine out of ten would be dusters.

But there were plenty of men to take the chance. Edgar B. Davis was one. He made some money in Sumatra rubber, and sank it all in a string of dry holes in Caldwell County, near Austin. He still believed there was oil there. He sold everything—even the furniture in his office—to raise money for one more well. Finally, he borrowed $25,000 from the Magnolia Petroleum Company and gave his rig and his leases as collateral.

The loan fell due. It was extended. It fell due again. There was still no oil. Davis couldn't pay his drillers. He sat down and wrote Magnolia to step in and protect its interests. Then he went out to take a last look at his well. He saw a pillar of oil cascade up from the hole, into the Texas sky.

Sometimes boldness and persistence weren't enough. Then a little resourcefulness helped. It helped Pete Frost of Houston, just getting a start in the oil game. One day he heard of a wildcat being drilled secretly in the country. He borrowed a pair of dogs, shouldered a gun and headed for the site. There was a guard at the entrance.

Frost emerged from the brush. He fired three times at an imaginary rabbit and shook his head.

"Miss him?" asked the guard.

"Sure did," said Frost.

They fell to chatting about the vagaries of rabbit hunting. When the guard's attention was momentarily diverted, Frost lifted a tarp and sneaked a peek at a well gauge. It told him that the driller had hit oil. He left, leased all the available land in the vicinity, drilled his own well and became a wealthy man.

From Texas the derricks marched northward into Oklahoma, westward into New Mexico and California, and on up into Wyoming. Rich strike followed rich strike; legend heaped on legend. In Oklahoma City there was the Wild Mary Sudik, which blew uncontrolled for eleven days, showering oil on homes and farms a half-dozen miles distant. There were Oklahoma's threadbare Osage Indians, who, after oil was found on their land, bought Pierce-Arrows and Lincolns and then, if a tire went flat, traded them in for new Pierce-Arrows and Lincolns. And in California there was a geologist who said, "I'll drink all the oil there is at Long Beach." He'd have drunk about a billion barrels at latest count, because that's where a place called Signal Hill is located.

After a while, the oil fever settled into organized big-time industry. World War II came. Something terrible happened to Hiroshima. Out on the Colorado Plateau a new fever erupted. The source of infection this time was uranium.

Vernon Pick was the first to get rich in it. He was an electrical contractor in Minneapolis. When his shop burned down, he collected his insurance, acquired a trailer and headed for Mexico. On his way through the West he heard intriguing talk of uranium. He bought a Geiger counter and geology books and headed into the Colorado Plateau country. Nine months later and a hundred miles west of Moab, Utah, he turned up an ore bed that made him $10,000,000.

A few weeks later it happened to Charlie Steen. He'd caught the fever from reading an article in a mining journal. For two and a half years he scoured the wastelands, so poor at times that he had to steal coal to keep his family warm and couldn't afford canned milk for his baby. Then, with a borrowed drill, he took out some ore samples near Moab and brought them into town for testing. The counter needle went crazy. "We've struck it!" shouted Steen. "It's a million-dollar lick!" It was that, all right, and a good deal more.

So the third wave of prospectors came rolling into the West, with picks and jeeps, Geiger counters, scintillometers and hope eternal. Again, as with prospectors everywhere, some hit it big, some hit nothing and some hit in between. They were the advance guard of America's atomic future.

And they were something else, too. There, on the Colorado Plateau, the mid-twentieth century met up with the mid-nineteenth; the age of the atom found kinship with the age of the Conestoga wagon. Once again, men dug for treasure in the West. And, by their labors, they made a hundred years come full circle to link the West's present with its past—a robust and glittering past that began at Sutter's Mill.

Part 4

The TOTE

Preceding page:
"A Sharp Turn"
—from *Fifteen Thousand Miles by Stage*,
by C. A. Strahorn, G. P. Putnam's Sons, 1911

There were three waves of migration on this continent and the second was always the cattlemen. Ahead went the trappers and the Indian traders. . . . Behind the cattle came the farmers. . . . There were always cattle out ahead of the plows. And for a simplest reason. Beef and pork and mutton were the only crops in that land without roads which could take themselves to market. . . . Cattle made the first frontier where white men lived. And grass made cattle.

ABCHIBALD MAC LEISH– "Green River"

COLONEL EDWARD N. WENTWORTH

Their Critters

No cows, no cowboys. No sheep, no shepherds. No livestock, not much American West. Animal agriculture now provides about two-thirds of the total income for all the U.S.A.'s farms and ranches. We can hold to the same ratio in the story of the West. Just about two-thirds of it is a livestock story.

Yet, except for the turkey, every one of the domestic animals figuring so spectacularly in the development of the Great Plains, the desert bowl and the Pacific Slope was an import. The Indian, a skilled botanist, had little knowledge of animal husbandry. Somewhere in the Southwest, or the Mexican highlands, he developed the corn that was to be the mainstay of the American cattle and pig industries. He crossbred the beans that were to be a mainstay of cowboy and Mexican diets. Pumpkins, peanuts, potatoes, were all Indian inventions, too, ready and waiting for the white man's taking. But the flighty, stupid turkey and the dog that eventually trailed the red man from Asia, were the only domesticated animals in North America when the Spanish and English landed. The story of Western livestock, then, begins in the East.

We can trace the original "cowboy-and-Indian" story to the East, too. It is almost 1,000 years old. The Norsemen brought cattle, sheep, and poultry to Vinland (probably New England) in 1004 A.D. Leif the Lucky's brother-in-law, Thorfinn Karlsefne, headed the expedition. He began trade with the Indians, exchanging red cloth, spears and swords for furs. Then he grew suddenly cautious and forbade any more exchange of weapons. This, in a developmental pattern that was to become commonplace throughout the West, infuriated the red men. They attacked and, by sheer weight of numbers, forced the Norse back toward their boats. Suddenly, as though ejected from an Alley Oop time machine, a huge red bull charged from the center of the Norse defense line. He tossed Indians to right and left, and sent the rest screaming into the forest.

The records do not reveal whether one of Karlsefne's drovers, dressed in leather breeches, a mail shirt and a raven's head "stetson," thought up the idea and "spooked" the bull through the lines. Yet there, on the very threshold of the white man's invasion of the New World, rears the original cowboy-and-Indian story, waiting patiently for a convention of the Western Writers of America, Inc.

If any of the Norse stock did fall into Indian hands, no effort was made to domesticate them. Nor is there evidence that the episodes passed into Indian folklore in the Northeast. Even explanation of the Aztec god Quetzalcoatl as a tenth- or eleventh-century Norseman falls short on this point. The Norse were excellent stockmen. Yet no legend of horses, cattle, sheep, pigs, goats, or chickens appears in Indian folklore before the day in 1519 when Cortes' cavalry landed in Yucatan, and man-and-horse were mistaken for a new kind of animal . . . a living centaur.

Hence, the Indian adaptations to horses, pigs and sheep are all part of the European conquest of the Americas. The Apache horseman, the Navajo herder, the Cherokee pork-lover, were actually first steps in that direction.

Aurochs, the cousin of the bison who somehow never migrated to the Americas, split into many families in Europe. Spain, England, France, all had good cattle country. But the mountains of Spain and France were better suited to rangeland operations than the moors and forests of England. So our cowboy and ranch traditions trace their ancestry more readily through the Pyrenees and the plateaus of Castile back to the skilled cowboys from Carthage who used wild cattle to stampede the Roman cavalry. Across the Channel, the English followed the more sedate route of the Flemish dairymen and used cattle as milch animals and oxen.

This difference was to have several influences on the development of the American West. The Spanish were, essentially, pork-lovers. They raised cattle for hides, bone, tallow, and bullfights. The peasantry of England were more frugal. They slaughtered their oldest oxen, sheep and pigs late each fall, thus eliminating them as grain-and-hay consumers over the winter months.

So the smoky-blue days of Martinmas provided the Englishman's big fresh-meat feast of the year. Then he gorged himself on livers, kidneys, fresh sausage, spareribs and knucklebones. Mutton joints, hams, bacon, butts and sides were salted down or smoked over peat and birchwood fires for winter use.

The carcasses of the sinewy old oxen were hung outdoors in sheds, until mold and "aging" broke down the tissues and tenderized the meat. This process was usually completed by the end of December.

It was but a short step from these traditions to the Thanksgiving feast of fresh meat in the New World and the joints of "aged" roast beef, with a side of crisp Yorkshire pudding, as the entree at Christmas or New Year's dinner.

Both the European mainlanders and the English knew branding irons. They had been used from time immemorial to permanently mark slaves and criminals, just as the New England Puritan would calmly brand convicted whores and their consorts with the letter "A" for "adultery," and Cortes would brand all his Aztec slaves with "G" for *guerra*, i.e., "war." But, again, frugality and traditions come into play. The Spanish free-ranged their cattle, so used big, bold brands on the sides of the animals. The Englishman considered this wasteful, and branded his cattle with script letters on the butt of the tail, thus assuring himself of an unblemished "side" for leather.

These were the basic "rigs," then, that moved into the New World, along separate channels, between 1500 and 1625. The Spaniard trekked his long-horned, gaunt Andalusian cattle into Mexico, thence north to Arizona, New Mexico and California. The English landed on the North Atlantic seaboard with red Devon milch cows and fat, yellow Danish oxen. It was like lighting two fuses, 2,000 miles apart, that would sputter along over two centuries and finally explode into the fireworks display of the trail drives and western range after 1850.

The horse proved itself the most individualistic of all the Europeans' animals. It took off for the Great Plains and went native. Fortunately for the Indians—but not for the nineteenth-century whites—the horses that "went West" were Spanish. Spain was still groggy from an eight-hundred-year war with the Moors and their wonderful Arab cavalry. Thus Spain possessed the best race horses and cavalry mounts of Europe. Its rapid evolution into the redoubtable "mustang" was logical.

If English, rather than Spanish, horses had been the first to run away to the plains, the results would not have been the same. English horses were bred for the heavy equipage of armored knights. The Clydesdale and Suffolk are typical. They had the paunchy impressiveness, and Col. Blimp dignity, of a beer wagon. The bison could have yawned and trotted away from any Apache or Comanche silly enough to mount them. Again, fate intervened. The Barb horses reached the Great Plains first. Mexican, Texan, Arizonan, Indian learned to ride them. Then, far up the Pacific coast, the Cayuse Indians

A Running of Wild Horses—from *McClure's Magazine*, volume xxxv

began to breed a vigorous, speedy strain of the new animal, and traded the stock back among the Blackfeet and Sioux. So the herds thundering the Great Plains of the nineteenth century won three names . . . "Cayuse" for the Oregon tribe of breeders, "mustang" from the Spanish *mesteño*, "a grazer," and "bronco," the Spanish word for "wild."

The pig could have joined the Indian's family, too, if it wasn't such a consarned, ornery individualist. Hernando de Soto learned that in 1540. Rigged to repeat the splendors-and-booty of Cortes' Mexico conquest, De Soto landed on the west coast of Florida—presumably at Charlotte Harbor—in May, 1539. As a pork-lover, he brought along twelve sows and a boar. They happened to be the first pigs to land in what is now the United States. The following spring, nature having taken her course, no fewer than three hundred porkers joined a cavalcade of three hundred horses, six hundred soldiers, twenty officers and twenty-four priests who spent the next three years on a trek through Georgia, the Carolinas, Tennessee, Alabama, Mississippi and Arkansas.

The Spanish knew the trick that was to make pig-drives possible across the Alleghenies and prairies during the nineteenth century. Sows, left to their own devices, are almost impossible to drive. They dawdle, graze, root, snooze and send drovers into violent rages. But—sweet sex!—sows will follow a boar with the docility of a hundred freight cars following a locomotive. However, a boar is just about the most arrogant creature on four feet . . . when he can see where he's going. But, blinded, a boar is as gentle as a poodle. Pig-drovers, then, merely sewed boars' eyelids together with gut and led them along the trail. All of the sows chuffed along, too.

Everything was going fine for De Soto until he served roast pork at a ceremonial dinner to one of the Indian chiefs. The Indians had never tasted anything like it. It had bison steak, venison, roast tarpon and rattlesnake filet pushed clear off the menu. From there on out, any Indian would gladly swap three squaws and a hank of beaver for a pound of pork chops. "Every night," reported De Soto's chronicler, "they would come up to some houses where the hogs slept, a crossbow-shot off from the camp, to kill and carry away what they could of them."

Roast-pig drooling caused Indian executions and pitched battles all the way to the Mississippi. In one of them, De Soto lost eleven soldiers, fifty horses and more than two hundred pigs. Finally, he took to handing out pairs of sows and boars, with breeding instructions, as a sort of "Croix de Oink" to chiefs who guaranteed good manners while De Soto trooped through the territory. Yet when the "virtuous, intrepid Captain Don Hernando de Soto" died in Arkansas and his property was distributed, more than three hundred pigs remained in the cavalcade. Most of these went to the Indians, and some eventually ran wild.

Thus it may be that to De Soto, the South and Southwest owe countless generations of the lean, long-legged, slab-sided "razorback" and "alligator"—mongrel pig that can jump a four-foot fence, eat its fill of rattlesnakes and copperheads, and hold wildcats, wolves and even bears at bay.

More than three hundred years later a rugged and unconquerable Dutchman named Pete Kitchen raised swine of the same strain in the Santa Cruz Valley of Arizona—and had experiences to match De Soto's. Pete was proud of his hogs. He processed and sold hams and bacon to every settlement from Nogales, Sonora, to Silver City, New Mexico. But, before the little pigs could go to market, their lives were in constant jeopardy. Repeatedly, Pete, his Mexican wife and his Opata Indian laborers had to stand off raiding Apaches with a hankering for pork. When a visitor, after seeing a sow limp around with Indian arrows in her hide, called her a "portable pincushion," commercial-minded Pete asked, "Don't you mean *porkable?*"

Economics prevailed over taste buds, however. The Indian of the West never took up with the pig, as he did with the horse and later the sheep and beef cow. Nor were there many Pete Kitchens beyond the Missouri. The pig is essentially a forest animal. Thus, although bacon and ham and salt pork were standard diet for miners, cowboys and the Army, the supplies were hauled in from the great corn-belt packing centers at Cincinnati and Chicago. Indeed, the pig became the basic reason for the Corn Belt. Pork production from Ohio to Nebraska and Missouri encouraged the big plow-up of prairie for corn acreage. Still today, the pig consumes more than forty per cent of the U.S.A.'s corn crop, while cattle consume only twenty to twenty-five per cent.

Cincinnati, as the logical packing point to turn Ohio, Indiana and Kentucky hogs into hams, bacon and fat-back for southern and western markets, quickly won the name of "Porkopolis." From her docks, steamboats loaded pork supplies for plantations all down the Mississippi as well as for the covered wagons' "jumping-off places" along the Missouri, the Arkansas and the Red rivers.

The assembly-line techniques of pork processing developed by the Cincinnati packers between 1810 and 1880 gave the manufacturers of Detroit the techniques for the assembly lines they developed in the automobile industry after 1900.

Ideas for the refrigerator car, and eventually the home refrigerator, came out of Cincinnati packing plants, too. And, oddest quirk of all, some of the packers' profits went to universities to finance archaeological excavations in ancient Greece and Troy, where, historians learned, the pig was first domesticated and swine herding began about 10,000 years ago.

By the time the pig reveled in Ohio cornlots, Mexican cattle and sheep were in Texas, Arizona and California, readying for the final move into the Great Plains. The crossing of the Alleghenies meant much for the feeding of American steers. The main avenues of approach were via the Mohawk River and the Erie Canal route to Buffalo, or the Ohio River from Pittsburgh. Much livestock traveled from still farther southeast via the Potomac, the Youghiogheny, and the Kanawha, with a southern contingent of cattle coming from south and southeast of Cumberland Gap. Soon a surplus of cattle existed in southern Ohio and Kentucky that caused a period of eastward droving to market. But the droving, in spite of its picturesqueness, did not last many years. Before 1850 it was necessary to go farther west for low-cost cattle that could be fattened profitably.

Then came the call to supply the great, lusty rush to the California gold fields. Stockmen and herds came from as far east as New York, Ohio, and Michigan and as far south as Texas and New Mexico. Very quickly, all wild game suitable for food in California was exhausted. Smart Eastern traders looked for profits in the food supply, rather than in finding precious metals. The Oteros drove cattle and sheep from New Mexico; Ira H. Butterfield and John D. Patterson drove cattle and sheep from New York.

The Gold Rush not only offered stockmen new markets for meat and draft animals but gave them opportunity to test new strains of sheep, cattle, horses, mules and burros in the Far West. A revolution in animal agriculture had been under way since the first years of the Republic. President Washington, Thomas Jefferson, Senator Henry Clay and Robert Livingston were among the leaders. Partly because of developments in England, partly because of fears for the future of American agriculture, they preached and demonstrated an upgrading of American herds.

George Washington took a special interest in mules and burros and conducted breeding experiments at Mount Vernon with the animals given him by the king of Spain and the Marquis de Lafayette. Later, Henry Clay continued the experiments. Thus, in time, the mule became the standard draft animal of the U.S. Army, as well as of the southern cotton plantations and the Southwest's mines and wagon trains. Then Missouri became the principal mule-producing state—probably because it lay astraddle both the Mississippi route south and the Santa Fe route west, plus the Army depots at St. Louis and Leavenworth.

Henry Clay, too, was one of the first American importers of Herefords, the chunky red-and-white beef animal developed in Herefordshire, England. He preached their virtues to Kentucky and Ohio stockmen who came to watch the trotters and pacers work out on the model one-mile track at his estate near Lexington, Kentucky.

Similarly, back in the Hudson Valley, Robert Livingston wrote long, glowing reports about the Merino sheep he had imported from Spain, and helped Elkanah Watson, the Pittsfield, Massachusetts, banker, promote his notion for an annual county fair to demonstrate superior animals, crops and farm production methods. The idea took. Out of Watson's scheme came the whole gaudy procession of state and county fairs and livestock expositions.

Steers from Indiana now began to replace those from Ohio in eastern markets. When the Civil War required that animals be moved by rail rather than by droving, the Chicago and St. Louis packing plants developed rapidly. By 1865, the regions for the supply of firm-fleshed cattle had moved into western Illinois and Iowa. The peculiar thing about this situation was that it was not man-made. There was no particular effort on the part of the westernmost feeders to make "solid" cattle at the same costs as their eastern competitors. The results were inherent in the new soils, the transportation conditions, and the westward movement of the market.

This was the situation when the Texans began their great drives of longhorns into Abilene, Fort Dodge, and other railroad crossovers. The saga years of cowboy-and-Indian, badmen-and-sheriff, swung into being. The cattleman made some changes in his lingo. The lasso became "lariat," the horse herd, "the *remuda*" and the halter—slightly varied in pattern—a "hackamore." The pommel of the saddle became "the horn" and the girth "the cinch."

Approximately 250,000 longhorns, gaunt and wild as bobcats, crossed the Red River into Indian Territory during 1866. The owners bunched them up in Missouri and Kansas until they could be sold directly to the packers or to corn-feeders from Iowa and Illinois. As the drives developed, herds went straight through to Wyoming and Montana for a year of grass-fattening before they hit the "high iron trails" to eastern feed-lots and markets.

After the railroads came through, cowboy crews developed the routine of splurging a good share of their pay in the "cow towns," then riding the boxcars south to start another drive. Some cattlemen developed "lead steers" who were as valuable as a half-dozen cowmen. Colonel Charles Goodnight's steer "Old Blue" was legendary for his know-how in leading herds up the trail, locating bedgrounds, and quieting the other animals during storms. Consequently, "Old Blue" always had a private boxcar for the trip home to Texas.

Between 1866 and 1895 ten million cattle and more than one million horses were driven overland from Texas to the railheads, pastures, and packing plants of the North.

The skinny, wide-horned creatures brought headaches, as well as opportunity, to the meat packers, too. Insofar as hides were concerned, the longhorn was a good investment. A hide still brought twenty-five to thirty per cent of the ranch price of the animal. But the beef was tough and gamey. Eastern butchers raised a howl against it, and housewives echoed them. Trainloads of "Western beef" stood on the New York and Boston sidings for a week or more, to sell finally for less than the freight rates.

Slowly, under the impetus of advertising and discounts, the butcher shops began to buy. The immigrants helped the situation. The Poles, Germans, Hungarians, Russians, Italians, pouring into east-coast ports all brought national appetites with them. Each wanted his home-style sausage, wiener, frankfurt, bologna and cured meats. Most of the recipes called for involved formulas of grind, blend and cure. Most were heavily doused with spices; a few called for wines.

Chicago, St. Louis and Cincinnati packers became heavy buyers on the spice and condiment markets. Longhorn beef rolled east in links, loaves and squares. Refrigerator cars were invented that permitted the carcasses to "age" and tenderize en route. But the situation called for an improvement in breeding stock, too. Shorthorns and Herefords from eastern show herds began to move into Texas, along with the ropes, pails, stoves, blankets, hats and other equipment needed for the cowboy rigs. And, from Nebraska west, the cattle kings came to their pommeled thrones.

John Wesley Iliff of Colorado was a stocky, well-built ranchman, whose

A Drive to the Market—from *Oklahoma!*, by Payne, Couch, Osborn & others, 1885

abundant hair and full beard made him look like a twin brother of his distinguished contemporary, Ulysses S. Grant. Iliff's success stemmed from his far-sighted pre-emption of extended water frontage along the Platte River, a move which permitted him to send his cattle foraging for free grass over a region covering an area larger than the state of Massachusetts.

The son of Thomas, a well-to-do farmer and devout Methodist, John Wesley was born in Zanesville, Ohio, in 1831. When he graduated from Delaware College, his father offered to buy him a neighboring farm for $7,500. John replied, "No thanks, Father. Just give me $500 and let me go West." He traveled to northern Kansas and took such jobs as were available in a small town on the Oregon Trail. After three years Iliff and two friends, hearing of the gold strike in Colorado, bought a stock of groceries which they hauled to Denver and quickly disposed of at a profit.

But he thought he saw a better chance in the cattle business, so, in 1862, he invested all he had—$2,000—in a small herd. Then, despite the warnings of friends, he moved out to the buffalo—and antelope—plains northwest of Denver, prepared to dispute with hostile Arapahoes and Cheyennes possession of their favorite hunting grounds.

As the herd thrived, Iliff began quietly to homestead and buy land along the Platte. As was usual in those days, he also arranged for his cowboys and friends to stake out other claims. After these were proved up, he bought them for such generous sums as to delight cowpokes working for $30 to $50 a month. Under Colorado water law, cattlemen who arrived first automatically had the first water right. Enterprising stockmen everywhere believed that by taking over open country and using it to raise stock they were doing the right thing.

John Iliff lived with his cattle, rode the open range, followed the roundup, slept and ate with his men. He paid his hands good wages but would not tolerate drinking, declaring that "cows and whisky do not mix." He never carried a gun, but would stand no nonsense from troublemakers. In a fight between Iliff and a cowboy, a hand reported:

> "Both men were game, fought hard and asked no favors. The cowboy gave Iliff the worst of it. In order to prevent his eyes from getting black . . . slices of raw beef were plastered over both eyes, which, however, did not prevent the flesh above and below becoming badly discolored. At the end of the fight Mr. Iliff shook hands with his opponent, told him it was 'all right,' and he had no hard feelings. . . ."

After closing government contracts for furnishing beef to army posts, Iliff left for New Mexico to gather stock. There he met the famous Texas Panhandle pioneer, Charles Goodnight. Years later the two men were called "symbols of a great expansion, leaders in an industry which remade the map of the West and the history of the continent. They possessed similar qualities of imagination, foresight and disregard of danger."

In spite of hostile Indians, droughts and grasshoppers, Iliff continued to build up his herds. Meanwhile, forty miles east of Trinidad, Goodnight had established a range onto which he moved a large number of longhorns. Of these Iliff purchased 10,000 for $40,000. In February, 1868, 1,300 of them, pointed north, passed fifty miles to the east of Denver, the first large movement of cattle into northern Colorado and Wyoming.

The natural increase in Iliff's herds ran from seventy to eighty per cent, with gathering and shipping costs for 25,000 cattle only sixty-five to seventy-five cents per head. Iliff himself wrote:

> "In Colorado and Wyoming . . . I consider the summer-cured grass superior to hay. . . . The per cent of loss in wintering here is much less than in the states where cattle are fed on hay and corn. . . . I am confident . . . that this Trans-Mississippi country can defy all competition in the production of wool, mutton, beef and horses."

John Iliff never slowed up, untiringly riding the range or dashing over rough trails in a specially built buckboard. But strenuous attention to business, aggravated by drinking too much alkali water, hastened his death, which came on February 8, 1878, at the age of forty-seven. Goodnight lived to be ninety-three. The Iliff estate, appraised at over $1,000,000, included more than 20,000 acres of pasturage carrying 50,000 cattle, from which were annually marketed an average of 13,000 head.

In 1874, the Laramie County Roundup of the Wyoming Stock Growers through their Association had ordered, planned, and regulated the sorting of the cattle, even though they had no legal power to enforce their regulations.

Ten years later, the Wyoming legislature provided a law which gave some authority to the Associations themselves. This law was of great importance in ranch history. It made the cattleman's local and state Associations semipublic institutions, with legal authority over the stock industry of the territory, and with power to enforce their regulations as to roundups and brands. It also provided the Associations with a certain punitive power against stock growers who would not comply with their rules, since it refused them admission to the Associations. The law also provided that any person in the stock business who complied with the by-laws was eligible, provided he had not been convicted of a previous felony nor possessed a reputation notoriously bad.

After railroads became more important as marketing agents, the Associations established brand inspectors, both when the animals were finally sold at the market and also at the point where the livestock were loaded for shipment.

Another spectacular event of the 1870's was the development of great cattle companies under British capital. These built up principally in Texas, Wyoming, and Montana, and for a time were a financial godsend to the investors. Unfortunately, in order to make the investment most alluring, a number of companies with unscrupulous managers in America sold off enough of the capital stock of the herds to make what seemed like a very great dividend to the foreign investors. Consequently, there was considerable trouble in the mid-eighties.

In 1886–87 occurred the worst drought, followed by the severest winter, ever recorded in the cattle business. Thousands of cattle perished on the range. Only three or four of the soundly managed corporations survived. The cattle boom was utterly deflated. More cattle were brought up over the

A Cowboy Roping a Steer
—from *McClure's Magazine*, volume xxxv

Texas Trail, but the lush days were past. Local banks were as flat as the ranchers themselves. Eastern financing institutions were slow to discount Western notes. Even though the security for notes constantly increased in value as the animals grew larger and fatter, Eastern financiers shied away from them. Fence-cutting wars in Texas and Oregon made Eastern bankers uncertain of their collateral. The Lincoln County War in New Mexico plus the Johnson County War in Wyoming left a bad taste in the mouths of men accustomed to providing capital only on a highly secure basis.

Even at the close of World War I and for a decade thereafter, laws designed to furnish credit to individual owners through government banking proved the only way in which credit could be expanded promptly.

When the bad winters first came, some cattlemen thought they were going to get rid of sheep competition because they did not think the animals could stand the cold. To their surprise, practically all sheep came through (even in the disastrous season of 1886–87). Many experienced stockmen who had insufficient credit to start up again with cattle could get together enough money for a small band of sheep. Finally, the growers found that cattle and sheep supplemented each other when run together under one ownership— the cattle grazing the lowlands and sides of the hills or mountains, and the sheep grazing the uplands and higher valleys.

Geneticists, animal husbandmen, and other scientists from the land-grant colleges and the U.S. Department of Agriculture soon brought a multitude of new efficiencies to the stockmen. The Shorthorn and Hereford quickly adapted to the mountain pastures of the northern Great Plains. By 1906, the first shipments of humpbacked Brahma cattle were landing in Texas and other Gulf Coast states, where their immunity to ticks and heat had been widely advertised.

Each new breed of cattle in the West now became another reason for forming an association, or "club." In time, the breed associations—Angus, Shorthorn, Hereford, Devon, etc.—became as vociferous, and sometimes as politically powerful, as the Granges and Farm Bureaus.

So, the grass empire of the Great Plains and the deserts and mountains settled into the mundanities of technology. Yet they did it as individualists, in ways that were typically Western. And through these ways, they produced more beef, more lamb, more leather and wool, than ever before.

That is the story today, tomorrow and the day after. So it was and so it will be. The West is the land of grass and livestock. As this is written, the Federal government urges the return of another 12,000,000 acres to grassland. And that, plus normal rainfall and modern science, can mean another six to twelve million head of livestock against the blue skies west of the 98th meridian. The West was, and is, the West because man and livestock are in partnership.

A steamer was attempting to grasshopper its way over a sandbar. Her engines were straining, her paddlewheels churning madly and every member of the crew was holding his breath as the vessel crept inch by inch over the bar. A woodchopper living in a solitary cabin on the riverbank chose this moment to come down to the stream's edge for a pail of water. As he turned away with a brimming pail, his action caught the captain's eye. "Hey," roared the fuming skipper, "You put that water back."

JOS. M. HANSON–"Conquest of the Missouri"

HOWARD R. DRIGGS

The Toters

"WATERWAYS IN THE EAST; wagonways in the West." The slogan pretty much tells the story of transportation on the great trek to the West before 1870. First there was travel along deer trails, patted down by moccasined feet and then by the hooves of horses. Slowly moving streams, pleasant lakes along the Atlantic Slope and the Mississippi with its eastward branches, were, however, an invitation for birchbark canoes, flatboats, keelers and other craft. Where the streams narrowed and danced near the sources, there were always the portage paths along which the Indians and others could easily make their way. Pupils of the Portage Path School in Akron, Ohio, once took delight in showing me the Indian trail that linked the Cuyahoga River, on which Cleveland is situated, with the Tuscarawas River, leading towards the Ohio and "Old Miss."

In later years, the Erie Canal was opened, with locks to ease boats from the head of the Mohawk Trail, on the Hudson, to frontier Buffalo. The history of the East is intimately connected with its waterways. The West is largely a different story, especially beyond "the wide Missouri." Rivers of the West are generally not navigable. Remember, Denver boasts of being "a mile high." Its Cherry Creek and the South Platte naturally come dancing down a long slope all the way to the Missouri.

Lewis and Clark followed "Big Muddy" with their clumsy Mackinaw boats, across shifting sandbars and trees juggernauting down the long slope from Yellowstone. It took about seven months to reach their first winter quarters, at what they called Fort Mandan in present South Dakota. There they made lighter craft and, when the ice broke in 1805, struggled on upstream into the swift, narrowing tributaries. On foot, with a few pack-horses, they made it over the crest of the Rockies, the Bitterroot Range, then down the Clearwater, Snake and Columbia rivers to the Pacific. Hard going every mile.

As for steamboating on the Missouri, Francis Parkman gives us this picture of his trip from St. Louis to Independence, the first jumping-off place where pioneers gave up the river for the covered-wagon trains:

"Our steamboat, *The Radnor*, was laden until the water broke alternately over the guards. The upper deck was covered with large wagons of peculiar form for the Santa Fe trade, and her hold crammed with goods for the same destination. . . . The boat struggled for seven or eight days against the rapid current of the Missouri, grating against snags, hanging for two or three hours at a time upon sandbars."

No wonder the westbound travelers took to the wagonways. In 1906, when Ezra Meeker, at seventy-six years of age, decided to impress on Americans east and west the matchless story of American pioneering, he used an ox-team and the covered wagon as symbols. Making a sound prairie schooner out of three old ones that had crossed the continent fifty years before, and training a pair of stout young oxen, he set forth on a west-to-east journey along the old Oregon Trail. Finally he reached New York State, scared the mules drawing boats along the Erie Canal, and at last reached upper Broadway in New York City.

Policemen promptly arrested him for driving cattle on the streets. An ancient ordinance forbade it.

"All right, boys," said the dauntless Ezra. "You take the cattle."

The officers couldn't handle the critters. An appeal was made to the mayor, who ordered, "Give the old pioneer the freedom of the city."

Next morning, in triumph, Meeker drove his ox-team and covered wagon all the way down Broadway. The police escort had to call out the reserves to help get the outfit out of the crowds around Wall Street. They gave a sigh of relief when the team and wagon with its bewhiskered driver were on the ferry to New Jersey. Meeker and his rig reached Washington. President Theodore Roosevelt came out to see him and to approve warmly his effort to save the Oregon Trail.

"What do you think of the automobile?" reporters asked Ezra.

"Great invention!" the veteran shot back. "Kills more folk than Injuns ever did." Then he added, "Another thing about the contrivance that disturbs me is that it is making people forget they have legs."

"Surely you wouldn't do without the auto?"

"No, no, of course not. Mark of progress. Can be useful and add comforts if the drivers will only use horse sense in handling it."

"What about its helping tourists to learn about our country?"

"It can give good help. But look here, young feller, if you want to get the feel of what it took to pioneer America, you can't just whiz over it. You'll have to do some walking along interesting stretches of old trails, and around the storied landmarks. I footed it every step of the way from Iowa to Oregon in 1852. My wife and our baby boy rode in the covered wagon. Didn't hurt me to hoof it."

Three centuries before Meeker, Cabeza de Vaca left the first impressive story of hoofing it across the American West. Cast up on the Texas shore, enslaved by Indians, he became a kind of medicine man and itinerant trader among the desert tribes. Through seven years, pack on back, Cabeza wandered over the vast, untamed realm, carrying primitive commodities and bartering for others to take back to his captors. At last escaping, he made his way to Spain, and wrote a book telling of his strange adventures.

More than three centuries later, Yarabe, a Gosiute Indian of the Utah desert, won a bet by outracing on foot an Overland stage.

"It was a twenty-mile run," said Nick Wilson, driver of the stage, "and it was nip and tuck between my six-horse team and that Injun. He finally beat us by 'bout a quarter of a mile. Most of the durned Gosiutes I knew," Nick went on, "had tough feet, wiry legs and good lungs. Sometimes they managed to trade for a pony, but usually they killed and ate it. 'Twas better than lizards, grasshoppers and the like eatin' them waste places generally allowed."

It was a different story with the Comanches, Sioux and other Plains tribes. Spanish horses, ranging out of Mexico, put mustangs under these redskins. They soon became expert riders, chasing buffalo, and widening their raids on weaker tribes and white settlements. They became adept, too, at horse stealing.

Another advantage of the "Injun ponies," as they were often called, was in primitive transportation. The animals were trained—some of them—at dragging what the French called a *travois*. This was made by taking down the tipi poles, then tying the tips of them with buckskin thongs to the "squaw saddles." The skin or canvas covers of the conical tent were placed on these poles to make a carry-all for robes, utensils and the smaller papooses. Indian mothers usually rode on the ponies pulling the travois. The contrivance was a great help in moving from camp to camp on the plains, and to convey at the same time the hard-to-get lodge poles.

Another animal—the humble burro—brought to America by the Span-

"Emigrants Crossing the Plains"—from *Picturesque America*, volume II, 1874

iards, played a colorful role in the developing story of the Southwest. Around the adobe huts of the Mexicans and the hogans of the Navajos, it was a household pet. Children rode it. Grownups made it a beast of burden. In after years, the prospector—with burro—wandered through the mountains hoping for, and not infrequently making, the "lucky strike."

Mules descended from the Spanish jacks and brood mares had an important part, too. These long-eared—often ornery—animals may first have been introduced in Missouri by Captain William Becknell when, in 1821, he opened the Santa Fe Trail. At any rate Missouri took an early lead in breeding up good stout mules for work as pack and draft animals. Their place in the United States Army is notable—the theme of many a song and story. As a boy, I saw mule teams with the rider in his saddle on a wheel mule, using the "jerk line" to handle the lead team of heavily laden wagons and trailers being drawn skillfully along canyon roads. The "twenty-mule team" was not uncommon.

Captain Becknell made his historic venture right after Mexico gained its freedom from Spain in 1821. Leaving Arrow Rock on the Missouri River in September, he led a train of pack horses loaded with American goods across the prairie and through Raton Pass to Santa Fe. The New Mexicans gave the traders from the northland warm welcome. Guns, knives, copper utensils, cotton fabrics and other articles—spread out on the plaza—were quickly sold. Bags of silver, serapes, turquoise jewelry, leather goods, Spanish mules and horses were doubtless procured in this bartering. Only forty-eight days were needed to make the round trip. The profits were large. It was the start of frontier trading over the Santa Fe Trail.

Pack-train travel, started by Becknell, was only of short duration. In 1824 he turned to the "prairie schooner"—so named because with its white canvas it suggested a ship of the plains. These wagons carried more goods. They were more easily protected from raiding Comanches than pack animals. Behind a barricade of parked covered wagons, teamsters and outriders of the caravans, holding rifles, spoke a language the redskins could understand.

The story was soon duplicated by the traders along what became the Oregon Trail. General Ashley first used pack animals to carry goods to the rendezvous held at strategic places in the Rockies. On his last fur-trading venture Ashley returned to St. Louis with several hundred horses packed with rare pelts. Elected to Congress, he sold out to the Rocky Mountain Fur Company.

In 1830 this company, too, turned to covered wagons as its means of transportation, and opened the wagon road to the eastern end of what became the South Pass gateway of the Rockies. Two years later, Captain Bonneville took a caravan of wagons through the Pass to the Green River, following the wheel trace left by Ashley's one cannon of some years before. Dr. Marcus

Whitman persisted in 1836 in trying to get a wagon over the western end of the Oregon Trail, and did make it with a cart to Fort Boise. It was not until 1840, however, that the wagonway on to the Columbia was traced with wheels. Two dauntless mountain men—Joe Meek and Bob Newell—did it with wobbly wagons drawn by Injun ponies. In them rode their Indian wives and children.

In 1843 came the "Great Migration"—1,000 men, women and children—bound for the rich realm of Oregon, west of the Blue Mountains. Other caravans of home-seekers followed into the Far Northwest. In 1847 the Mormon pioneer vanguard opened the way to the arid region near the Great Salt Lake, and with magic of irrigation made the desert blossom. Thousands of families in the "homes on wheels," drawn mostly by oxen, crowded the westward trails during open months to help win the West—and add new stars to our flag.

Where did the covered wagon, or prairie schooner originate? Lancaster County, Pennsylvania, maintains it was the birthplace of the useful vehicle. Indirectly, Ben Franklin, in his *Autobiography*, lends support to the claim. When General Braddock, heading for what is now the Pittsburgh region, needed conveyances for the luggage and supplies of his British army, Franklin helped by advertising in Lancaster.

The Pennsylvania Dutch farmers along Conestoga Creek responded by providing 150 wagons, with arched canvas hoods and boat-shaped bodies sloped from each end toward the middle. This, they knew, would keep payloads from shifting on the hillslopes.

Later, the Conestoga wagon became the popular carrier along the Philadelphia-Pittsburgh Pike and west into Ohio. Peddlers used them to carry their jangling loads of pots, dress goods and trinkets. They stocked a reeking black cigar, too, that settlers nicknamed "the Conestoga," then shortened to "stogie."

But the "prairie schooner" nickname for the wagons came, it seems, straight out of New England. The schooner was a two-masted sailing ship invented in 1705 in Gloucester, Massachusetts. Its name derived from the word "schoon" meaning "to skim." The schooner became the most popular fishing boat out of Boston, Ipswich, Salem, Marblehead and the Maine ports. Between 1795 and 1860, hundreds of thousands of New Englanders migrated west. It is logical, then, that some homesick fisherman gave the name "prairie schooner" to the boat-shaped wagons "sailing" bravely across the Great Plains sea of grass.

For motive power, pioneers of the plains and mountain region generally used oxen. There were reasons. Oxen were cheaper. They were more tractable. Thieving Indians couldn't run them off as easily as horses and mules. Also, oxen did not require so much grazing ground; they could get along with grass and herbage closer to the campsites. Lastly, they afforded beef—a better food—when they reached the new homeland. The thousands of oxen driven west with covered wagon trains were a source of invaluable food supply for not only the settlers but the miners in various gold fields and silver camps that sprang up over the West.

After the crest of the wave of covered wagon migration had passed in the early 1850's, another picturesque drama of early transportation came with the Handcart Pioneers. Converts of the Mormon Church, mainly from Great Britain and Scandinavia, lacking means to buy wagons and oxen, decided to pull and push their goods across the plains and mountains with two-wheeled carts. The plan had been suggested by Brigham Young, who saw in it a less costly way of getting to their Zion in the valleys of Utah, and to make the trip even more quickly than the first caravans did.

Approximately 3,000 signed up for the venture. In 1856, two of the companies got off to an early start on the long trip. It was first to Boston from England by ship, then by rail to the terminus at Iowa City, Iowa. Then about 1,300 miles more had to be walked with the handcarts. These were ready for the eager emigrants. Off they started with their caravan of hand-carts, plus a few prairie schooners to haul those who might fall ill. These two companies got through without serious delay. They were met in Salt Lake by a brass band.

Tragedy befell two other companies. The ocean voyage went smoothly enough, as did the trip by rail. But when the terminus of the Rock Island Line was reached at Iowa City, hopes were dashed. The handcarts were not ready. Six precious weeks passed before the emigrants could start for Zion. Some of the practical ones urged that they stop and get work among the farmers in Iowa to win food for the winter. These were outvoted by the en-thusiasts, determined to get through that year. Rations fell to a low point. Wheels made of green timber began to wobble. Finally half the handcarts were left behind in the speed-up to get through the South Pass before winter. They did not make it.

An early snowstorm struck the half-fed, weary travelers. Many died from hunger and cold. All might have perished, had not a rescue train manned by husky young Mormons fought their way east through snow-drifts, gathered the survivors into covered wagons filled with food, buffalo robes and blankets, and hurried to the warmer valleys.

Mule-drawn Army wagons first appeared in the Southwest in 1846 when Lieutenant Colonel Phillip St. George Cooke took them with the Mormon Battalion from Santa Fe to San Diego. Eleven years later Captain Lew Simp-son led a caravan of like wagons loaded with supplies for the troops heading to Utah, through the South Pass. For about three years thereafter, a steady stream of freight caravans kept going through the mountain gateway on to

"The Pony Express"—from *The Great Salt Lake Trail*, by Inman and Cody, 1898

Fort Bridger and to Camp Floyd, built at an oasis on the eastern edge of the Great American Desert. Then came the Civil War. Camp Floyd became a "ghost town."

Floyd was a busy place through its palmy days. It was one of the main stations of the Pony Express and of the Overland Stage. In his book *Roughing It*, Mark Twain gives a vivid portrayal of the trip he took with his brother on a stagecoach from the Missouri River to Carson City, Nevada. They caught some sleep on top of mail bags in the coach. Once, in daylight, they had a glimpse of a Pony Express rider speeding East with his messages and mail. They saw also the builders of the telegraph line—one group working westward, the other eastward—with Salt Lake City as their goal. Those that reached there first would get a prize. The boys from the East won the race by about two days. Then on October 24, 1861, the two met. Wires were connected above the office on Main Street in the city by "America's Dead Sea." Shortly after this a message, flashed across the wires from California to President Abraham Lincoln, expressed "loyalty to the Union" and determination to stand by the Government in its day of trial.

With the completion of the transcontinental telegraph line, the Pony Express service of 1860–61 came to an honorable close. There were Pony Riders, of course, on shorter, branch lines—some such pony delivery of mail and messages is still going on in remote parts of our country. Indeed ox-teams are still being used in the Green Mountains, the Rockies and the Sierras. The same is true of mule-drawn freight wagons, and of stagecoaches. Old methods of communication and of transportation persist where modern means and methods cannot well serve.

As for the Overland Stage, the transcontinental runs along the line of the Pony Express and the looping telegraph wires were kept going until, with the driving of the "Golden Spike" on Promontory Point just north of Great Salt Lake, the first transcontinental railroad was made a reality. Passengers and mail, as well as express and freight, could then be carried by rail "from sea to shining sea."

And there was drama of sterling quality, too, in the building of the railroads up the Big Hill and across the mountains and desert. The hulloo for them began during the Gold Rush of the Forty-niners. No sooner had the iron horse proved effective on eastern lines than men of vision—and need—began to urge their extension across the continent. In 1834, before New York and Boston were connected by rail, Samuel Barlow of Massachusetts was promoting the idea for an "Atlantic and Pacific" line.

Congress appropriated funds for the so-called "Pacific Surveys" in 1853. Jefferson Davis, then Secretary of War—also responsible for the brief experiment of a Camel Corps in the Southwest—acted by sending out detachments under courageous, efficient leaders to chart routes for railroads from Missouri to California and Oregon. That their task was well done is attested by the fact that today the Northern Pacific, Santa Fe, Denver, Rio Grande & Western, Union Pacific, and other lines follow, in the main, these surveys. The Union Pacific and Central Pacific jointly were first to complete their line.

"It was a race," one pioneer wag put it, "between the Paddies and the Chinks—and the Paddies won." Lusty sons of Old Ireland, in other words, did a large share of the pick and shovel grading between Omaha and Ogden, then pressed on to the meeting point in the desert. Chinese laborers on the western end performed like tasks in getting over the Sierras and along the Humboldt River.

There were others, of course, who put their strength and skill into the effort. One group of Mormon leaders took the contract to grade 500 miles of "high iron" for the Union Pacific; another about the same length for the Central Pacific. They sublet sections of the work to smaller groups. The writer's own father with three others took on one mile in Echo Canyon. These Yankee boys didn't like pick and shovel work, so they put their wits to work. One of them, a blacksmith, bolted a strip of iron to a slab. Chains were attached, handles set. A team of horses pulling the slab caused it to scoop dirt up onto the grade. Out of this pioneering, it was said, the "tongue scraper"—often called the "Mormon Scraper"—was devised. It is still used where bulldozers are not available.

William H. Jackson, the pioneer photographer, played an interesting role during this railroad building. Riding back and forth along the line with his wet-plate camera, he recorded the great enterprise with on-the-spot pictures. Many of the colorful personalities, scenes, events and story-spots are in his collection. Once, while he was showing these photos, the question came, "Where is the one of the driving of the Golden Spike?"

"Oh, I wasn't there," Jackson grinned. "You see, I had a more important assignment that day. At the Pawnee Indian Agency in Nebraska, I had met a beautiful young lady whose father was the Indian Agent. Well, we became engaged, and set May 10, 1869, as our wedding day. Then they chose the same day for the Golden Spike ceremony—well, what would you have done?"

The new day for travel and transportation had dawned in the West. Pioneer beginnings were past, with the excitements of the Moguls, the Mallards, the "big fellows," the "puddle jumpers," throughways and DC-7's all springing from these sturdy roots.

What comes next? Who knows.

From *Harper's New Monthly*, June, 1883

*Don't . . . meddle with old unloaded firearms; they are
the most deadly and unerring things that have ever been
created by man. You don't have to have a rest, you don't
have to have any sights on the gun, you don't have to take
aim, even. No, you just pick out a relative and bang away,
and you are sure to get him. A youth who can't hit a
cathedral at thirty yards with a Gatling gun in three-quarters of an hour, can take up an old empty musket and bag
his grandmother every time, at a hundred.*

SAMUEL L. CLEMENS

WILLIAM B. EDWARDS

Shootin' Irons

MANY A FAST GUNFIGHT tightened the "wide loop" a man dropped over somebody else's steers. The gun was the final judge in disputes of land, water, title,
gambling debts and "wimmen." It served to equalize all. The small rancher
loomed just as bulky as the man who controlled 100,000 acres, if each carried
one of Sam Colt's arbiters on a hip. The gun was a necessity to the western
frontier's rough and ready life.

The cowboy's most important gun was a Colt. Two reasons exist for
this. Firstly, popular writers seem for a half-century to have been unable to
spell "Merwin & Hulburt," "Forehand & Wadsworth," "Bacon," "Manhattan," or any of a hundred other brand names of firearms popularly used on
the frontier. The second reason was a very good one: Samuel Colt himself
made sure that his name got into local print. Writing in 1860 to his agent
James Dean Alden in Arizona, Colt said:

"I am noticing in the newspapers occasionally complimentary notices of the Sharp & Burnside Rifles & Carbines, anecdotes of their use
upon Grisly Bears, Indians, Mexicans, &c.&c. Now this is all wrong—it
should be published Colts Rifles, Carbines &c. When there is or can be
made a good Story of the use of a Colt's Revolving Rifle, Carbine, Shotgun or Pistol, for publication in *The Arizonian* the opportunity should
not be lost, and in the event of such notices being published you must

181

always send me one hundred copies. If there is a chance to do a few good things in this way, give the editor a Pistol or Rifle compliment, in the way it will tell—. You know how to do this & Do not forget to have his Columns report all the accidents that occur to the Sharps & other humbug arms. I hope soon to see the evidence of your usefulness in this line of business."

The evidence, testifying to Alden's "usefulness," is still with us today. Every cowboy cap-pistol is an imitation "Colt." But cowboys and other frontiersmen were not limited to Colts. At the time of the War of Texan Independence and the Mexican War, a great variety of arms were used on the frontier. Foremost were the short, "plainly finished rifles" which modern terminology has corrupted to "plains rifles." They were shortbarreled rifles, with a wood stock which extended only part way beneath the barrel. Usually they had a rib welded from the forestock to the muzzle beneath the barrel. Attached to the rib was a pair of iron ramrod ferrules. Such guns were of "small bore," usually .40 to .50 caliber, and rifled with seven grooves intended for a round patched ball. These rifles were made for hard service and hence were utterly plain in finish, without foofaraw. The use of the word "plain" to modify "rifle" caused some early arms historians to invent a category of rifle called the "plains rifle." They assumed the word meant a type of rifle used exclusively on the Great Plains. This was not the case. Common American sporting rifles of the 1840's and later were sold in all types of design— half-stock, full stock, round, octagon barrels, all calibers—and all advertised as "plain" rifles.

In the early days of the fur trade, short, light muskets of rough finish were constructed in England and America for swapping with Indians. Some of this type of arms, commonly called "fusils" or "fukes," were made at Springfield Armory for official U.S. government trading enterprises. They were short in the barrel, usually of musket bore—about .60 to .70—and with cheap, pin-fastened stocks. The brass or iron bands fitted to genuine military arms added unnecessarily to the cost. Locks were crudely fitted and finished, but they were very serviceable. On the left side of the stock, opposite the lock, was a brass sideplate shaped like a dragon. While the gun was rough, the safety factor was high. Indian guns were proved with double charges of powder and three lead balls well wadded. The idea that they were "long in the barrel to be traded for a bigger pile of beaver skins" is completely false. One of the few long-barreled "fukes" was measured against a pile of beavers at $6 a "plew." Nearly 500 beaver pelts, worth $3,000 in the 1840's, was piled up to equal the long-barreled gun. The Indian would never trade the equal of $3,000 for a cheap musket. He could kill a white man cheaper.

These Indian guns were used by some early frontiersmen. Other types of fusils were also carried. Correctly, the fusil is not a trade gun, but a light, graceful, well-finished musket for officers to carry. An officer's fusil, such as those carried by Lewis and Clark on their trip west, was a fine little gun. Some were fitted with good London locks with rainproof flash pans, safeties, and other advantages. Before the wide use of rifles, these fusils were popular. They could be loaded with ball for bear and other large game at short range; or they could handle shot for bird shooting.

When the whites who first settled Kentucky became nervous and felt civilization crowding in on them, they moved farther west. Taking with them their long Kentucky rifles, they accidentally founded a new school of gunsmithing. At Independence, Missouri, where the wagon teams made up for all points west, gunsmithing flourished. A man deciding to strike out for parts unknown was well advised to put his rifle into first-class order. One of the common faults of a flintlock gun was the erosion of the flash vent between pan and powder. Enlargement of this hole was known to reduce the force of the shooting, causing erratic ignition and inaccuracy.

A common way to correct this was to chop off three or four inches of barrel at the breech and fit a new plug and drill a fresh touch hole. The muzzle, too, might be cut off for an inch since the rifling was most likely damaged or worn from loading with a ramrod that slapped against the side of the muzzle on entering.

When a gunsmith had got finished with the Kentucky it was much shorter and often the barrel needed to be refitted to the stock. An easy way to fix it was to copy a style set by the special half-stock rifles made at Harper's Ferry Arsenal for the Lewis and Clark Expedition. Following a general military vogue, since the dragoons' short rifles were fitted with stocks that went only halfway up the barrel, the so-called "plains rifle" developed from the cut-down and refitted "Kaintuck."

Perhaps the leading exponent of the "plain American rifle" was the shop of Hawken in St. Louis. There the famous Hawken rifle was made, built to the curved-butt, octagon-barrel, American rifle pattern, but with a barrel of unusual weight and a stock which went halfway to the muzzle. Bores ranged from a big .44 up to .50 and .60 calibers, rifled. All the work was done in the Hawken shop. Some English locks are found on these rifles, but it is generally considered that most were made by Hawken's own workmen at St. Louis.

Proprietors of the factory were Jake and Sam Hawken. Their shop was opened about 1815. In the 1820's business really began to boom. Those were the days of the mountain men and the rendezvous. Many a Hawken was packed a thousand miles along the beaver traps, or used in "civilizing" an Indian. These rifles were used by Kit Carson, Mariano Modena, Bill Williams, and others of the beaver-hatted breed. The heavy barrels, tipping the total weight to sometimes fifteen pounds, made the rifles valuable after they were shot out and obsolete. Dozens of them were eagerly bought up by the iron-starved gold hunters of '49, who would even trade new Sharps carbines for them. The barrels made fine crowbars!

The Hawken rifles were not alone on the frontier. Indian trade rifles and carbines made at Springfield Arsenal, or by the Pennsylvania gunmakers, were in great quantity. Some continued in business until long after the Civil War, selling percussion muzzle-loading rifles to frontiersmen. Inevitably, some of these rifles were used by men whose daily living came to be cattle.

Carrying a rifle on horseback was a difficult matter until the invention of the cavalry-type saddle scabbard. Full-length buckskin scabbards were often used, which followed the pattern of the frontiersman's dress. Fringed and beaded, they might have been made by his squaw, or obtained in trade. A sling carried the rifle over his back, muzzle down, inside the scabbard. The ends would fold over or tie, to keep rain out. An easier and cheaper way to carry the rifle was directly across the saddlebow, often balanced only on the knees. This was precarious, and a flat strip of leather was sometimes used to secure the gun. The strip had two slots, one at either end. The first slot was dropped over the saddle horn. Then the rifle was laid across it, and the other end was looped up and over onto the horn. To bring the rifle free, the rider grasped it and pulled it up, the loop of the leather slipping off the horn. A leather breech cover was sometimes used with this rig, with lacings which could be loosened easily. Tightened down, the cover protected the flintlock or percussion mechanism from the effects of rain.

Pistols during the early period of the cowboy West, from the 1840's in Mexican California on to the 1860's, were in fair quantity and variety. Predominant was the "Colt," but originally in greater numbers were the plain American and Mexican-Spanish horsemen's pistols. Called popularly "horse pistols," these were single-shot arms, flintlock until about 1840-45, percussion after that. The U.S. Army Models of 1819, 1826 and 1836 were predominant, the last most common. R. & D. Johnson, Simeon North, Asa Waters, and Henry Aston are gunmakers' names associated with these pistols. All were of nominal "rifle" caliber, firing a half-ounce round ball—therefore about .54 inch bore. Barrels were fastened by steel loop bands which surrounded stock and metal halfway to the muzzle. Locks were conventional flint with rounded double-necked cocks, and brass flash pans. The ramrods were of steel, slung with a permanent swivel below the barrel muzzle. This made it possible to reload while on horseback, without losing the rod. A pair of such weapons was issued to the cavalryman. In the opening of the frontier, many cowboys and Texas Rangers carried a brace of these guns in holsters slung at the pommel of the saddle, or stuck onto a waist belt with side belt hooks. These arms were American patterns. The Spanish types used in the Southwest closely paralleled them in design.

In 1836 a momentous incident occurred in Western gun lore. A "Mr. Rathbun" went from New York to Texas. He took with him a sample hand-made revolver pistol constructed by Sam Colt's personal gunsmith, John Pearson. The Pearson-Colt was the first of a succession of Colt revolver designs to have a great bearing on the future of the young Republic, and of the West.

In 1839 a large invoice of Colt Paterson revolvers and carbines were ordered by the Texas Navy. Some of these guns were lost in the fortunes of war. Others were peddled by officers of the Navy to pay for food and provisions locally when they put into friendly foreign ports. But some were saved. These last remained in Navy stores when President Houston ordered the Texas Navy to be beached in 1843–44. Captain Jack Hayes evidently learned of these and obtained the revolvers for reissue to his Texas Rangers.

In June of 1844 Hays with fifteen other Rangers, including Sam Walker who later became famous for designing a special "Colt," were on a scout for Comanches. They discovered some eighty mounted braves, who taunted them and dared them to come and fight. The Indians had never heard of repeating guns, and thought the Rangers had only their usual issue of a brace of horse pistols and a plain rifle or musket. But the Comanches' self-superiority was shaken as the Rangers charged behind a wave of lead, their five-shooters blazing. Half of the Indians were killed and the others so frightened they retreated, leaving their dead. This engagement, memorialized as "Hays' Big Fight," marked the first significant use of Colt's revolvers in land warfare.

Gradually more Colts came to be used in Texas. But not enough in time to save the company from failure. When Walker at the commencement of the Mexican war traveled east to recruit a regiment and buy Colt revolvers, he discovered the factory had been closed years before. The inventor was penniless.

The original guns had some defects in their design which, Walker felt, should be corrected if any more were to be made. From the ideas of Walker, Colt created a new revolver, a heavy four-pound .44 six-shooter later known as the "Colt Walker model." A thousand of these guns were made by Colt to arm the Texas regiment for Mexican War service. Then another thousand were ordered by the Army, and still more.

Colt set up in business in Hartford, Connecticut, and, by 1851, was producing three basic models of revolver. These were the modified Walker or "Dragoon Holster pistol"; the Model 1851 Navy .36, which was designed on the urging of Colonel Jack Hays; and the small pocket .31 caliber "Model 1849" revolver. The discovery of gold in California speeded up the movement westward. Pioneers who trekked across the vast grasslands, the Great

American Desert, needed protection from Indians, and weapons to use for hunting. Congress, in March, 1849, passed an act to aid the emigrants. One clause in it allowed them to buy at low government cost ($25) the Army's Colt revolvers. These could be obtained at St. Louis Arsenal or Baton Rouge, Louisiana, one to a traveler.

The prospect of buying guns cheaply caused two thousand Easterners going west to buy out the government supply of Walker and Dragoon Colts. These 2,000 were Sam Colt's advance sales messengers. Their use contributed to the reasons why the Colt company today is as much a part of American history as it is a gun factory. The demand grew for good revolvers. "The Indians of the Sierra Madres are terrified into honest habits," wrote one miner in comment on the settlers' use of Colts.

Men in the gold fields demanded strong, reliable firearms, and they got them. Two types of guns became so widely used in the 1850's that no one thinks of the West without bringing to mind these guns. The first is the ubiquitous Colt. The second is the Deringer pistol.

Henry Deringer was a Pennsylvania German craftsman. He had specialized by the late 1840's in making single-shot percussion pistols of large caliber. His specialty was the "little pistol with the big, bad bite." With barrels often as short as one and a quarter inches and bores usually .40 to .44 caliber, the Deringer pistols were designed for effectiveness at short range—across the poker table, for example.

A man who could palm an ace could as easily palm a Deringer pistol. Toting a brace of these little guns became fashionable with gamblers and other gentry of the West. The pistols were inconspicuous, did not bulge a tight frock coat or waistcoat, and were ever ready. Deringer was a fine gunmaker but not too sharp on protecting himself against infringers. A former Deringer workman, Schlotterbeck, left the firm and set up in Philadelphia under the cognomen of Slotter & Co. Of course, he made Deringer-type pistols. They were in demand, and he had been trained to make them. He even hired a tailor named John Deringer and marked his Henry Deringer-imitation guns with "J. Deringer's" name. Despite lawsuits, Henry Deringer never really stopped these infringers from pirating his style of gun. Ironically, the spelling with two "r's" was invented by infringers to circumvent his injunctions. Thus "derringer pistol," became part of our language. It means any small, large-caliber pistol.

Many other firearms were carried in boots, tucked neatly into the small of the back, or concealed nonchalantly in the hand held at the side, while strolling a busy Western street. One of the most popular, yet one almost devoid of legend, is the tiny Smith & Wesson .22, their first model of revolver. A delicate, fragile seven-shooter with a silvered brass frame and blue barrel, this titbit pistol had sights so thin that, held at arms length of a normal reach, the blade foresight dissolved into the mists of distance. It was a thoroughly unusable pistol, except for two counts. First, it had a spur trigger. This was a trigger sheathed by a lug of the frame, so that only the trigger edge stuck out. A light pressure on this could fire the gun. Since it was not necessary to grope with one's finger to get it inside the trigger guard, these little pistols were very fast-handling. The second thing which made it useful was tetanus. It made the gun a killer all out of proportion to its size.

There is an old story told about these little pistols. They say a tenderfoot showed up in a saloon with one of the little Smiths in a tiny alligator-leather belt holster, about the size of a large watch fob. "Boy, don't you shoot me with that thing," exclaimed one of the frontiersmen. "Because," he went on, "I might get awful angry, if I *ever found out.*" It makes a good tale, but is far from fact. One desperado was brought to bay by a lawman who had the drop on him with a little Smith & Wesson. He meekly elevated his hands and walked back to jail. In those days, a cut could be deadly. Tetanus spores lived in the horse dung and filth everywhere. Certainly the Smith & Wessons had their share of popularity. Some 200,000 of them were made between 1857 and 1875. Honkytonk girls liked them, too.

Bigger Smith & Wessons were also used. The heavy-frame .44 American had limited issue to the U.S. Cavalry, as did the following Schofield Model, with an improved top strap latch invented by General John Schofield. But the Smith & Wesson revolver never caught on to the extent that the Colt dominated the scene.

The Russian contract is supposed to be the main reason that Smith & Wesson lost the American Western market by default. From about 1870 to 1875, Smith & Wesson were busy turning out revolvers for the Russian government. This contract supposedly occupied their plant so intensively that there was no time to spare to make guns for sale in the West. But this is only partly true. The real reasons were the Colt "Allies."

During the Civil War, five or six major sporting goods firms became closely associated with Colt. They were known as the "Allies," and signed annual contracts whereby they undertook to sell Colt firearms at fixed discounts. These discounts were more favorable to them if they handled Colt guns exclusively. Since in the Colt firearms line there was a revolver for every need, the Allies did a good job of selling Colt guns and a poor job of pushing other lines.

The Allies included such monster firearms firms as Hartley, Schuyler and Graham of New York. This was a company so powerful that it bought up the Remington works lock, stock and barrel in the 1880's, and did millions of dollars' worth of business with the government during the Civil War. With so aggressive and powerful a jobber setup, Colt guns were well distributed. But Smith & Wesson, although their guns were sold by many firms, never made the special concessions of price which were necessary to get top billing. They concentrated often on export markets. While "Colt" today is a synonym for "revolver" throughout the English-speaking world, "Smith & Wesson" is almost as well known in the Latin countries, especially South America.

Thousands of single-shot muzzle-loading and breech-loading muskets went west after the War. But the major long guns of the post-Civil War period were the Sharps and the Winchester. Remington single-shot rolling block rifles were used to a limited extent, and feeble attempts have been made by Remington fans to boom the gun into a romantic, glamorous position occupied by Winchester. General Custer carried a Remington on the Black Hills expedition. But Remington in the 1870's was far more interested in selling its excellent rifle to a couple of million foreign soldiers, rather than blanketing a rapidly settled nation with sporting guns. It was partly this inattention to home business which put the Remington company, diversified with a number of products including the famous Remington typewriter, in such a financial strait that they could be bought out by Hartley & Graham.

While the Winchester will be long remembered as the rifle of the Indian wars, mostly unjustly and incorrectly, there is no doubt that the Sharps was the champion sporting rifle of the Western era. Winchester paid it a compliment when John Browning in 1879 designed the single-shot Winchester, styled as an "improvement on the Sharps."

Christian Sharps began his career in 1848 when his first dropping-breechblock gun was patented. One of the first such rifles made was a prized possession of fanatical border-state fighter John Brown. When Brown sought to create a slave insurrection a decade later, he turned to the Sharps rifles. Carbine versions of the gun, made in Hartford, were shipped west in wooden cases marked "Bibles." A wooden shipping box of Bibles has an astonishing resemblance to twenty carbines in a chest. The Rev. Henry Ward Beecher, an ardent abolitionist, was associated with the Kansas aid committee (Massachusetts Emigrant Aid Committee) which paid for these weapons. Sharps carbines came to be known as "Beecher's Bibles." With 200 of these in the hands of his Kansans, Brown attacked the U.S. Arsenal at Harpers Ferry, Virginia. The Sharps carbines caught the popular imagination from that time on.

The Sharps was one of the strongest breechloading designs ever made. After the war, when buffalo hides became big business, the Sharps boomed to popularity. It could be chambered for the heavy calibers needed to shoot buffalo. With metal cartridges like the modern kind, its mechanism did not foul up and it could shoot indefinitely. Such noted frontiersmen as Bill Tilghman and Tom Nixon wore out barrels in their pursuit of bison and money. At the battle of Adobe Walls, Billy Dixon took a chance shot at three Indians "about a mile off," waited a few seconds as the heavy, slow-moving Sharps slug curved through the air, and then saw the middle of the trio fall from his horse, and the other two bear him away. The shot contributed to the survival of a few of the buffalo hunters besieged at the old house.

The Sharps Company was too closely geared to the buffalo hunting trade. When the buffalo were killed off, the firm could not make the transition from single-shot to repeater, although in 1879 their last catalogue referred to a "new model gun." This was the Lee bolt-action magazine gun, designed by James P. Lee and eventually built by Remington. It grew into the famous Lee-Enfield used by the British armies. The Lee-Remington was made from 1880 to 1909, and in every popular caliber as a sporting rifle, but it has never become linked with the saga of the West. Today the Remington Lee is virtually unknown, while its competitor, the lever-action Winchester, reigns supreme.

The Winchester started with Smith & Wesson. Horace Smith and Dan Wesson had developed and marketed a lever-action pistol, with a tube magazine beneath the barrel. It was also made in a short carbine and rifle style, but the pistols were more popular. Oliver Winchester about 1854 bought out the two partners, who then turned their talents to revolver-making. Winchester, who had a going business making shirts in New Haven, pumped money into the company. Finally he obtained the services of a top-notch mechanic, B. Tyler Henry. He redesigned the lever-action Smith & Wesson rifle to use metallic cartridges.

The M1860 Henry rifle became one of the important weapons of the Civil War. While not Army issue, it featured in many spectacular forays of volunteer troops, especially Kentuckians. The firepower of the Henry made men armed with these guns virtually invincible against ordinary musketry. The factory claimed that "a resolute man, on horseback, armed with one of these rifles, positively cannot be captured."

A thousand Henrys and ammunition were sold by the factory to the Mexican revolutionary, Juárez, the "Lincoln of Mexico." Credit was nil. Factory representative Thomas Emmitt Addis traveled with the rifles to Monterrey to pick up the cash, $54,000 in silver. Addis hired a coach and rode behind the driver and guards, his cocked Winchester ready, and a long scarf pin in one hand, jabbing himself in the thigh to keep awake. Nearly dead from fatigue, he reached the border and banked the money, then waited weeks for his raw, bleeding leg to heal.

At the end of the war the Henry was slightly redesigned into the Winchester Model 1866. With a bright brass frame, it became known as the "yellow boy" or "yellow belly," and was widely acclaimed by men in the West to whom a rifle was as vital a tool as the plow and the mattock.

Billy the Kid owned a "yellow boy." Buffalo Bill Cody earned one at the time he also earned his name. In 1870 there was a rival contender for the title of "Buffalo Bill," one William Comstock. At Fort McPherson, Cody and Comstock held a contest, which resulted in Cody's killing more buffalo than Comstock. The latter got his buffs to running and the dead animals were strung out over the plain. Cody started his herd milling in a circle and every one was dropped almost within sight of camp. At the finale Cody brought a huge buffalo bull running into camp toward the pavilion erected to shade the officers and ladies from the sun. Cody dropped the buffalo almost at their feet as they scrambled for safety with one shot from his single-shot breechloading Springfield, "Lucretia Borgia." Apparently the officers felt that "old certain death" needed a partner—a repeater. They obtained a Winchester Model 1866 and had it inscribed "William F. Cody, Champion buffalo hunter of the plains."

To those who have not lost herds in the frozen grasp of a norther, the snow might be considered "thrilling." To those who have not seen the sand eating at the edge of tillable land, the desert might be considered "colorful." And to the armchair Westerners of today, in the guns of the Western age, there lingers on a glory and excitement which they never had in their day of use. Look at the Colt with its cylinder dented from fence staples. Should a cowboy carry a hammer? Look at the Winchester with its iron-shod butt cracked from pounding coffee, or loosening up the jerked beef so it could be chewed. The guns of the West had little glamour in their day. Colt, Winchester, monkey wrench—all tools of the trade.

Part 5

The SAGA

HOMER CROY

They Built the Saga

ONCE UPON A TIME the West wasn't any more glamorous than New Jersey,
then, all of a sudden, it became the most glamorous place in the world.
How did this come about? Who were the people who put the popcorn
on the Christmas tree?

The first man was none other than Wild Bill Hickok. He wanted
money. He hired three ropers and told them to bring him in half a dozen
buffaloes on the hoof. This, sure 'nuf was a new kind of hunting. The
amazing thing is that the men did actually rope and get to the railroad
yards six of the maddest buffaloes ever seen on the Great American Plains.
The men clapped them into freight cars. In no time, the buffaloes were in
Omaha. In the meantime, Wild Bill had hired four Comanche Indians and
had bought a cinnamon bear and a monkey.

Wild Bill was now in the show business. He got the outfit on a train
and finally to Niagara Falls, which, he figured, was eager to see how life
was lived in the Wild West. He called his show "The Daring Buffalo Chase
of the Plains." Wild Bill had no arena to exhibit in, so he hired a vacant
lot and hastily had a wire fence run around it so that the buffaloes would
not get foolish ideas in their heads.

Drawing a pistol from his belt, Wild Bill fired into the air. The buffaloes flinched, but didn't move a hock. The Indians gave a war whoop and waved their blankets. Away went the buffaloes in a fast walk, tails switching in resentment. The cowboys galloped up, firing enough blank cartridges to frighten the Five Civilized Tribes. The monkey ran up a pole and clung there, his teeth chattering. The cinnamon bear turned pale. At last, by honest effort and co-operation, the cowboys and the Indians got the buffaloes into a run. The perverse animals ran once around the enclosure, then lowered their heads and stood like hairy Rocks of Gibraltar. The bear was brought out and led around, so the people could see one of the terrors of the West. The monkey worked for peanuts, becoming—it developed later—the best-paid performer on the lot.

The show was over. Wild Bill had the cowboys pass the hat, for not a single ticket had been sold. A few men tossed in some money. But most of them suddenly remembered they had told their wives they would be home early.

The Indians said they wanted to go home. Wild Bill had no money with which to send them. The Indians threatened to scalp him unless he raised the money. Wild Bill had long, luxurious hair, and did not want to be scalped. Finally he sold the six buffaloes to a butcher in Niagara Falls, then went down to the depot and bought tickets for the ungrateful Indians. After that, Wild Bill and his intrepid cowboys got on a freight and left for the glamorous West. Thus came to an end the first Wild West Show. The date was June 22, 1870, six years before the Battle of the Little Bighorn.

Wild Bill went back to Hays City, Kansas, and hired out to clean up the outlaws. It was a snap, compared to the show biz.

Twelve years passed before anything else happened in the outdoor show line. And this came about by chance. Buffalo Bill bought a ranch at North Platte, Nebraska, not too far from where Yellow Hand had made his fatal error, and named it "Welcome Wigwam." His wife came out to look it over, said, "You're welcome to it," and went back to her steam-heated tipi in St. Louis.

But Buffalo Bill liked the place and expected to settle down for the rest of his life. Who knows the inscrutable ways of fate? The local chamber of commerce decided to celebrate the Fourth of July in a big way and to call the affair "Old Glory Blow-Out"—nobody but a Chamber of Commerce could think up a title like that. They asked Buffalo Bill to run the thing. Full of local pride, he said he would. He decided that instead of shooting off some firecrackers and having a pretty girl recite "The Spirit of '76" with gestures, he would put on a real show—horses, buffaloes, sharpshooting, and Indians.

He bought the Deadwood Coach, had it fetched to North Platte, and put on a stage "holdup" that made strong men turn pale. Then he had a buffalo chase, being careful not to depend on a wire fence. (And no hat-passing—let the Chamber of Commerce worry about that.) A poor defenseless pioneer family was attacked by bloodthirsty savages. But the bloodthirsty creatures paid dearly, for some soldiers, who happened to be lounging at the Fort, came on the double-quick and shot them down like dogs.

The show was a whacking success. It was really a tryout for an idea that Buffalo Bill had been nursing for years—a big outdoor Wild West Show with Indians, cowboys, good people and bad people, and lots of noise. Right then and there the Wild West Show was born, and the place was North Platte, Nebraska. A monument, please. That format is used today and always will be as long as grass grows and rivers run.

Buffalo Bill threw the name Old Glory Blow-Out into the South Platte and called his new show "The Wild West Rocky Mountain and Prairie Exhibition." But this was a little too much. After a time, he shortened it to "Buffalo Bill's Wild West Show." So great, so sensational, was the success of the show that our Bill took it to London and there, May 12, 1887, put on a command performance for Queen Victoria. This was just eleven years after Yellow Hand had bit the dust, which shows how fast the Wild West idea was moving.

And now, just as everything seemed peaceful and quiet, came the writers—a bunch to be regarded with profound distrust. They took up the West and made it Wild. There wasn't a good Indian between Omaha and Great Salt Lake. Ned Buntline—one of the outstanding liars of the world —gave William F. Cody, the Iowa lad, that name of "Buffalo Bill." Right then and there, *history* was made. And, for that matter, so was Cody. Ned Buntline began writing dime novels about Buffalo Bill like mad. Each one praised Buffalo Bill to the skies; also the West. Pulp by pulp, the legend of the Wild West was growing. Soon it would have roots as deep as the General Sherman tree in Yosemite Park.

Charles Bragin, 1525 West 12th Street, Brooklyn 4, New York, is the authority on dime novels. He has enough to fill a hay barn. He says the first Buffalo Bill dime novel was written by Ned Buntline in 1869 and the last one appeared in 1933. During that time 1700 dime novels appeared about our Bill.

And now came another one of them writers, this specimen being Prentiss Ingraham, from Natchez, Mississippi. He was for three months press agent for Buffalo Bill. The result was fatal. He began writing dime novels about Buffalo Bill; in fact, he wrote some of the novels that Buffalo Bill signed. He wrote, in all, 200 dime novels about Buffalo Bill. I copied down the title of one of them: *Adventures of Buffalo Bill from Boyhood to Manhood. Deeds of Daring and Romantic Incidents of the Life of William*

F. Cody, the Monarch of the Bordermen. He was, it would seem, not a follower of the Short and Snappy School. (This book was published December 14, 1881.) Now and then some truth got into the book. The lack of truth did not worry the reading public. This public wanted Right to triumph and every Indian to die with a well-placed shot. Ingraham gave the public its money's worth. His Indians were riddled with well-placed shots.

Another of the legend-builders was Edward L. Wheeler, who wrote eighty dime novels about "Deadwood Dick"—a pitifully small number. And so, now, we have three men writing as fast as they could about the Glamorous West where men were men and women had no sense of shame.

I fell into the toils of one of these glamour writers. One day a man on horseback came over the hill, tied up at our hitch rack, and came into our farmhouse in the Great Plains section. We gathered around him like children around Santa Claus, so glad we were to see somebody new. He was, it developed, selling a "subscription book." The title of the wonderful book was *Thirty Years on the Plains and in the Mountains,* and it was by William F. Drannan.

The man opened up the book and read part of it aloud—the most exciting, the most thrilling stories I'd ever heard—mostly stories about "renegades." I didn't know what a renegade was, but I knew he was bad.

Finally Pa bought a copy and the man climbed on his horse and went away. Ma started to read the book aloud to me. It was the story of William F. Drannan himself. He told how his parents had died, and how he had to go forth into the world and take care of himself. My parents were strong and husky—maybe I could run away and go to the Wild West where exciting things were happening. I was living in the Wild West, but I didn't know it. I thought it was pretty dull, especially when I had to take the basket and go out to the hog lot and pick up corn cobs for the kitchen stove.

The book told how Kit Carson took a liking to the boy and invited him to travel with him. The boy met the most wonderful people: Jim Beckwith, Jim Bridger, and Frémont. Kit Carson asked the boy to call him "Uncle Kit." Oh! if only I could meet Uncle Kit. I didn't know Kit was dead and buried; I thought of him as being just around the corner. Some day I would meet him and watch his jaws silently chewing tobacco.

The other day I pegged down to the library and looked up the book that once so thrilled me about the wonders of the Wild West. Here is one of the stories:

One day when the boy was traveling with Uncle Kit, he went out to kill a mountain sheep. Suddenly, a few yards ahead of him, he saw a panther. He "drew a bead" and killed the panther. The boy heard a strange cry and, holding his rifle to his shoulder, moved slowly toward the strange

"Hunting Buffaloes"—first reproduced in 1870

sound. To his astonishment he saw a panther cub. He took it back to the
cabin and fed it—he does not tell on what. The cub grew rapidly. The boy
trained it so that it could count up to ten. The boy would call out a
number and the cub would pat its paw on the floor to correspond to the
number. But, strive as he would, the boy could not train the panther to
count above ten. The boy would romp with the panther until the panther
got tired; then the panther would lick the boy's face with its tongue and go
contentedly to sleep.

Finally the boy took the panther to Santa Fe. One day an Englishman
named Mr. Mace saw the young panther and offered the boy $100 for it.
The boy had never seen so much money at one time before in his life,
and sold the cub. The Englishman led the panther away—a touching sight,
no doubt. A few days later the boy saw the young panther in a cage.
When the panther saw the boy, the panther cried pitifully. The boy regretted deeply he had sold the pet which was so devoted to him. The boy
tried to buy the pet back, but the cruel Englishman flatly refused. The
matter was settled by the boy having to leave with Uncle Kit on a beaver-
trapping expedition, leaving the sorrowing panther behind.

I was thrilled by this story of the West and wanted to get a panther
which could count to ten and would, after a romp, lick my face. But I
was never able to bring this about.

I believed every word of it and so did, I'm sure, thousands of other
boys. We didn't know it, but the book was setting for us the pattern of
the Wild West.

Other books came pouring from the presses, all singing the song of
the Glamorous West. These books were sold not only from house to house,
but on railroad trains, everywhere. And they all carried the same central
theme: the land where the men shot with the speed of a hummingbird's
wing and asked questions afterward. Such heroes were everywhere. Billy
the Kid was an example—Billy who could shoot so fast with his Bisbee
Colt—"the fastest gun in any man's hands."

Along in 1902, came Owen Wister with *The Virginian*, which set the
pattern for all cowboys—tall, lean, laconic. And that's the way they are
today. If an author turned up with a fat, talkative, jolly cowboy, the editors
would pull down on the author and shoot him as full of holes as a flynet.

The pattern was being set more and more firmly. Then came the
artists who set it as firmly as a child's initials in a block of sidewalk ce-
ment. The first artist of any considerable stature was Rufus F. Zogbaum,
who was a military artist, attached, most of his professional life, to the
Army. He journeyed west to do some military pictures and came back with
a Wild West painting called "Hands Up!" It depicted a stagecoach robbery,
and was printed in *Harper's Weekly*, August 29, 1885—yes, that early.

A year later came his "Painting the Town Red," also in *Harper's Weekly*. This showed four cowboys coming down the street a mile a minute on their horses, shooting right and left and having a wonderful time. In the foreground was a Chinaman who wasn't having a good time at all. The reproduction made eyes bug. This painting did more than any other piece of magazine art to set the standard for the American cowboy. If an artist bobbed up with a painting, or a drawing, that did not depict the cowboy as Zogbaum did, then that artist was an imposter and should be booted out of town.

In 1901 came "The Defeat of Roman Nose" at the Arikaree Fork of the Republican River. The picture was by Carl Forsyth and set for all time and eternity (almost) what a battle between whites and Indians looked like. Later artists followed the details set down by Forsyth and, to this day, they bob up in Western paintings.

Other artists were painting the American cowboy as a kind of Little Lord Fauntleroy with spurs. The cowboy, as these artists depicted him, could not rope a steer from a haywagon. Then—oh then!—came Frederick Remington. His first realistic cowboy appeared in *Harper's Weekly*, October 9, 1886, and was entitled "In from the Night Herd." It was a masterpiece, and sent Little Lord Fauntleroy home from school, weeping copiously.

Suddenly cowboy pictures in the magazines became popular. But they were all sired by Zogbaum and Remington. People knew the look of the West—they'd seen these pictures and that settled the matter.

Even cowboys, who didn't look any more like the pictures of them than they did like Daniel Webster, began to think the pictures really looked like them and stood on street corners looking picturesque.

Then came the most important, the most breath-taking, picture of all. It is the greatest Wild West picture of all time and has been viewed by more people than "Washington Crossing the Delaware." But it didn't start off with a boom; in fact it dragged its moccasins. It was called "Custer's Last Fight" and was painted by Cessily Adams. He had high hope for it and scraped up enough money to hire Sioux Indians to pose for him in his studio in St. Louis.

When he got the painting finished, Adams rushed around to the art galleries of St. Louis, who were as cold as a frosted tomahawk and would have naught to do with him. Just another Indian picture, they said: thanks for thinking of us. Finally he had to sell it to a saloon, the pit of artistic aspirations. The saloon was near Eighth and Olive Streets, St. Louis, and there it hung on the wall, back of the bar. But it didn't bring in any great number of art lovers and the saloon got deeper into debt. Finally the Anheuser-Busch Brewing Company took the painting over on the debt that the saloon owed the company. The price that the brewing company allowed the saloon off on the indebtedness was $10,000 (the whole sum the saloon owed was $35,000). Cessily Adams was heartbroken; the painting he had started with such high hope was now saloon art—not only that but was being jockeyed around to settle a debt.

Anheuser-Busch let it lie around a year, not knowing what to do with the picture. Somebody suggested they could make lithograph reproductions and send them out free of charge to their customer saloons. The company got ready to do this, not thinking much of the idea. The saloons, finding they didn't have to pay for the lithographs, were enthusiastic about the idea. Soon Custer was fighting behind ten thousand bars. Men who had never paid the slightest attention to art, thirsted for more.

In fact the author of these lines began to study art this way—the art becoming dim as the study went along. But in a few days he would be back for another go at art and to mourn, as all true Americans should, the dreadful fate suffered by brave George A. Custer. (The date that the brewing company sent out the lithographs was 1886; the picture had been painted a year earlier.)

The Seventh Cavalry (Custer's own) now pined to have the painting. The brewing company presented it to them at Fort Riley, Kansas, with enough beer to raise the Little Bighorn River to flood proportions. And there the painting remained for about three months, then was sent to Fort Grant, Arizona, which promptly—of all things—lost it. After a time the painting was presented to Fort Bliss, Texas, to our heroic soldiers stationed there.

In no time the painting was in a warehouse in Fort Bliss. Officers heard of this and rescued it from such shocking indignity and brought the painting—now world-famous—to the Officers' Club in Fort Bliss. The club promptly burned down. This ended the career of the painting which had risen from the saloons to respectability. (The date the club burned down was June 13, 1946. The painting was seventy years old.)

The painting had a tremendous effect on establishing the West as a dramatic, exciting place. It helped pass along the idea that Indians were savages and should be shot on sight.

But all Western art wasn't on-the-spot reporting. Even the dignified house of Currier and Ives got out two etchings telling the story of the Wild West. One was "The Last Shot"; the other, "The Emigrant Train." Western art had got to Fifth Avenue.

Song helped fasten, even more securely, the legend that the West was a jolly place. The covered wagon people sang "Oh! Susanna" at their campfires and danced to it, hopping over the buffalo grass as best as they could. But that wasn't all; they changed the destination from Louisiana to California. This is the way it went:

"I'll scrape the mountain clean, old girl; I'll drain the rivers dry.
I'm off to California, so Susanna, don't you cry.
Oh! Susanna. Oh! Susanna, don't you cry for me,
I'm off to California with a washbowl on my knee."

No great improvement on Foster and certainly a strange place for a washbowl. But that was all right with the covered wagon people—they were going to California where everything was perfect and every mountain was made of hard rock candy.

It was not long until cowboy songs came. The greatest was "Git Along, Little Dogie." It was supposed to be sung by a herder to the rhythm of the movement of his horse. The East didn't know what a "dogie" was. But pretty soon every school child tall enough to chin a blackboard knew that a "dogie" was a motherless calf and that it had to live on grass. This, in turn, distended its stomach. When its stomach was opened, the contents had the appearance of dough, and so it was called "Dough-gie." This was simplified, in spelling, to "dogie" and thus a great saddle song was born. (The song itself was a little "dogie," because no one ever knew its father or mother.)

Other splendid songs turned up, all passing along the wonder of the West. One was "Bury Me Not on the Lone Prairie." It sprang up like a dandelion on a widow's lawn; none knew whence it came. And this was true of "Good-bye, Old Paint," which has delighted ten thousand barbershop quartets and some audiences. Two other famous ones are "The Old Chisholm Trail" and "Little Ah Sid," the latter telling the sad-humorous tale of a Chinaman caught in the meshes of white society.

And then came the greatest of the West-booming songs—"Home on the Range." For years no one knew who wrote it, or anything about it. Now I am right proud to set down here the part I played in establishing the story of how the "Home" was written. It made me blink, when I got into the matter, to find that the song had been written not far from my home and that it had been sung by the prairie people right where I lived. And that they had danced to it. But my parents hadn't, for they were strict Methodists and believed that anybody who danced was going to Hell. And sometimes, today, when I see modern dancing, I think they were not far wrong.

But back to the home of the "Home."

The first thing I turned up was that four states claimed to be the birthplace of the song (Colorado, Arizona, Oklahoma and Kansas). In fact, an ebullient congressman from Colorado had it written in the *Congressional Record* that Colorado was the state. His local patriotism exceeded his knowledge.

At last I learned that the song had been written at Smith Center, Kansas, in 1873, by a doctor who had fled from La Porte, Indiana, to escape a scolding wife, and who must have put his very soul into the line "'Where seldom is heard a discouraging word." (The old doctor had five wives during his lifetime and lived to be eighty-nine before he went to the Home on the Range. He is buried in Fairview Cemetery, Shawnee, Oklahoma, and there you may go today if you wish to see his grave.)

In the song, the old doctor had his highs and lows. Here's one of the latter:

> "Oh, give me the gale of the Solomon Vale,
> Where light streams with buoyancy flow;
> On the banks of the Beaver, where seldom, if ever,
> Any poisonous herbage doth grow."

The last line is surely the worst bit of verse a well-intentioned poet ever left behind. Thank goodness, the people who later worked over the song threw the poisonous herbage into the Beaver.

Dr. Brewster Higley, at dusk, sat on a fallen tree and wrote the poem. I was all apant to see the picturesque cabin where the old gentleman had lived and, after a time, I found myself there. I was shocked. It had been turned into a henhouse. Thank goodness the doctor is in Heaven and does not know to what low estate his cabin has fallen. (*Note:* I have before me a letter from W. E. Lee, editor of the Smith County *Pioneer*, who tells me the ancient log cabin has been restored and that no hen dares to go near it. Thank God, I say, and I am not anti-hen.)

My part in running down the story is too long to go into here; it is, however, dealt with at some length in my book *Corn Country*, beginning on page 164.

Here are the vital statistics of the song: the music was composed by Daniel E. Kelly, a miller, at Gaylord, Kansas, a couple of jumps from where the doctor lived. The poem was first published in the *Smith County Pioneer* in 1873, about a year after the doctor put it on paper.

The local people began to sing and dance it (not being Methodists and, seemingly, having no fear of Hell).

I interviewed, in Shawnee, Oklahoma, the son of the old doctor, who told me the story of how his father had written the song, and showed me manuscript copies of other songs his father had written, but not the original manuscript of the song; this was burned up in a "wagon fire." He called his father "Pa," which shocked me that the author of so great a song should be spoken of so casually. He said, "Pa was always writin' songs. His best one was 'Army Blue.' He also wrote 'A Dream in Which I Saw

My Mother.' That was good, too. My mother said if he spent more time doctorin' and less time writin' poetry the family would have got along better."

"Did your father make much money out of 'Home on the Range'?"

"He never made any money out of it."

The song was not put into print until a year before the doctor died. He never saw a copy of the printed song. When the old doctor died he was so little known that the Shawnee paper merely wrote, "An Aged Physician Passes." Later, when I uncovered the story, the paper came out with an enthusiastic piece about the doctor and the great honor to the town —with never a peep about me.

John A. Lomax saved the song from oblivion. One day in 1908 he turned up in a colored saloon beyond the Southern Pacific depot in San Antonio, lugging an old-fashioned Edison recording machine about the size of a hay wagon. The Negro proprietor had been a camp cook and for years had sung the song up and down the Chisholm Trail. Lomax found him behind the saloon, under a tree, asleep—and intoxicated. Lomax punched him in the ribs and told him what he wanted.

"Come back tomorrow," mumbled the singer.

And this Lomax did, and under a mesquite, where he had first found him, the record was made. Henry Leberman, a blind music teacher in Austin, put the rubber tubes in his ears and set down the music. Lomax published the song in 1910 in *Cowboy Songs*. And that, very briefly, is how a great Western song was born and passed along to the world.

Years passed. The idea that the West was a glamorous place was set into the American consciousness like a brand into a steer's hide. The West was different from any other place in the United States. If you said a rude word to a lady in Charleston, South Carolina, she would swoon; in Charleston, Arizona, she would whip out her hogleg and shoot you as coolly as she would a sidewinder.

The legend kept building. Unexpected twists came. Arthur Chapman (father of John Chapman, drama critic for the New York *Daily News*) was conducting a column in the *Denver Republican*. One day in 1912, he read in the papers that at a convention of state governors being held in Buffalo, New York, the men got into an argument as to exactly where the West began. This gave Arthur Chapman an idea and he sent upstairs a poem which he called "Out Where the West Begins." It was just part of the day's work. The next day, however, the managing editor got up from his desk, went over and said, "That was a fine poem, Arthur." (That made newspaper history; there is no other authentic record that a managing editor ever got up from his desk, went to a man on his staff, and congratulated him. Old newspapermen talked about it in hushed voices.)

You will recall the opening:

"Out where the handclasp's a little stronger,
Out where the smile dwells a little longer—
That's where the West begins."

It leaped into popularity. It appeared on half a million post cards, it was made into records, became a song set to music. And it appeared in the public school readers in Colorado. Children were required to memorize it. In fact, the first time I ever saw John Chapman was in his father's home in Denver. The lad had come back from school with a scowl as big as a towel. "What do you think, Ma!" he said. "Our teacher says we've got to learn Dad's poem by heart. I wish he'd never wrote the thing." (I think I am quoting him correctly.)

It was made into a pillow—that is, the poem was burned by pyrography into leather pillows, for no home in that day considered itself up-to-date unless it had a jaunty leather pillow on the sofa. But things were not as good as they seemed. At that time there was no automatic copyright law; if an author did not copyright his work before it was published, then the moment the work was printed it went into public domain and anybody could batten upon it. And that is exactly what happened to "Out Where—." Arthur Chapman himself never got a penny out of it, except when he lectured and used it as part of the program. But he never learned it by heart; he had to fish the poem out of his pocket and read it aloud.

Thus the legend grew that the West was wonderful, a glamorous, an exciting place. The movies gave it an assist; so did radio, and now television is running its cattle all over the range.

I've not been able, in the short space tossed me, to take up the endless ways the legend has been spread. (A whole book could be pecked off about this.) If I had to set down the five men who put the popcorn on the tree, I would nominate—

Buffalo Bill
Ned Buntline
Prentiss Ingraham
Cessily Adams
Frederic Remington

Many will not agree with this selection. In fact, as I read it over, I don't agree with it, myself. If I'd said a dozen, then I'd have room to turn around. But five it was and five it will remain.

Anyway, it's a glorious story; there has never been anything like it and every American with anything in his veins redder than carrot juice should be proud of it.

Pioneers or frontiersmen are a class of men peculiar to our country and seem to have been designed especially to meet the exigencies of the occasion.

JOHN C. DUVAL

J. F. WEADOCK

They Lived the Saga

As VARIED IN THEIR CHARACTERS as the land itself, the people came from many places and many backgrounds. In the Southwest, those who stayed were fused by their environment into a common pattern as the demands of the desert and mountain country pressed them into a single mold. Men and women alike, few but the strong remained. The fearsome and the weakling fled.

So it was in the early days of Arizona Territory, in 1873, when Governor A. P. K. Safford was attempting to prove that "with about 3,000 cavalry and 1,000 infantry I could, within a year, eradicate the difficulty." The difficulty of which the governor wrote so plaintively to Washington was the Apache people, who were turning the horizon red with the flames of blazing ranch homes and staining the ground with the blood of the owners.

In an interview with a New York reporter, the governor told the story of the wife of a member of the Territorial Legislature which was in session at Prescott. She had remained at their mountain ranch a few miles out of the frontier settlement while her husband struggled with the creation of a legal code for the Territory. The Apaches attacked the ranch. The wife went to work with a double-barreled shotgun and "was not," according to the governor, "by any means unsuccessful in disposing of some of her enemies." But as dusk fell she ran short of ammunition, so she "dispatched a small Mexican boy to her husband, informing him of the occurrence and requesting an additional supply of ammunition." The interview fails to record whether or not the husband returned with the boy or whether he just sent the ammunition and stuck to his politicking.

"Dissolute Cow-Punchers"—from the *Century Magazine*, October, 1888

Law came slowly to the Southwest. Frontier justice lacked many of the refinements of the more settled areas. There were many frontier officers whose names became a part of the saga of the times. But not so often mentioned were the justices and judges. There was a justice of peace in Globe named George Allen. He found a couple of fellows guilty of murder and sentenced them to be hanged, without bothering about any higher court. He then saw to it that the sentence was carried out. When some folks argued that this was a bit hasty, he replied "They were going to be hung anyway, and I just made it legal. I wasn't going to have any lynchings in my district!"

Jim Burnett, of Charleston, a rowdy mining camp not too far from Tombstone, decided the layout needed a justice of peace and that he would be a good one. So he set up shop and went to work. The camp was booming. Between the miners, prospectors, cowboys, gamblers and rustlers,

Burnett and his self-appointed constable did all right. Over in Tombstone the county supervisors heard about this court and decided that Burnett could keep the job. But they would send him some regulations to operate by. Also, the supervisors opined, it would be a fine thing for Burnett to send down the county's share of the fees.

Burnett disagreed on what the supervisors considered the county's share and issued his ultimatum in the form of a letter to the board. In it he said, "Hereafter the precinct of Charleston will look after itself with no help from the county." He sent the message off to Tombstone and continued to hold court, pocketing all of the fees as before.

But there was a shooting scrape that Burnett couldn't settle. He got crossed up with a fellow named Greene and the argument ended in gunsmoke. Greene shot first. The Charleston court was without a judge. Ironically enough, one chronicle of the times reported that Burnett died because of one thing he hadn't committed. Later evidence seemed to indicate that he was innocent of the act of which Greene accused him, although guilty of many others.

There was another early judge, an erudite gentleman from Alabama, named Edwin F. Jones. He looked like a Confederate colonel was supposed to look. In his twilight years, he functioned as both a justice of peace and U.S. commissioner. One day in his court a husky cowhand was on the witness stand, testifying in a case concerning a stolen calf. He was being grilled by a waspish defense attorney who was putting on quite a show for the six-man jury. He implied, in a nasty way, that it was possible the wrong man was being tried and that the witness could have been the one that got tangled up with the wrong calf.

The cowboy took it for a time but he was getting pretty red about the neck. Finally he turned to Judge Jones and asked, "Your honor, can I ask you a question?"

"Certainly," said Judge Jones, "go right ahead."

"Well, your honor," said the cowboy, "just suppose a man was to hit a man in your courtroom. What do you figure the fine would be?"

"Now that," replied the judge, as he stroked his mustache to hide a smile, "is a touchy question. But I'd say if the circumstances you refer to are the ones I think you mean, and the man you refer to is the one I think you mean, I'd say the fine would be about a dollar and then I would remit the fine."

The cowboy grinned and started to get out of his chair. The defense attorney hastily withdrew and said, "That will be all. I have no more questions."

There were some bang-up divorce cases in those courts, too. I found the record of one in the old courthouse at Tombstone when the county seat was being moved to Bisbee. The record was that of a divorce sought by the wife of a character known as Buckskin Frank Leslie, a gambler and bartender, also somewhat notorious as a pistol shot. He had married one of the dancing girls at the Crystal Palace who had yearned for a quieter life and sought it in matrimony.

However, she told the judge, from whom she sought the divorce, she had not found it. It appeared that Buckskin Frank was not much of a husband. He failed to come home at nights, hanging out at the Crystal Palace even though she was no longer there. When he did come home he would be drunk and would raise general Hades around the house. All of this, she said, she could stand. But what was getting her down and frazzling her nerves was his other habit. On these occasions Buckskin Frank would demand that his wife stand against the wall of their bedroom while he with his .44 shot her outline in the plaster with bullets.

It was not only wrecking the plaster, the woman opined, but it was wrecking her as well. The judge agreed and granted the divorce.

But not all of the rugged characters of the early towns and camps were of the rougher elements. There were other folks around who, in their own way, had a lot of iron in their makeup. They had to have in order to do the things they did in that time and place.

In early Tucson, which had more saloons per block than it did any other business, was Mrs. Josephine Hughes, wife of L. C. Hughes, newspaper publisher and later governor. Mrs. Hughes was an exponent of temperance. This was not unique, since many women agreed with her. But Mrs. Hughes did more than believe in it. She not only made the Woman's Christian Temperance Union a going concern in thirsty Tucson, but established a chapter in Nogales, Sonora, Mexico, as well.

There was a traveling preacher in the '70's, whose name is dropped from the record. He arrived in Charleston when that restive camp was the headquarters of a group of citizens not noted for their piety. Curley Bill Brocius, the bull of the woods of the moment, was not what one would call a religious man. His main business was to acquire cows, regardless of ownership, and sell them to any who wished to buy.

The circuit rider felt that Charleston was in need of spiritual guidance. He decided it was going to get it and looked up Curley Bill. No one knows just what he told him. But Curley took a liking to the salty little parson, and promised to be at the meeting and to bring some of his friends. The little parson went to work and, for the better part of an hour, gave them the best he had. The sermon, one old-timer recalled, laid heavy stress on the error of coveting the goods of a neighbor, including his ox, I assume. It must have touched a responsive chord. Brocius passed the hat, and sent the parson on his way rejoicing—with laden pockets.

It was down in the Big Bend that I heard the story of the doctor who spent a lot of his time patching up folks along the international border between Texas and Mexico. His friends kept warning him that he couldn't go roaming around like that, without getting into trouble. But Doc, who patched up border officers, rangers, smugglers, and rustlers with equal facility, was not alarmed.

"No one is going to bother me," he said, "they know I keep my mouth shut. Besides none of these boys are going to let me get hurt. Hell, within a week they may need me themselves!"

Some folks seem to think that personal valor comes only in large packages. Which isn't always true. A big fellow with a broad strip of lean in his bacon can get along in some rough company. It was so in the early days of the Territory when John Slaughter, of Texas, drifted into Arizona with his young bride, a few vaqueros and a herd of longhorn cattle. He settled along the border on the old San Bernardino grant and immediately a lot of folks with a yen to gamble began giving odds that he wouldn't last long enough to get acquainted, much less get a calf crop.

That was their mistake. Slaughter never qualified as a large man. When I knew him in his later years, he wouldn't have weighed 140 pounds soaking wet. But he evened things up by toting a 10-gauge Greener shotgun across his saddlebow, and kept it loaded with buckshot. The long loop boys soon learned that he would use it, too. His dictum to rustlers was short and to the point. It was "Get out or get shot." After a few had tested this, and got buried finding out, Cochise County folks talked Slaughter into becoming sheriff so that he could apply Slaughter's "law on rustling" on a county-wide basis. He did just that. Soon word got around that the new sheriff wasn't much interested in bringing in prisoners. A number of well-known local characters moved to Colorado.

Another little man who made big tracks in those days was Billy Breakenridge, a deputy under Sheriff Johnny Behan. Billy was never hefty enough to get out of the welter division. But he did all right in huskier company. The sheriff was ex-officio tax collector. It was no easy job. Much of the citizenry was transient. A lot of the remainder didn't believe in paying taxes anyway. Billy's boss tossed the task of collecting from the outlying precincts into his lap. The sheriff, of course, took care of the town folks who were more stable and easier to find.

This left Billy with the rough-and-ready element of Charleston, Gleason, Galeyville and other stopping points along the border where a large number of citizens made a living handling other folks' cattle, horses and personal funds without the owners' consent.

Billy thought the matter over and decided to have a powwow with Curley Bill. A short time before, the outlaw had been wanted for assault with a deadly weapon. Breakenridge had brought him in. But he had also seen to it that Brocius received a fair hearing. Witnesses rounded up by the deputy had testified and Brocius was freed, the court deciding he had acted in self-defense. Billy figured Curley Bill owed him a small favor. It was worth trying.

Brocius listened to Billy's problem about the taxes and agreed to help. It tickled his fancy to ride with the little deputy and in one isolated camp after another make his associates pay up on what the deputy declared to be a fair assessment on all personal property found in their possession, including livestock. In each instance, Brocius recommended immediate payment. Collections were good. Breakenridge returned to Tombstone with his saddlebags well filled.

Brocius, however, thought Billy was carrying this thing pretty far when, on their return, he was told to ante up his own share. He paid.

Ben Regan of Florence, one of the owners of the fabulous Silver King mine, left his mark, too. He was a saloonkeeper and his own bartender, since in those days some of the trade paid in gold dust. A bartender with a broad thumb could make a neat profit for the house—or himself—as he "took a pinch" to pay for a round of drinks. In being both owner and bartender Regan figured he would prevent any leakage from the till as well as from his kegs. In addition to these duties, Regan served as undertaker for the town. Then, being a religious man, he often acted as a lay preacher. In a booming community such as Florence it can be seen that Regan managed to be kept right busy.

It is related that one night, before he became a part owner of the Silver King, Regan was handling the custom in his bar when a soldier recently discharged from Fort McDowell wandered in to spend a portion of his final pay and to try a hand at poker. The soldier's luck wasn't good. He soon lost most of his stake. But he had taken enough drinks to make him quarrelsome. Deciding that his losses were not all on the level, he pulled a gun and started to tree the entire saloon.

Regan warned him that a certain amount of argument would be considered boyish fun and frolicking, but this was going too far. The soldier made a pass. Regan hauled a gun from under the bar and shot him. The soldier died.

Regan was no man to slight his duty as he saw it. He closed the bar, removed his apron and went to work knocking together a coffin. Getting it into shape he placed the defunct warrior in it, then called a Mexican wood hauler to bring his wagon around to the saloon. Together they loaded the coffin and went to a spot in a sandy bar along the Gila where the digging would not be too tough. They prepared a grave and lowered the box into it. Regan, in his capacity of lay preacher, said a few well-chosen words and paid the Mexican to fill the grave. He then returned to open the bar, setting up drinks for all who had attended the obsequies.

When Regan struck it rich with his share of the Silver King sale he disposed of his bar and left Florence for San Francisco, where he turned his attention to religion and good horses, the latter of which he was very fond. There were hundreds more—miners, merchants, cowmen and soldiers, all of whom added to the pattern that is the Southwest. They were all different in many ways, but they were, and are, all alike in one. They came to live in a hard but lovely land, and they remained to make it their own.

"Modern Comanche"—from *Harper's New Monthly*, May, 1891

For Western life ain't wild and woolly now;
The cowboy knows a lot besides more cow;
He can two-step, do hemstitching,
And do hay or baseball pitching—
For Western life ain't wild and woolly now.

"Western Life"

S. OMAR BARKER

The West Today

BIG IS THE BRAND OF THE WEST, today as yesterday. Northwest, southwest or smack through its mountainous middle, once you have sampled the vast, varied expanse and savored the spirit of that rambunctious region lying, roughly, between the ninety-sixth meridian and the Pacific Ocean, the impression of almost fabulous bigness will be one you cannot escape.

It's not all Texas, either, though the Lone Star does stretch out like a giant steerhide over a right smart patch of country in which are located several of those "biggests" that we westerners sometimes brag about. Take the famous old King Ranch, for instance. U.S. Highway 77 uses up about eighty flat Texas miles to reach through it. Set Delaware down in it and there'll still be room for Rhode Island. Its Running W brand is official on enough range for 120,000 head of big red Santa Gertrudis cattle and 12,000 horses, with some 600 home-on-the-ranch vaqueros, mostly of Mexican extraction, to look after them.

Among other legitimate Texas brags are the biggest state capitol, biggest oil field, more goats than Missouri has people, more sheep than the population of Pennsylvania, and more big hats than neckties. Oddly enough, however, it is in Oklahoma's Wichita Mountains National Wildlife Refuge that you will find the biggest living heard of Texas longhorn cattle.

To list all the "biggests" in the West would wear out both a typewriter and the reader's patience. Yet wonders on a grand scale are such an inescapable aspect of Western geography that I must venture to list a few of them.

In Colorado you can get lost in the biggest batch of tall mountains in the nation, including forty of the fifty highest. Wyoming claims the oldest National Park (Yellowstone) with its biggest geyser (Old Faithful). If you're salt hungry, maybe Kansas will let you lick awhile in the biggest salt mine, at Hutchinson. In Montana (Glacier National Park) are the biggest ice cubes; in Utah the biggest copper-mining hole-in-the-ground (Bingham Canyon) and the most gigantic natural bridges; in South Dakota the biggest man-made sculpture (Mount Rushmore); in Idaho the deepest river gorge (Snake).

New Mexico boasts of the biggest caverns (Carlsbad), the oldest archeological relics, and the biggest Indian festival (Gallup). Arizona takes pride in the biggest cactus (saguaro) and the incomparable Grand Canyon. In California, in plain sight of each other, are the lowest spot (Death Valley) and the highest (Mt. Whitney) in the United States, plus the world's biggest trees (redwoods) on up the coast. Oregon and Washington operate the biggest sawmills and grow the biggest apples. In Nevada it is not hard to find some of the biggest wide open spaces as well as wide open casinos.

These are only a few of the visible "bigs" we Westerners claim the right to brag about—and sometimes do. We also raise big beef and fine horses, uncork the saltiest rodeos, shoot big game, catch big trout, harvest big wheatfields, cuss big dust storms, and delight in big distances.

But we like to believe that a more important bigness of the West, past and present, is its bigheartedness. Maybe that's not the right way to say it, for there are plenty of bighearted people everywhere in America, even under the artificial enamel of protective sophistication in muscle-bound Manhattan. The difference is that the West, with its heritage of pioneer neighboring so recent and its elbowroom still adequate, feels no need for any protective shell over its fundamental friendliness.

I heard an old cowhand put it this way: "You can rub out cow trails with highways, swap sagebrush for cities and free grass for filling stations, but you can't cure the West of bein' 'howdy country'—not yet awhile, anyhow!"

On a sky-blue day last summer a family of Ohio tourists pulled off a Western highway to look at some pronghorn antelope several hundred yards from the road. Presently a shiny limousine pulled up behind them. Three men got out, one in the uniform of a state policeman, one in the cowboy boots and slim-styled pants of a ranchman, one in slacks and a tail-out sport shirt. What they had stopped for, it turned out, was to lend the tourists a pair of binoculars for a better look at the pronghorn, much to the delight of three eager children.

Of course Westerners don't spend all their time looking for favors, small or large, to do for strangers, but it is significant that, for the West, there was nothing at all remarkable about a state policeman, a county sheriff and a state governor stopping to help total strangers enjoy a better look at antelope. And of course they would have been even more certain to stop if the tourists' car had appeared to be in trouble.

I believe it is no libel on the rest of the United States to say that nowhere else will you find the same easy, friendly informality in all human contacts that is common custom all over the West—except possibly deep in the hustle-bustle of a few of its bigger cities.

I have said the West is big, and it is—too everlasting big for either its well-known or its wayside wonders to be ticked off in detail in these pages. State tourist bureaus, chambers of commerce, tourist agencies and the companies that sell gasoline will gladly furnish reams of specific sightseeing information to any inquirer. I can only try, here, to present sort of a brief buzzard's eye glimpse of what the big, outdoor, once wild and woolly, West is like today.

First, let's face it: the modern West is a vigorous part and parcel of a dynamic, progressive nation, with a fair share of the country's highways, railroads, airports, cities, power plants, factories, motels, hotels, hospitals, supermarkets, service stations, sea ports, high schools, colleges, radio and TV stations, automobiles, football teams and juke boxes—and maybe a little more than its share of atomic and nuclear installations.

The old wild and woolly West of rowdy cow towns, roaring mine camps, dusty covered wagons, frontier forts, buffalo hunters, open range cowboys, and longhorn trail herds is gone. But the hardy heritage remains. There is still room for wide-open spaces, and the flavor of the Old West still lingers.

It lingers in the fact that the West is still cow country. On hundreds of off-the-highway ranches, wind-tanned cowpokes, not of the drugstore or movie variety, still do a big share of their cow work on horseback. Brands are still laid on with red-hot iron. There are still catch ropes on the cowboy's saddle, though less used now than in years gone by. In many a Western town, sweat-stained, curl-brimmed hats, lean-legged Levis and the tapping sound of high-heeled boots are as common as cow tracks in a corral. Nor are these, in most cases, worn for show-off. Just ranchfolks come to town.

From the green hills of Wyoming to the thorn thickets of the Texas Gulf Coast, from the plains of western Kansas and Nebraska to the ancestral *haciendas* of California, from the high mountain parks of the Rockies to the cactus half-deserts of Arizona, from the rimrocked mesas of New Mexico to the flats of eastern Oregon, grass and the critters that eat it still manage to keep the buckaroo breed from plumb petering out.

One way in which Westerners try to hang onto their horseback heritage shows up in hundreds of organized Sheriff's Posses and Mounted Patrol Companies, in which every member keeps a horse and knows how to ride it, owns a six-shooter and knows how to shoot it, and holds himself ready to turn out on call for any emergency from policing rodeo-day traffic to helping hunt escaped convicts, fugitives from the law, or lost babes in the woods.

The ancient and honorable tradition of horse-straddling with the forked end down is also kept alive throughout the West by resorts and dude ranches that feature trail trips where automobiles (thank the Lord) still cannot go. Numerous vast primitive areas in Western national forests are permanently restricted to horse and foot travel only.

Each summer, Wilderness Trail Rider groups from all over the country take two- and three-week camping trips by horseback into such rugged primitive areas as the Upper Pecos in New Mexico, the San Juan Mountains in Colorado, the Uinta Mountains in Utah, and many others. It is also in such remote areas that the West's finest big-game hunting is enjoyed by those nimrods hardy enough to pack in by horse, mule or shank's mare.

For the West-visitor who lacks the time, money or hardihood for roughing it, there remain plenty of national forests, parks and monuments accessible by wheel and plainly shown on road maps. Add to these the long stretches of open plains, of juniper-and-piñon-dotted foothills, semi-deserts of sagebrush, greasewood, yucca and cactus through which various Western highways pass, with no human habitation in sight for mile after mile, and you become aware that the West, with all its modern developments, is still a land of wide-open spaces.

For the West-visitor steeped in the rambunctious history and legends of pioneer days, a phantom flavor of the frontier still lingers in scores of ghost towns. Some of these, like Bodie in California, Candelaria in Nevada, and Dewey in Idaho, are completely abandoned. In others, like White Oaks, New Mexico, a few hardy die-hards still live among the empty shells of former glories. In still others, like Tombstone, Arizona, and Virginia City, Montana, history-minded inhabitants faithfully preserve the aspect of olden times for all to see.

Typical also of the West's laudable desire to keep alive the memory of its pistol-pointin' past, are the many regional and roadside museums where the traveler nostalgic for signs of the Old Wild and Woolly he has read so much about can pause to gaze and ponder on old guns, old saddles, old branding irons and innumerable other relics of frontier garb and gear. You may be astonished to find "Billy the Kid's six shooter," or "The gun that killed Billy the Kid," on display in a dozen different roadside museums; but however imaginative the text of some of their tags, you will find most articles shown to be genuine relics of the rawhide era.

Old West museums that are painstakingly authentic include the Alamo
in San Antonio, Frontier Times Museum at Bandera, Texas, the Old Palace
of Governors at Santa Fe, the Charley Russell Memorial Studio at Great
Falls, Montana, the Pony Express Museum at Sacramento, California, the
Panhandle-Plains Historical Museum at Canyon, Texas, and many others.
My choice of them all for *cow country* record is the one at Canyon, where
the fine murals of Harold Bugbee help tell the story of the Plains.

Even without museums, the West-visitor who brings his imagination
along may well conjure up ghostly wagon trains from still visible ruts of the
Oregon and Santa Fe Trails, and hear phantom bugles sound for ghostly
cavalrymen on parade amid the tumbled ruins of old frontier forts. Notable
among these is old Fort Union, once guardian of the Santa Fe Trail, near
Las Vegas, New Mexico, now a National Monument.

Oldest of all the ghost towns, of course, are the ancient cliff dwellings
and time-ruined pueblos of the Southwest's first inhabitants. These are given
added interest by the nearness of the present-day pueblos of their sun-
browned descendants, the Pueblo Indians, whose corn grows in many hues
and whose ceremonial dances are rhythmic rainbows of mystic meaning.
Elsewhere the Sun Dance of the Sioux tribes, the Yei-bei-chai of the
Navajos, and the Devil Dance of the Mescalero Apaches are equally
thrilling.

Oddly enough, the first white pioneers to gain a foothold in the
West came in from the south, not the east. They were Coronado and his
conquering *caballeros* from Spain, via Mexico, in 1540. By 1608 the Spaniards had set up their capital at Santa Fe and settled down to stay. Their
descendants are still here, a large and respected part of the citizenry of
the Southwest. Their proud but easy-going culture, their folkways, and
their love of *fiestas* have greatly enriched our Southwestern heritage, as
well as earning for New Mexico the pleasant nickname of "The Land of
Mañana." Their language and ranching customs have given the cowboy
a large share of his cow-work vocabulary, in words like lariat, corral, hackamore, *remuda*, etc. Hispanic tradition lingers, too, in the time-mellowed
Spanish Missions of California.

If I have seemed to neglect the Pacific Slope in this brief report, it may
be because that region's march into modernity has been perhaps more
rapid and more complete than that of the more definitely cow-country
West. Yet with all its fine cities, busy harbors, alluring beaches, fabulous
orchards and huge lumbering industries, the Slope is also a region where
unforgotten traditions of hardy pioneering help keep the new West
Western.

Along with its modern hustle, its bigness, its easy informality and a
lingering flavor of the wild and woolly, another notable quality of the

West is sudden contrast: green fields and orchards smack up against gray desert, with only an irrigation ditch between; flat plains abruptly blocked by implacable mountains; sagebrush and jackrabbits inside a city limits; vast blue lakes backed up by huge dams in the midst of desert; a cowboy towing a horse trailer behind a Cadillac.

The atom, nuclear fission and uranium have created still greater contrasts. Los Alamos, brain-and-nerve center of the superscientific future, sits on a mountainside within night-light view of the oldest capital city (Santa Fe) in the United States, and only a few miles from both, empty cliff dwellings and inhabited Indian pueblos where the basic ways of tribal life have changed but little in four hundred years.

In the desolate but picturesque Colorado Plateau country where Utah, Arizona, New Mexico and Colorado corner together, uranium, most modern of metals, is being mined canyon by canyon and cliff by cliff alongside innumerable deposits of the bones of prehistoric monsters a thousand million years old!

The West today can be all things to all people: industrial development, or the glimpse of a lone coyote skulking through the sagebrush; an ultramodern motel, or a primitive *adobe placita* hidden in the hills; prize potatoes in Idaho, or a javelina hunt in Texas; the glamour of Hollywood, or Kit Carson's grave in Taos; the delicate bloom of desert cactus, or a salmon run in Oregon; the Pacific Fleet at Bremerton, or burros dozing under a New Mexico cottonwood; oil derricks, or a matched calf roping on Sunday; cattle, corn, and cotton, or high mountain trails and summer snowdrifts; a swift black highway from here to yonder, or a thousand dusty side-roads to adventure—and maybe getting stuck—among remote canyons and mesas.

The stagecoach days are gone. The thundering herds have given way to less rambunctious breeds. The blue gauze of gunsmoke has drifted over the hill. The heroic haze of hoof dust no longer signals a stampede. But something of the old-time magic still lingers.

How can the West-visitor best find and feel it?

One way or another it will be all around him if he will forget the daily mileage and take time to look, to see, and to behold with understanding. Let him venture to explore side roads. Let him stop over in the smaller towns—and ask questions. Let him now and then hoof it off the main drag a little. Let him "git a horse." Most of all, let him frame some knowledge of the Old West with reconstructive imagination.

On many a ranch there are still branding days, seasonal roundups, cow-horse *remudas*, broncs to bust, yearlings to dehorn, steers to ship. Unfortunately for the West-visitor, ranchmen cannot welcome everybody who would like to watch "the doin's," for the obvious reason that there would be too damn many of 'em. But if you should sometime happen to "get lost" on an *unposted* side road, I doubt if many ranchmen would run you off—provided you kept plumb out of the way. There are also guest ranches that run cattle and put their dudes on horses to "help" with the cow-work—which is just as genuine as if it had no audience. However the West-visitor manages to see it, the old cowhand was right: whether at a city filling station or in the wide open spaces, most of the West today is still "howdy country," where an inquiring stranger can ask most anybody and get a friendly answer.

Appendix

The WEST YOU CAN ENJOY

The 150 Places to See in the West

THERE ARE HUNDREDS of excellent guide books to the American West. The AAA, the state information bureaus, the chambers of commerce, and the oil companies have seen to that, as well as such books as the Rand McNally Road Atlas. The series of State Guides put out by the Federal Writers Projects of WPA days are still un-excelled for detail. There is only one fault with this lavish library of Travel West.

They offer too much and are overpowering in their richness.

Hence the list that follows is intended as a taste-panel, rather than a compre-hensive guide, for travelers west. The editors went to members of the Chicago, Denver, Tucson, New York and Washington Corrals of the Westerners. We asked, "Give us the names of the 100 places that should be seen *first* in all the states west of the Missouri River." Their selections hustled in—some as marked maps, some as complete manu-scripts. Check and whittle as best we could, we found that Westerners favor 150, rather than 100, places "to be seen first" in the West.

Here they are, arranged by states. Little attention has been given to the obvious. You cannot ignore Fort Worth, Kansas City, Los Angeles, San Francisco, Seattle or Portland when you get out there. But all these big cities deserve detailed guides, and you'll find them at bookstores, gas stations and in the chambers of commerce.

Only a few privately operated ventures are mentioned in this list. Emphasis instead is on the National Parks areas, each of which was set aside for excellent reason.

INFORMATION – The National Parks Service (Department of the Interior, Wash-ington 25, D.C.) provides descriptive, illustrated leaflets that are available free at nearly all areas, or obtainable on request at the Washington address.

At the areas themselves everyone from superintendent to rangers will answer questions and give you every reasonable attention. Obviously it is impracticable for them to give each one of the millions of visitors to Yellowstone Park a personally con-ducted tour. But you can be sure the red carpet was rolled out for each of the forty-two visitors who got to Yucca House, Colorado, within one recent year.

State historical societies exist in nearly all states. Information, printed and personal, is their business. Their museums are always useful, as are many maintained by county historical societies, municipalities, and a few private persons. The museums that exist in most of the National Parks areas are primary guides to the understanding of those areas. Chambers of commerce also exist to give out information, and many of them do an excellent job. The railroads were the original source of much information about the West, and still produce useful literature. Some offer conducted tours. State highway departments and touring bureaus issue excellent maps. The road maps of the oil com-panies are unexcelled. In many cities travel bureaus, sometimes maintained by newspapers, assemble all types of information as do the auto clubs.

THANK YOU! A platoon of busy citizens contributed long, and unpaid, hours to this list. They deserve a public "Thank You." The first of these hat-tips goes to Nevada. There we approached the state's best-known literary figure to write the piece about Virginia City. Despite four book contracts, a variety of magazine assignments, speeches and a weekly newspaper, the copy was prepared and delivered three days after the query was mailed. With it came a typed note that reads, "Obviously this can't carry my byline as its contents will indicate. It is just an entry in your directory of places to see in the West. Beebe." So be it.

Others who rate special thanks are: Don Russell, J. H. Euston, Leigh P. Gerrard, Delos P. Grant and Arthur G. Murdock of the Chicago Corral; Maurice Frink, 1956 Sheriff of the Denver Corral and Executive Director of the Colorado State Historical Society; Herbert E. Kahler, 1956 Sheriff of the Potomac Corral and chief historian, National Park Service; and authors Reginald R. Stuart, S. Omar Barker, Charles Way-land Towne and Colonel Edward N. Wentworth.

ARIZONA. – *Tucson*, the "Old Pueblo" dates from 1776 when *soldados* of the *presidio* danced their señoritas across the torch-lit *placita*. Within the site of the *presidio*, artifacts and foundation walls have been unearthed, proving occupation scores of centuries ago. The *State Museum* shows the pioneer studies in tree-ring research. Its Navajo sand paintings are outstanding. *Tucson Mountain Park*, twelve miles west of the city, includes the "Arizona" movie set of Old Tucson and the exciting *Trailside Museum*, a display of Southwest plant and animal life. *San Xavier del Bac*, founded by Padre Kino in 1700, is nine miles south. Papago Indians have worshipped since 1797 in the present church, called the finest example of Spanish-mission architecture in the United States.

Tucson has an elevation of 2,400 feet and an annual rainfall of less than nine inches— and the temperature is high even in the shade provided by citrus, eucalyptus, oleander and olive trees. In contrast with the University of Arizona's fifty-six buildings on eighty-five acres is *Saguaro National Monument*, seventeen miles east of Tucson. On its 64,000 acres loom massive, columnar specimens of the granddaddy of all cacti. In nearby *Colossal Cave*, where train robbers once hid out with their loot, underground waters have carved a Devil's Head, Frozen Waterfall, Praying Nun, and Pillars of Hercules.

Organ Pipe Cactus National Monument preserves plants of the Sonoran desert, found nowhere else in the United States. It has 516 square miles of rolling hills, mountain range, and alluvial plain along the Mexican border. From Tucson go west by way of Sells and the Papago Indian Reservation. It is twelve miles east of Ajo. The Papagos stage tribal dances and rodeos annually. Ajo is a copper-mining town, as are San Manuel and Bisbee. *Tumacacori National Monument* is another of Padre Kino's missions, dating from 1701. The Church of San Juan de Tumacacori stands—with a new roof; the unroofed circular mortuary in the cemetery and the unfinished bell tower are as the Fathers left them. It is forty-eight miles south of Tucson on U.S. 89.

Tombstone, "the town too tough to die," still boasts the Bird Cage Opera House and Boothill Cemetery. A rip-roaring "Helldorado" in October stages the "OK Corral Fight" in which Marshall Wyatt Earp figured. Tombstone is seventy-two miles south of Tucson on U.S. 80. *Bisbee*, another copper town, is twenty-six miles further. Then twenty-five more miles bring you to *Douglas*, copper-smelting border town opposite Agua Prieta, Mexico.

Chiricahua National Monument, an area known to Cochise and Geronimo, is a Wonderland of Rocks in the Chiricahua Mountains, a verdant, forested island in a brown sea of desert. It is a short distance off U.S. 666. North fifteen miles is Cochise's Stronghold, and nearby is Apache Pass, where Cochise first took to the warpath, and the site of Fort Bowie.

Casa Grande National Monument in the Gila River valley is a roofed-over ruin, once a fourteenth-century watchtower, built of huge mud bricks. It was first seen by Padre Kino, who reported it in 1694 as a "four-story building, as large as a castle and equal to the finest church in Sonora." It is on Ariz. 87, two miles north of Coolidge.

Phoenix has the *Arizona* and *Heard Museums*, both strong in Indian exhibits, and the state capitol, with statues of such robust heroes as Bucky O'Neill and Frank Luke. Indians peddling pottery may suggest a look-see at *Komatke*, a Pima village on the Gila River Reservation (thirty miles southwest) with its one-room dwellings of ocatillo and saguaro ribs plastered with mud. *South Mountain Park* and *Hieroglyphic Canyon* (eight miles south) has pictographs of wolves, horned sheep, lizards, men, and geometric designs duplicating those on the sidewalk-peddled pottery. Camelback Mountain, say the Indians, was once one of Uncle Sam's camel corps, which, defying the gods of thunder and lightning, was turned to stone.

Tonto National Monument includes two accessible and well-preserved fourteenth-century cliff dwellings—one is visible from the parking area. It is on one of the ridges running north from Superstition Mountains. The Apache Trail (Ariz. 88) also leads to Roosevelt Dam and to Globe. *Montezuma Castle National Monument* in the Verde Valley is a large cliff dwelling about 90 per cent intact and original. It is on Ariz. 89, five miles north of Camp Verde. *Tuzigoot National Monument* consists of the excavated ruins of a hilltop pueblo of 1000–1400 A.D. and a museum housing the entire collection recovered from the site during excavations in 1933–34. It is across the Verde River from Clarkdale on U.S. 89A.

Petrified Forest National Monument contains the greatest and most colorful concentration of petrified wood known in the world. Huge logs lie about on the surface. Newspaper Rock has a great variety of petroglyphs and there are many more of these mysterious Indian drawings in the area. Just across the highway is one of the most colorful parts of the Painted Desert. The monument is on U.S. 66, east of Holbrook twenty-five miles.

Meteor Crater is one of the world's largest craters, formed by a giant meteorite some 40,000 years ago. It is privately operated, seven miles south of U.S. 66, near Winslow. *Walnut Canyon National Monument* preserves some 300 small cliff dwellings. You can walk into about twenty-five of them in a fifty-minute trail trip. It is reached by a short detour from U.S. 66 *Sunset Crater National Monument* is dominated by a 1,000-foot-high volcanic cinder cone in dull red and orange. Tree rings and archaeological data put the eruption at 1046–1071 A.D. There are many small spatter cones, black cinder dunes, and slag heaps of lava in the area, some of which look as though they barely had time to cool. It is north of Flagstaff on U.S. 89 to a turn-off into four miles of unimproved, rough and seasonally difficult road. *Wupatki National Monument* contains many well-preserved ruins of red sandstone pueblos that date from an Indian "land rush" that followed the Sunset Crater eruption—the cinders held water, improving productivity. Go back to U.S. 89 to a turn-off a few miles north, since the connecting road between Sunset Crater and Wupatki is not advised.

Canyon de Chelly National Monument in the northeast corner of Arizona marks the area where Kit Carson rounded up the Navajos and made a permanent peace. It is typical Navajo country, but also has remains of several prehistoric peoples. Turn north from Gallup, New Mexico, by way of Window Rock (the Navajo capital) and Fort Defiance, or from Chambers, Arizona, by Ganado and Chinle. Both roads are bad—and long. *Navajo National Monument* has three of the largest and most intricate of known cliff dwellings, representing thirteenth-century Pueblo culture. Betatakin, the most accessible, has been excavated and restored. Keet Seel is the largest cliff ruin in Arizona. Inscription House is named for an undeciphered inscription believed to be Spanish. The monument is competely surrounded by the Navajo Reservation on the edge of a "roadless area" nearly a hundred miles from any paved highways. Turn off U.S. 89 north of Cameron to the northeast and keep going.

Pipe Spring National Monument was a Mormon fort built in 1869–70, named when William Hamblin, known as Gunlock Bill, bet he could shoot the bottom out of a tobacco pipe without touching the rim—and did it. It was later a ranch headquarters. It is fifteen miles southwest of Fredonia (U.S. 89) by a fairly good graded road.

Grand Canyon National Park is of course one of the world's greatest natural wonders, and there is no need to discuss its superb attractions here. James Ohio Pattie, trapper and mountain man, was the first American to see it, in 1826. Major J. W. Powell in 1869 was the first to succeed in a boat trip down the Colorado River. His scientific explorations did much to make it known. And there was Captain John Hance, who built the first cabin on the canyon rim and marked most of its trails. He it was who had a horse he thought could jump Grand Canyon if he had a good start. So he went back three miles, galloped full speed to the rim and took off. "I wasn't half way across before I saw he couldn't make it," Hance tells the story. "We hadn't taken a big enough start. So we just turned around and went back."

CALIFORNIA. – *Death Valley National Monument* marks an area where some pioneers first saw California at its worst and fastened on it such names as Funeral Range, Furnace Creek, and the Black Mountains. After the Jayhawkers and the Bennett-Arcane party—whose rescuer, William L. Manly, was also the historian—Death Valley gained further fame through the lost Breyfogle mine, the Lost Gunsight silver lode, 20-mule-team borax, and Death Valley Scotty. Now it can be visited in comparative safety by several routes. *Joshua Tree National Monument* is another desert area of deserted mines, notable for the scarce Joshua-tree, a member of the yucca family with spectacular flowers. The best route is U.S. 60, 70, and 99 to a point fifteen miles east of Banning, thence to Twentynine Palms and the main entrance. *Lassen Volcanic National Park* marks another pioneer trail. Peter Lassen piloted emigrants over a cutoff from the Humboldt with Mt. Lassen as his landmark. Mt. Lassen was in eruption from 1914 to 1921, the most recent volcanic activity in the United States. It is fifty-two miles from Redding on Calif. 44.

Yosemite National Park, established in 1890, was set aside by the Federal government as a "public trust" in 1864. Yosemite Falls, El Capitan, and the giant sequoias are its features. Other stands of the big trees are to be found in *Sequoia* and *Kings Canyon National Parks* near Fresno. *Muir Woods National Monument*, only ten miles north of Golden Gate Bridge, has the only stand of redwoods in the National Park System. *Pinnacles National Monument* is notable for its spirelike crags, volcanic in origin, once a refuge of the bandit Tiburcio Vasques. It is just off Calif. 25, about thirty-five miles south of Hollister. *Cabrillo National Monument* at Point Loma commemorates the discovery of the coast of California by Juan Rodríguez Cabrillo on September 28, 1542. There is a memorial monument and plaza. The old San Diego lighthouse, used from 1855 to 1891, is on the grounds. The monument is within Fort Rosecrans Military Reservation but open to the public. *Santa Barbara Mission* is the best preserved of the Franciscan missions in California. It was founded in 1786 by Father Junipero Serra. Paintings in the church were brought from Spain in 1793. *Lava Beds National Monument* is far north in California—virtually on the Oregon line—and not far from Crater Lake and Oregon Caves. It was the scene of the Modoc War of 1872–73. Here General R. R. S. Canby was killed during a peace parley. For their part in that killing Captain Jack, the Modoc leader, and three of his followers were hanged. Before that there was desperate fighting among the cinder cones, craters, and natural trenches. It is reached on Calif. 39 from Tulelake, California, or Merrill, Oregon. Just above *Sacramento* is the Eldorado of 1849 with its many ghost towns and near-ghost towns.

COLORADO. – *Denver*, mile-high capital, founded in the Gold Rush of 1859, is a center for state tours. Its museums offer the overview of its history, culture, and background. These include the *Colorado State Museum*, maintained by the State Historical Society; the *Denver Museum of Natural History*—from dinosaurs to ducks and from Indians to uranium; the *Denver Art Museum*; and *Chappell House*, with its collection of Indian arts and crafts. The *Grave of Colonel William F. Cody, Buffalo Bill*, on Lookout Mountain, is west of Denver, near Golden (U.S. 40). There is a Memorial Museum.

Trail Ridge Road and Rocky Mountain National Park. The High Trail follows the route of the Utes and Shoshones and after them the fur hunters over the Great Divide to the buffalo plains. It is part of U.S. 34 from Loveland to Granby. From Estes Park village to Grand Lake is fifty-five miles of mountain park and high ridge road, reaching well over 12,000 feet and traversing Rocky Mountain National Park—405 square miles of the Front Range of the Rockies. There are sixty-five named mountains within the park reaching altitudes of more than 10,000 feet. The highest is famed Longs Peak, 14,255. On the High Trail you will cross three divides, two of them more than 11,000 feet: Iceberg Lake, Fall River, and Milner. Like the Indians and the mountain men, you will see the full sweep of the continental divide and both sides of Mummy Range. The Medicine Bow Range lies along the misty, northern horizon, toward which Cache la Poudre Valley points. The Gore Range is at the southern limit of vision and the Never Summers Wall, with its snow ramparts, to the west. On the tundra slopes above Iceberg Lake (12,-183 feet) you can feel the everlasting frost only eighteen inches below your feet. Far down is the emerald valley of the Colorado River, so green that it belies its name, which means red, its meandering valley strung with beaver ponds. The park boasts five glaciers and 700 varieties of wild flowers.

Central City. This "oldest living gold camp" is in the "Little Kingdom of Gilpin," a county that in the 1870's poured out $2,000,000 a year in gold. Ignore your fellow tourists from "the Plains" and listen for the rumble and clank of six-horse ore wagons on Eureka Street and the tramp of booted feet. Can't hear them? Too bad! But look to the hills that wall in the town, stacked with stilted buildings, gashed with tunnels and drifts, heaped with yellow tailings piles. The twisted streets follow the gulches into the hills with fabled names: Silver Hill, Quartz Hill, Bobtail Hill, and on top the Glory Hole, 500 feet across and 900 feet deep, where they blasted out the gold. The *Coeur d'Alene Mining Museum* preserves the original shaft, the hoist that operated the ore buckets, the mine tracks and the ore cars that used to run on them, the original steam engine and air compressor, and the blacksmith forge where the drills were sharpened. Tours leave from the *Teller House*, where you may dine in Victorian opulence in the gilded second-floor dining room. During the festival season you can see a play at the Teller Opera House. Here Edwin Booth, Emma Abbott, and Joseph Jefferson played. The original hickory chairs are here with famous names carved in their backs. The "Face on the Barroom Floor" is railed off in "The Elevator," the old bar of the Teller House. Central City is thirty miles west of Denver on U.S. 6 and Colo. 199.

Leadville, another famous mining town; here the State Historical Society maintains Healy House and Dexter Cabin, museums depicting household life in the silver mining era, 1870–80. Leadville is 114 miles from Denver by U.S. 6 and Colo. 91.

Colorado Springs, founded in 1871 by General William Jackson Palmer, was built for the leisure and culture of the nabobs. Industry was not to darken its sky, or commerce to disturb its serenity. The storied, lordly hostelries, the Broadmoor and the Antlers, lately refurbished, bear out this purpose. Round about lies the older West. Just at the edge of the city is the *Garden of the Gods*, with its Balanced Rock and other strange red formations. Ute Pass is now traversed by U.S. 24. *Cheyenne Mountain* was Captain Pike's lookout. From here he deemed his great white peak forever unscalable. Now you can take the Pikes Peak auto highway to the top, long ago reached by cog railway. Looking down from Cheyenne Mountain, you will see the old right-of-way of the Cripple Creek Short Line Railroad, with grades so steep that five locomotives were needed on ore trains. Now this is a wide, safe highway over which you can drive to *Cripple Creek*, once the "greatest gold camp of the world." It dug $25,000,000 in its best year, 1901, and $412,000,-000 all told. Colorado Springs is 108 miles south of Denver on U.S. 85/87. Cripple Creek is west on U.S. 24, south on Colo. 67.

Pike's Stockade, a replica of the fort built by Captain Zebulon Pike in 1807 in what was then Spanish territory, is maintained by the State Historical Society east of La Jara, Conejos County, 232 miles from Denver on U.S. 285 south of Alamosa.

Old Fort Garland, is a restored army post of the period 1858–83, commanded by Colonel Kit Carson, 1866–67. It has adobe barracks, soldiers' theater, dioramas, and historical relics; 206 miles from Denver. Take U.S. 85/87 to Walsenberg and U.S. 160 west forty-nine miles.

Bent's Fort on the Arkansas River and Santa Fe Trail was a famous adobe trading post, 1833–52, in Otero County between La Junta and Las Animas on U.S. 50.

Great Sand Dunes National Monument has the highest inland sand dunes in the United States, paralleling the heavily forested, snow-capped Sangre de Cristo Range. It is reached by Colo. 17 north to Mosca, then east on Colo. 150. No accommodations, except camp grounds.

Mesa Verde National Park is the major archeological preserve of the Federal government. It has hundreds of ruins of ancient villages and cliff dwellings, representing cultures that flourished in this region from the time of Christ until about 1300 A.D.—the Basket Makers in the earliest period to about 700 A.D., and the Pueblo Indians in the later period. Only a few of the hundreds of ruins have been excavated. Cliff Palace, largest and most famous, was first seen by two cowboys, Richard Wetherill and Charles Mason, in 1888. This huge cave dwelling has 200 living rooms and twenty-three kivas and may have sheltered 400 people. It is reached by U.S. 160 or north from Gallup, New Mexico, by U.S. 84/285. *Yucca House National Monument*, near U.S. 84, has similarly interesting ruins, and *Hovenweep National Monument*, on the Colorado-Utah line, contains four groups of prehistoric towers, pueblos, and cliff dwellings. It is not, however, accessible by highway.

Black Canyon of the Gunnison National Monument contains a ten-mile section of the spectacular gorge of the Gunnison River, notable for its huge isolated granitic masses. The north rim is reached from Colo. 92, just east of Crawford by a fourteen-mile graded road. The south rim is seventeen miles from Montrose, east eight miles by U.S. 50 and nine miles north by graded road. At Montrose the State Historical Society maintains the *Ute Indian Museum*, a memorial to this tribe and its Chief Ouray. *Wheeler National Monument* is notable for its weird and picturesque rock formations, due to eccentric erosion and volcanic action. It is in Mineral County near the famous mining town of Creede on Colo. 149, which turns off U.S. 160 west of Del Norte.

Colorado National Monument comprises an area of fantastically eroded and vividly colored highlands along the Colorado River on either side of Grand Valley. It includes areas appropriately named Monument Canyon, Independence Rock, Devil's Kitchen, and Monolith Parade. Dinosaur remains have been found in its sandstone formations. The eastern entrance is four miles from Grand Junction, on U.S. 6, U.S. 24, and U.S. 50. The north entrance is three and a half miles from Fruita, on U.S. 6 and U.S. 50. And speaking of dinosaurs, there is *Dinosaur National Monument*, 203,965 acres on both sides of the Colorado-Utah border, which has many fossil remains. This is up in the far northwest corner of Colorado, where Green River joins the Yampa. Turn off U.S. 40 at Maybell for thirty-two miles of Colo. 318 marked as "graded."

IDAHO. – Indian Wars against the Nez Percé in 1877, the Bannacks in 1878, the Sheep-eaters in 1879, were fought in Idaho. The troops found themselves in country that was unmapped and little known. Some of that country is as little known and inaccessible today as it was in 1879. Particularly is that true of the country of the Sheepeater War, the Salmon River valley, the "River of No Return." If you are foolhardy enough, you can hire a boat to take you down the Salmon River. But you cannot find one to take you back. Airplanes fly over the forested mountain mass of central Idaho, but much of it is seldom seen from ground level.

A glimpse of the primitive that still marks much of Idaho can be seen at *Craters of the Moon National Monument*, so named because the general appearance of the area is more suggestive of the surface of the moon than of much else on earth. It is seventy-five square miles of all varieties of volcanic activity—cinder cones, lava cones, lava flows from the Great Rift, a series of fissures, lava tubes producing caves and natural bridges, lava bombs, tree molds, and pit craters. It is on U.S. 26 near Arco. For contrast, there is *Sun Valley*, sophisticated winter sports capital, notable for its ski runs, near Ketchum, on both U.S. 93 and the Union Pacific R.R.

KANSAS. – *Council Grove*, outfitting point for the Santa Fe Trail, took its name from the 1825 council held here with the Osages to make a treaty. A "Madonna of the Trail" statue points the way of the pioneers. The old *Kaw Mission*, built in 1851, was the first school for white children in Kansas. It is preserved as a state museum, administered by the Kansas State Historical Society—which also has an outstanding museum at the Memorial Building in Topeka. *Pawnee Rock*, most spectacular of Santa Fe landmarks in Kansas, was a lookout point for Indians, and scene of several fights. It is a state park, within sight of U.S. 50N between Great Bend and Larned. *Dodge City* was founded in 1872 by buffalo hunters. That year, too, the Santa Fe R.R. made end-of-track here. Then for fourteen years Dodge City was the "Queen of Cow Towns" with Wyatt Earp and Bat Masterson among those hired to keep the peace. Its history may be seen at *Beeson's Museum*, built up by the late Merritt Beeson, son of "Chalk" Beeson, sheriff and owner of the Long Branch Saloon. *Boot Hill* also has relics of those days. *Fort Dodge*, built in 1864, became a Soldiers' Home. Much of it is still in use. At Cimarron, a riverside park marks the *Cimarron Crossing* to "the Cimarron Cut-Off" of the Santa Fe Trail. A preserve near *Garden City* has a large buffado herd, a fitting memorial to Charles J. "Buffalo" Jones, who did much to save the buffalo. First of the cow towns was *Abilene,* now more famous for the *Eisenhower Memorial Museum,* since this was the boyhood home of President Dwight D. Eisenhower. Wild Bill Hickok was marshal of Abilene, and also of Hays, another cow town with its *Old Fort Hays Museum* in the guardhouse of that frontier outpost. *Wichita,* airplane manufacturing center that takes top rank in the making of private planes, recalls its cow town beginnings with a reconstruction of a Cow Town, to which some of the original buildings have been moved. Bob and Grat Dalton and Bill Power are buried in Ellinwood Cemetery, *Coffeyville.* They were shot down while trying to hold up two banks at once. The *Dalton Defenders Museum* is on the plaza. The *Dalton Gang Hideout and Museum* at Meade was traditionally used by these bandits; you enter it through a "secret" tunnel. At *Fort Scott,* the *Headquarters House,* completed in 1843 and used during the Civil War, is preserved as a museum. The *Kansas Tourist Guide,* published by the Kansas Industrial Development Commission, 1025 Kansas Avenue, Topeka, is one of the best, and outlines many more spots worth seeing—region by region and town by town, with full directions on getting there.

MINNESOTA. – *Pipestone National Monument* preserves an area that was neutral ground to the Indians, the quarries where they obtained the red stone used for their ceremonial pipes or calumets. The stone is called "catlinite" because it was first described by the artist George Catlin, who traveled among and painted the Indians from 1829 to 1838. The monument is in the southwest corner of Minnesota at the north edge of the city of Pipestone, on U.S. 75, Minn. 23 and Minn. 47.

MONTANA. – *Custer Battlefield National Monument* commemorates a fight which, in proportion to its size, certainly takes the lead for verbal argument and the utilization of black ink on white paper. It was on June 25, 1876, a day of dust and smoke and blood, when the Seventh U.S. Cavalry, led by Brevet Major General George A. Custer, attacked the Sioux hordes on the Little Bighorn. The Seventh came to enforce policy; the Sioux to defend their traditional hunting grounds. Both failed. If they proved anything, they proved themselves men, both red and white. On that quiet hill among the white markers, you may understand more about such things than you learn by reading or televiewing. It is at Crow Agency on U.S. 87.

Virginia City, Montana (not to be confused with Virginia City, Nevada), was a pioneer mining camp in 1863 with the discovery of gold in Alder Gulch. There the Vigilantes hanged Henry Plummer, one of the few cases on record where the sheriff actually was the leader of the outlaws—a familiar plot to all who go to movies or watch TV. They also hanged Jack Slade, a frontier character known to Mark Twain and Buffalo Bill. The ghost town has come to life for visitors with a *Memorial Museum,* as well as Rank's Drug Store, in continuous operation since 1864, the Bale of Hay Saloon and the Variety Theatre, where melodramas are given in season.

Glacier National Park has superb mountain scenery, sixty glaciers, and Blackfeet Indians. It adjoins Canada's *Waterton Lakes National Park,* the two together forming *International Peace Park.* It is on U.S. 89, U.S. 2—and the 49th parallel of north latitude.

Big Hole Battlefield National Monument preserves a portion of a major battlefield in the retreat of Chief Joseph and the Nez Percés from Wallowa Valley in Idaho over the Lo Lo Trail to Bearpaw Mountain, where Chief Joseph surrendered with the pathetic statement, "From where the sun now stands, I will fight no more, forever." Colonel John Gibbon commanded the troops in the desperate fight at the Big Hole. There is a foot trail to the rifle pits, the soldiers' memorial monument, and the Chief Joseph Memorial. The monument is twelve miles west of Wisdom and twenty-one miles southeast of U.S. 93.

The Charles M. Russell Room in the State Historical Society Building at Helena has more than forty works of the cowboy artist, whose home for so many years was at Great Falls. Its *Gallery of Western Art* in the same building has a fine collection of the work of E. S. Paxson and other Montana artists. A Historical Museum, Historical Library, and Research Center are other facilities.

NEBRASKA. – *Scotts Bluff National Monument* commemorates a landmark and favorite campsite on the Oregon Trail, traveled by so many emigrants between 1843 and 1869. The bluff rises 800 feet above the trail in a region of treeless plains. Ruts of the old trail can be easily followed for more than a mile around its base. Neb. 86 follows the route of the Oregon Trail along the North Platte River and passes other landmarks of similar erosion: *Jail Rock* and *Court House Rock* near Bridgeport; *Chimney Rock*, perhaps most famous of all, rising 200 feet in a spire above its 300-foot base, and *Castle Rock*, near McGrew. U.S. 87, north and south, reaches the city, which spells its name as Scottsbluff.

Homestead National Monument, near Beatrice, commemorates the Homestead Act and consists of the first claim filed under that act. Daniel Freeman, a Civil War soldier, was on duty at Brownsville on December 31, 1862, and was ordered to St. Louis the following day, when the act became effective. He routed out the assistant registrar of the land office from a dance and persuaded him to file the claim just after midnight. An original homestead cabin—not Freeman's, which was destroyed—is a museum exhibit. The area is on Nebr. 4 about four miles northwest of Beatrice, and accessible from U.S. 77 and Nebr. 3.

Omaha, founded in 1854 with the opening of Nebraska Territory, was a gateway to the West. Winter Quarters, nearby, and Mormon Pioneer Memorial Bridge recall that the Mormons camped here after being driven out of Nauvoo, Illinois, before starting their trip to Utah. Bellevue, a suburb to the south along the Missouri River, near present-day Fort Crook, has a marker for the beginning of the Oregon Trail, which once started here. The first transcontinental railroad started west from Omaha, and the *Union Pacific Historic Museum* at the home office of that railroad is well worth a visit.

NEVADA. – *Virginia City*, twenty-three miles south of Reno, Nevada, over a splendid hard-top all-season highway, is one of the few authentic, unrestored and altogether atmospheric souvenirs of the Old American West. Unlike other synthetic "Western" towns that make a bid for the tourist trade, Virginia City is not a restoration, a fakement of frontier structures, or a collection of miscellaneous jails, saloons and can-can parlors staffed with ancients and gaffers with Central Casting whiskers. It is a mere microcosm of its once booming self with a population of 25,000, but its 400 permanent residents live here, drink, roar, quarrel and conduct businesses on a twelve-month basis. Virginia City is not a stage-set; it is the McCoy.

Virginia City in the sixties and seventies was the setting of the fabulous Comstock Lode of gold and silver which produced nearly three quarters of a billion dollars in hard wealth in those years, built San Francisco as the glittering cosmopolis of the West, in part financed the Union cause in the Civil War, and created ordinary millionaires by the score and a number of really rich millionaires. It never was a cow town. To approach it in the expectation of hair pants and Bull Durham doings is a misapprehension. It was a rich mining and banking and railroad community of six-story hotels, grand opera and evening clothes, mansions of the nabobs in Millionaire's Row, and the mecca of every traveling celebrity of its bonanza years from President Grant and the Duke of Sutherland to Adah Isaacs Mencken, Baron Rothschild, Adelina Patti and David Belasco. It was as stage manager of Piper's Opera, still standing to this day, that Belasco first fell in love with the stage. The late Maude Adams made her first stage appearance there.

To repeat, Virginia City was an urban, frock-coated metropolis, whose fabled International Hotel boasted the first elevator west of Chicago. It never saw a cowpoke, and in its heyday a cowboy on his horse in C Street would have been as much a curiosity as he would have been in Delmonico's. The town's only connection with cowpokes is indirect, for here were invented and first made the copper-riveted canvas pants known today as Levis. They were first devised for hard-rock miners and not for Texas waddies.

Virginia City today is not a museum piece to be merely looked at as a historic curiosity. It is an animated and in some ways uninhibited twenty-four-hour-a-day Nevada resort town with several hotels in summer months, three or four restaurants, and eighteen gorgeous saloons, three or four of them with fine Victorian gambling parlors attached. People come to stay a day or so at Florence Edward's celebrated and only slightly Bohemian Silver Dollar Hotel, to play roulette and craps if the spirit moves them, and to drink the clock around at magnificent bars where once John Mackay, Mark Twain and other legendary frontier great wore the mahogany smooth. You can even get thrown in the gow, for sufficient cause, in the most commodious jailhouse in the West. It was built for a town of 25,000 more or less freewheeling characters.

Still published in Virginia City and the largest weekly newspaper in the entire West by Audit Bureau of Circulations count, is *The Territorial Enterprise*, on whose staff as a reporter in 1865 a red-headed drifter named Samuel Langhorne Clemens, who smelled strongly of bourbon, first signed a story with the byline: Mark Twain. Owned and edited by Lucius Beebe and Charles Clegg, *The Enterprise* today is still an uncommonly outspoken newspaper that finds itself quoted on a national scale and is something of a power in Western affairs. Its current edition is for sale everywhere in Virginia City and newsstand copies each include a comprehensive tourist guide and thumbnail sketch of the town's romantic history.

Strictly a museum piece, save when it was the actual setting for the première of the Columbia Broadcasting System's television program "Odyssey," is Piper's Opera, the third of that name and only one to survive Virginia City's successive conflagrations. Another attraction is the Catholic Church of St. Mary's-in-the-Mountains, said to be one of the notable ecclesiastical edifices of the West. Its various holy vessels are cast from Comstock silver. Some of the same metal is incorporated in its great bell, which peals out as it has for three-quarters of a century over the desolate Washoe Hills.

Virginia City has no single industry or manufactory of any sort. No mines operate nor any reducing mills where once its mine hoists and stamp mills reached for miles along the Comstock Lode. Its entire business is in tourists and tourism. It is a place to come and experience, not merely view. And if the drinks in the Delta, Sazarac, Comstock House, Brass Rail, Sawdust Corner, Washoe Club or other Victorian oases lay uncommon hold on you, remember that you're a mile and a quarter straight up and it's economical to drink at this altitude.

Hoover Dam is perhaps the greatest man-made wonder of the West; there is no doubt of its being the world's highest dam—726.4 feet. With a base thickness of 660 feet tapering to a crest thickness of 45 feet, the length of the crest from canyon wall to canyon wall is 1,244 feet, nearly a quarter-mile. Formed by it is Lake Mead, which holds enough water to cover the state of New York one foot deep. Lake Mead Recreational Area has been developed by the National Park Service.

The most publicized recreational area in the United States, *Las Vegas*, is also nearby. Patrons of Hell-on-Wheels at end-of-track while railroads were being built across the Plains would be astonished at the lushness of Las Vegas. *Reno*, the divorce capital, vies for notoriety.

Carson City, the state capital, is more modest. Its Mint has become a museum; it boasts a house in which Mark Twain once lived, and some historic mansions of silver-mining days.

Lehman Caves National Monument is a vast, intricate, and beautiful cavern system underlying the flank of 13,058-foot Wheeler Peak in the high desert country of eastern Nevada. A date 1878 in one of its chambers indicates its discovery shortly before that time by Ab or Absalom Lehman, whose horse stumbled into the cave opening. However, it was used by Indians for burials many thousands of years ago. It is five paved miles west of Baker.

NEW MEXICO. – If you enter New Mexico by the Santa Fe Trail you will come down from Trinidad, Colorado (U.S. 85), through *Raton Pass*, once guarded by Uncle Dick Wooten, retired mountain man who undertook to maintain a toll road, on past the landmark of *Wagon Mound* to Las Vegas. But the highway has wandered off from the trail, isolating its guardian fort, *Fort Union*, which can now be reached by eight miles of blacktop road. Here are the ruins of the largest frontier fort, dating from 1850, a remount and supply depot for troops during the Civil War. The ruins are being restored by the National Park Service for a national monument; Fort Union has been in the middle of a big cow ranch, typical of the Southwest's cow country.

At the end of the Santa Fe Trail, at the end of the Jornada del Muerto from Mexico, at the end of the long trail from California, lies La Villa de la Santa Fé de San Francisco. Behind the adobe walls of *Santa Fe* two cultures persist, the deep-burning Castilian and the sophisticated, cosmopolitan culture of modern literature and painting. But the pilgrim of the trails can roll back the centuries and see this a provident land, caring for its red-skinned and brown-skinned villagers. The snowy Sangre de Cristos on the east held back the Comanches. The rolling waters of the Rio Grande, the Great River, kept the valley green. The sun worked its spells of enchantment. Slow your city pulse to the tempo of the Tewa *tombés*–"drums like a slow heart beating." In the Plaza stands *El Palacio Real*, the seat of a hundred governors and captains general, Spanish, Mexican, and American, since 1610. The Acequia Madre still brings mountain waters to the town. You will not want to miss the Museum of International Folk Art, the State Art Museum, the Museum of Navajo Ceremonial Art, St. Francis Cathedral, San Miguel Mission, Guadelupe and Cristo Rey churches, and the capitol.

Taos may be reached north from Santa Fe through the black gorge of the Rio Grande, or from Raton through Cimarron, Eagle's Nest, and the Palo Flechado Pass, or south from the San Luis Valley in Colorado, just the way the mountain men drifted in to ease their hair and bones at the oasis of Don Fernando de Taos. Here were fandangos, fat doin's, and "Taos lightnin'" to scorch your gullet. Here today is beautiful mountain scenery. On cool nights the incense of piñon fires under the close, trembling stars is unchanged from olden days. The paintings of its artists—many, but not all—help you to experience the beautiful aspects of this country in all seasons. Spanish people have been in Taos for four hundred years; the mountain men came two hundred and fifty years later; the wagon traders still later; and the artists only fifty years ago. Now as then, the wide sage plain slopes up to the Sacred Mountain.

Capulin Mountain National Monument, in the northwest county of the state, is an extinct volcano with symmetrical crater and molten-lava river cooled to stone. From its summit you can see parts of Colorado, Kansas, Oklahoma, and Texas. Only seven miles away is *Folsom*, which gave its name to the "Folsom point," a weapon point that pushed back the prehistory of man in America for thousands of years—perhaps 20,000. Entrance to the monument is on U.S. 64 three miles from the junction of U.S. 87 at Capulin.

Bandelier National Monument commemorates Adolph F. A. Bandelier and the Pueblo ruins of Frijoles Canyon, scene of his ethno-historical novel *The Delight Makers*. Cliff dwellings, or talus villages, extend along the north wall of the canyon for two miles. El Rio de los Frijoles—the little river of the beans—is a rare permanent stream in this dry land. Its canyon is cut in the Pajarito Plateau, once a deep blanket of ash blown out by the crater of the Jemez Mountains. Here ancestors of the Keres Indians lived. They built the circular, once three-storied, community house called *Tyuonyi* on the valley floor and the cave homes on the talus slopes. Still to be seen are foundations of the homes, the holes in the cliff where roof beams fitted, and the carvings that marked the domains of the clans: Water, Snake, Sun. It is about forty-five miles from Santa Fe by U.S. 285 to Pojoaque, then on N. Mex. 4.

Chaco Canyon National Monument has eighteen major ruins of Pueblo civilization, including Pueblo Bonito, a five-story village, built in part as early as 919 A.D. Threatening Rock, a vertical cliff, ceased to threaten on January 22, 1941, when it fell, damaging twenty-one rooms of Pueblo Bonito. It is reached by U.S. 66 to Thoreau and sixty-five miles north by a graded road; or from the north by N. Mex. 55 past Aztec and *Aztec Ruins National Monument.* The Aztec Ruins are of a great prehistoric town of the twelfth century, built, not by Aztecs of Mexico, as once supposed, but by Pueblo Indians. There are thirty-six kivas, one of which, called the Great Kiva, has been completely restored. There are about five hundred rooms in all, a huge court or plaza, and much decorative masonry. Besides the road from Chaco Canyon, Aztec Ruins can be reached from the north by U.S. 550. *Gran Quivira National Monument* has eighteen ruined house mounds of Indian pueblos and the ruins of two Spanish missions, abandoned since 1678. It is reached by U.S. 60 to Mountainair and twenty-eight miles of N. Mex. 15; or by U.S. 380 to Carrizozo and fifty miles of N. Mex. 195. *Gila Cliff Dwellings National Monument* is thirty miles northeast of Cliff in the southwest part of the state.

From Taos on the north to Kuaua in the *Coronado State Monument* are eighteen living Indian pueblos. *Acoma,* the "city in the sky," can be reached by a steep climb to the top of the mesa; the nearby *Enchanted Mesa* is inaccessible. The Indians will welcome you—for a price—and show you their ancient church, the pools that provide their water supply, and the modern pueblo grocery store.

More typical, perhaps, is *San Juan Pueblo.* In 1598 San Juan de los Caballeros ("of the gentlemen") was Coronado's capital. On the wall of the governor's piñon-fragrant living room hangs a silver-banded cane, his staff of office, presented to his predecessor by the President of the United States, Abraham Lincoln. In March they dance the *Deer Dance.* Not suddenly, but as if they always had been, drum rhythms creep in. Steadily throbbing—not fast like war drums, but slower, deeper, powerfully felt through the earthen floor and the air. The people crowd the plaza with dark color. Like an arrow bisecting its center, the deer dancers, sixty strong, face the sacred Turquoise Mountain of the West, antlers tossing, legs driving hard against the red earth; rain rattles swishing, voices calling. The War Chief's hair is let loose for battle. A man of granite, he dances alone opposite the center of the file while the tombés boom and the deep-voiced chorus sings the words for pity and for help which always had brought down the deer from the mountain; sings the words of thanks for the life and the food and the raiment which the deer had always given men sacrificially. Thanks to the Sky and the Earth and the Spirits of the four World Quarters for health and long life and plenty of food for everyone to eat.

And so at Cochiti, Isleta, Jemez, Laguna, Nambe, Picuris, Sandia, San Felipe, San Ildefonso, Santa Ana, Santa Clara, Santo Domingo, Tesuque, Zia, and Zuñi.

Carlsbad Caverns National Park is a series of connected caverns of unusual magnificence. It was discovered by Jim White, a cowboy, in 1901, when he saw a dark, moving column issuing from the region. It proved to be alive, a moving stream of bats from down in the darkness of the caves. Each dusk, millions of bats fly through the great entrance arch. There are superb stalagmites, stalactites, helictites, and seven miles of underground corridors open to visitors. It is on U.S. 62, U.S. 285, and U.S. 80.

Billy the Kid. The trail of this notorious gunman is broad through New Mexico. At Mesilla across the Rio Grande from Las Cruces (U.S. 70) is one of the jails that failed to hold him (with museum). Of greatest interest is the old town of Lincoln and the *Old Lincoln County Courthouse* from which he escaped after killing his guards, J. W. Bell and Bob Ollinger. Every house in this one-street almost-ghost-town reeks of the Lincoln County War. More than twenty-five markers within two city blocks inform you of details and sites, (U.S. 70 and 380). Finally, at *Old Fort Sumner,* you will find the grave with its stone marked "Pals—Tom O'Folliard, died Dec. 1880; Charlie Bowdre, died Dec. 1880; William H. Bonney alias Billy the Kid. died July 18–" The souvenir chippers got the rest of it, but you know it is "1881." The city of Fort Sumner is at the junction of U.S. 60 and U.S. 84; the old fort is about seven miles over local roads.

NORTH DAKOTA. – *Fort Lincoln State Park.* This is Fort Abraham Lincoln from which General George A. Custer marched on the expedition that led to his Last Stand on the Little Bighorn. Foundations of the officers' quarters, barracks, and corrals are marked. On the bluff is a restoration of three blockhouses and palisades of Fort McKeon, established in 1872. Also in the area are restorations of the huge earth lodges of the Mandan Indians. Lewis and Clark camped here in 1804. Fort Lincoln State Park is four miles south of Mandan, on U.S. 10, across the Missouri River from Bismarck.

Theodore Roosevelt National Memorial Park. In 1883 Teddy bought the Maltese Cross cattle brand, then established Elkhorn Ranch, thirty-five miles north of Medora. The park consists of three areas, with headquarters in the South Unit near Medora. Medora was founded and named for the wife of Antoine de Vallombrosa, Marquis de Mores, who attempted a meat-packing business. The *Chateau de Mores,* a State Historic Site, is nearby, furnished just as he walked off and left it. This area is the heart of the North Dakota badlands, one of nature's paintboxes, with strata of red, blue, yellow, buff, grey, brown and coal-black. This area is on U.S. 10, U.S. 2, and U.S. 85. The North Unit is reached by U.S. 85. Ask about routes at Park Headquarters before trying for Elkhorn Ranch.

OKLAHOMA. – *Platt National Park* has taken rank among the first half-dozen of National Parks areas in annual attendance. Yet, outside of Oklahoma, few persons have ever heard of it. In the words of the National Parks Service official pamphlet, its "gently rolling hills offer a pleasing relief from the comparatively level surrounding country." It is an oasis in a land where there are few scenic recreational spots. It once belonged to the Chickasaw Nation and was first called Sulphur Springs Reservation. There are sulphur springs, bromide springs, and some of fresh water. It is reached from U.S. 77 at Davis and from U.S. 70 at Ardmore, south of Oklahoma City.

The National Cowboy Hall of Fame was chartered in 1955 to be established at a site chosen in Oklahoma City. The first five elected to the Hall of Fame were Will Rogers, Theodore Roosevelt, Charles M. Russell, Charles Goodnight, and Jake McClure. A nationwide architects' competition is scheduled for design of the final plan.

OREGON. – *Crater Lake National Park*, on the crest of the Cascade Range, has high rank as a scenic wonderland, for here is the deepest lake on the North American continent—1,983 feet—and fifth deepest in the world, resting in an almost circular crater blasted out by an extinct volcano. Near Medford, in southern Oregon, it is accessible from a number of highways. *Oregon Caves National Monument* is "The Marble Halls of Oregon" celebrated by Joaquin Miller. Guide service is required for tour of the caves. It is twenty miles over Ore. 46 from Cave Junction on U.S. 199 near the southern border of Oregon. *McLoughlin House* in Oregon City (U.S. 99 between Salem and Portland) was the home of Dr. John McLoughlin, chief factor of the Hudson's Bay Company, who befriended many American trappers and early emigrants. He started the house in 1845 and occupied it until his death in 1857. Members of his family lived there until 1880. It has been restored and has some of the original furniture. The site of *Fort Astoria* at the end of the Oregon Trail is owned by the city of Astoria and is under the jurisdiction of the State Historical Society.

SOUTH DAKOTA. – *The Black Hills.* This is an area about a hundred miles north and south and about fifty miles east and west. You can take a circuit drive around it in about eight hours, but better make it eight days—or even eight weeks. *Deadwood,* gold camp of 1876, has its *Adams Memorial Museum,* and on *Mount Moriah* the graves of Wild Bill Hickok and Calamity Jane (buried Martha Jane Canary). At Lead is the *Homestake Mine,* greatest gold producer in America. At *Mount Rushmore National Memorial* (two miles off U.S. 16) Gutzon Borglum sculptured gigantic heads of Washington, Jefferson, Lincoln, and Theodore Roosevelt. (At Thunderhead Mountain, Korczak Ziolkowski is at work on a gigantic statue of *Crazy Horse.*) Custer State Park (on S.Dak. 87) has 1,200 buffalo, one of the largest herds in the country. Its State Game Lodge was President Coolidge's *Summer White House* in 1927. *Wind Cave National*

Park (ten miles north of Hot Springs on U.S. 85A) is a limestone cavern noted for its rare and unusual boxwork, resembling pigeonholes. Cave trips take from one to one and a half hours. *Jewel Cave National Monument* (fourteen miles west of Custer on U.S. 16) is named for the dogtooth calcite crystals that coat its walls. (Fossil Cycad National Monument nearby is not open to the public.) You will also want to see Mount Harney, Bear Butte, Inyan Kara, the Cathedral Spires, the Needles, Spearfish Canyon, Sylvan Lake, and the many other beauty spots of the Black Hills. U.S. 16 leads directly into the Black Hills east and west as does U.S. 87 north and south. U.S. 212 is at the north edge, and U.S. 20 a few miles to the south.

Badlands National Monument has 150,103 acres of fantastic peaks, pinnacles and palisades, utterly barren, and almost worthless to any form of life since the days of the three-toed horse, the saber-tooth tiger, and the titanothere, whose remains have been found here. It lies along U.S. 16.

Slim Buttes, site of the battle where General George Crook defeated the Sioux and Cheyenne on September 9, 1876, and, in the words of State Historian Will H. Robinson, "a little known wonder region." To the south of the battlefield monument are seventy-one square miles of Custer National Forest. This area had nine residents when surveyed in 1895 and has only few more today. It is a region of buttes, precipices, and escarpments. Turn east at Buffalo from U.S. 85 to S. Dak. 8, which passes the monument. For further experiment take the Rex Cross Trail north from the Reva Gap picnic ground and other Forest Service roads.

TEXAS. – *The Alamo.* San Antonio is a gracious town, holding the Shrine of Texas Liberty to her heart while old Fort Sam Houston and Kelly and Randolph Fields have taken up the Alamo's burden for later generations. Travis, Bowie, Crockett, and their comrades had their bones burned in the plaza here. Santa Anna's bloody flag of "No Quarter" flies from San Fernando Cathedral a few blocks away. The Alamo, a hymn and a prayer of the Old West, is maintained by the state, and in the heart of downtown San Antonio. The original mission is intact, surrounded by beautiful gardens. A museum and a library adjoin it. San Antonio's river parkways set off many relics of its Spanish past—the old Governor's Palace, La Villeta village, and *San Jose Mission National Historic Site*, founded in 1720. The Menger Hotel has never changed its barroom, where Leonard Wood and Theodore Roosevelt recruited their Rough Riders.

San Jacinto Monument commemorates the battle in which the Texas forces commanded by General Sam Houston with their battlecry "Remember the Alamo" defeated a Mexican army and captured Santa Anna, wooden leg and all. Markers point out scenes of the action. The base of the 570-foot monument contains an ideally arranged museum of Texas history. Within range of Sam Houston's flintlocks, but jumping a century and more, is the battleship *Texas*, veteran of World War I and World War II, in retirement, but still afloat and fully equipped and gunned. Launched in 1914, the *Texas* was in the Sixth Battle Squadron of the Grand Fleet in World War I, while in World War II she bombarded Casablanca, North Africa; the coast of Normandy in the great invasion; and Iwo Jima and Okinawa in the Pacific. The battleship is open to the public. San Jacinto Monument, maintained by the state, is twenty-two miles east of Houston on Tex. 225.

Beaumont boasts a sixty-foot monument with the modest inscription "On this spot on the tenth day of the twentieth century a new era in civilization began." This is no boastful Texan exaggeration, for here, on January 10, 1901, the *Luca Gusher, Old Spindletop No. 1* blew in. The world has been traveling on oil power ever since. Beaumont is down near the coast in the southeast corner of Texas and is reached by U.S. 90, 96, 287 and 69 and Tex. 124.

"The Law West of the Pecos" was Judge Roy Bean, whose combination Jersey Lily bar, billiard hall, law office, and justice court is maintained at Langtry. It was Judge Bean who at an inquest fined the deceased the amount found in his pockets for carrying a concealed weapon, also found in his effects. Langtry is just west of the deep gorge

of the Pecos River on U.S. 90.

Palo Duro Canyon State Park is a geologic paradise of white, yellow, green, blue, and red formations eroded into a deep cleft running southward through the Panhandle. Here the Comanches and Kiowas held forth; here was one of the last stands of the buffalo, and here Charles Goodnight's dugout may still be seen, called the "cradle of Panhandle civilization." Palo Duro is named for a small hardwood shrub that grows in the canyon and was used by Indians for making arrows. The park entrance is twelve miles east of Canyon on Tex. 217.

Frontier Times Museum at Bandera, owned and operated by J. Marvin Hunter, has a most remarkable collection of old Texas relics in the heart of the hill country some forty miles northwest of San Antonio. The special attraction is that Marvin Hunter, author and editor, a genial gentleman in his eighties, knows in detail the history of every item and enjoys answering questions. *Bandera County* is in the blue hill country, with blue skies and far blue distances, live oaks, clear streams, and tonic air. You can see dinosaur tracks in the rocky stream beds where the Herefords drink, and your horse may kick up fossils of sea clams and other creatures from the ancient seas. Bandera in Bandera County is on Tex. 16 north from San Antonio.

El Paso, farthest west in Texas, is just across the International Bridge from Juarez, largest Mexican city on the border. At Fort Bliss, headquarters for guided-missile, rocket, and anti-aircraft training, is a replica of the original *Fort Bliss* (museum open 10–5 Saturday and Sunday). *Ysleta Mission*, built in 1682, is on U.S. 80, twelve miles east. *Socorro Mission church*, built in 1681, is three miles away on a crossroad, and eight miles further is *San Elizario*, presidio chapel at the site of the Salt War.

UTAH. – Salt Lake City dates from 1847 when Brigham Young proclaimed to 148 pioneer Mormons, "This is the place"—and a city rose out of the desert, nurtured by their faith and genius. The first stop is *Temple Square*, a ten-acre plot open daily. (A Bureau of Information is just within the south gate.) Each weekday at noon a free organ recital is given in the huge dome-roofed Tabernacle, where everyone is welcome. It was completed in 1867. The Temple, which took forty years to build, from 1853 to 1893, is reserved for sacred ceremonies and may not be entered by non-members. *The Seagull Monument* in Temple Square recalls the birds that miraculously saved the early settlers from a plague of grasshoppers. The Beehive and Lion Houses, Brigham Young's residences, are offices of auxiliary organizations of the church. Pioneer relics, such as the first piano hauled across the plains by ox-team, are shown at the museum in the capitol.

Bryce Canyon National Park includes interesting exposures of the Pink Cliffs formation, whose rocks are among the most colorful of any forming the earth's crust. From Rainbow Point, at the southern end of the park, you can see most of its area— Black Birch Canyon, Agua Canyon, and Willis Creek, and to the south "the land of the purple sage," Navajo Mountain, Kaibab Plateau and the Trumbull Mountains. *Cedar Breaks National Monument* to the west is another in the Pink Cliffs formation. *Zion National Park* has as its chief feature the great multicolored Zion Canyon. Here are the deep red of the Vermilion Cliffs and the brilliance of the Great White Throne. Bryce Canyon is seventy-five miles east of U.S. 89, turning off seven miles south of Panguitch. Cedar Breaks is twenty miles east of Cedar City, which is on U.S. 91. Zion is on Utah 15, reached from U.S. 89 (via a remarkable solid-rock tunnel) and U.S. 91. *Arches National Monument* contains more natural stone arches, windows, spires, and pinnacles than any other known section of the nation. It is near Moab in south-eastern Utah and is accessible from Utah 93. *Timpanogos Cave National Monument* is a series of scenic caverns in Mount Timpanogos high in the Wasatch Mountains. It is seven miles south of Salt Lake City and may be reached from U.S. 50, U.S. 89, and U.S. 91. *Capitol Reef Natural Monument* is notable for its colorful sandstone cliff of gothic appearance and the Fruita Natural Bridge, on Utah 24 between U.S. 89 and U.S. 6 and 50.

WASHINGTON. – *Mount Rainer National Park* features the most superb landmark of the Pacific Northwest. Mount Rainer is 14,408 feet high and all but a few of its most rugged crags and ridges are mantled by glacial ice. It occupies about one-fourth of the park area, also notable for great fields of avalanche lilies, western anemone, marsh marigold, mountain buttercup, paintbrushes, lupines, veronica, valerian and mountain dock. The park is accessible by a number of roads from Tacoma and Seattle. *Olympic National Park* on the Olympic Peninsula is a wilderness of coniferous rain forests, wildlife, alpine flower meadows, glaciers, lakes, and streams in one of the most rugged mountain masses in the country. The west side of the park has the wettest winters in the United States, usually topping 140 inches a year; the east slope of the park is the driest on the coast except for southern California. It is readily accessible from Olympia.

Whitman National Monument commemorates the massacre by the Cayuse Indians of the missionaires Dr. Marcus Whitman and his wife Narcissa, in 1847. They came to Wailatpu in 1836, bringing the first wheeled vehicle over the Oregon Trail. Mrs. Whitman and her companion, Mrs. Henry H. Spaulding, were the first women to travel the trail. The grave of the massacre victims, a memorial shaft, and foundation ruins of the mission buildings may be seen. The museum has some relics uncovered by excavations of the site. It is six miles from Walla Walla.

Fort Simcoe at Mool-Mool is an Historical State Park restored to commemorate a fort established in 1856 and important in the war against the Palouse, Spokane, and Coeur d'Alène Indians. It became the Yakima Indian Agency in 1859. Some of the original buildings are preserved. A Westerner, H. Dean Guie, has written a history of the post, *Bugles in the Valley*. Fort Simcoe is near Yakima.

WYOMING. – *Yellowstone National Park*. Ever since John Colter tramped through, watchful and alone, on his way to Manuel Lisa's fort at the mouth of the Big Horn in 1807, this has been the supreme American attraction. It was the first of all National Parks; for many years after 1872 it was the only one. From Colter's descriptions it became known as "Colter's Hell." Jim Bridger saw its wonders in 1830 and raised the ante. Bridger's "lies" were not believed either, so he made them taller. His "glass mountain" (Obsidian Cliff) is still there. So are Old Faithful and the many other geysers, Fountain Paint Pot, and one of the supreme sights of the continent, the falls of the Yellowstone.

Early visitors to Yellowstone Park fled as Chief Joseph of the Nez Percés hurried women and children, screened by warriors, to Targhee Pass. General O. O. Howard followed, killing his horses to bring the Indians to a stand.

Now summer crowds of tourists make it almost as difficult to see Yellowstone's wonders, but the park's vast areas still have little-visited "trails of wonder" in this last stand of the buffalo and the grizzly.

Colorado has been called the "Mother of Rivers," but Wyoming sends its waters into the Pacific, the Gulf of California and the Gulf of Mexico. In the Teton Wilderness Area just south of Yellowstone Park lies *Two Ocean Pass*, where Pacific Creek, feeding the Snake, and Atlantic Creek, tributary of the Yellowstone, lie close together. From this "Summit of the World" of the Shoshone Indians, your mind may follow the waters of the turbulent Snake, looping south, then north and west, boiling through Hell's Canyon into the Columbia and following that majestic river to the Pacific, while the Yellowstone waters swing north and east, draining the short-grassed high plains into the Missouri—the "Big Muddy" of the mountain men.

More accessible is *Togwotte Pass* (9,658 feet) on U.S. 26 some thirty miles east of Moran. East of the pass Buffalo Fork of the Snake and a branch of Wind River rise in a cluster of glacial lakes. Fabled *Green River*, carrying the name of the fur trappers' favorite hunting knife, rises on the high slopes of Gannett Peak (13,785 feet) the highest point in Wyoming. East across the Continental Divide, not far away, Bull Lake Creek has its source below a glacier on Fremont Peak. A raindrop falling on this divide may travel south in Green River and the canyons of the Colorado to the Gulf of California; or by way of Bull Lake Creek, Wind River Canyon, the Big Horn, Yellowstone, and the Missouri to the Gulf of Mexico.

Grand Teton National Park lies directly south of Yellowstone Park. Jackson Hole, the fur trappers' rendezvous, is always a surprise; no wonder the ragged and odorous fur brigades enjoyed their lusty meetings there, as recorded by Thomas Moran on canvas. (His painting "The Rocky Mountains" is in the Metropolitan Museum, New York.) Jackson Lake may be thrashed with speed boats; Leigh Lake not so likely. The view of Mt. Moran is worth hiking to see.

Devils Tower National Monument. Wyoming boasts not only the first of National Parks, but also the first National Monument, in Devils Tower; its fiftieth anniversary was celebrated in 1956. This huge fluted monumental shaft was known to the Sioux as *Mateo Tepee* meaning "Grizzly Bear's Lodge." It rises to a height of 1,280 feet and from its apparent base 865 feet, like a tree trunk a thousand feet around. Its formation is a geologic mystery. It is seven miles north of U.S. 14, twenty-nine miles from Sundance and thirty-three miles from Moorcroft, in the northeast corner of the state.

Fort Laramie National Monument marks what many will regard as the most famous of all forts in the West. It was a center of the fur trade from the time Fort William was erected here in 1834 by William Sublette and Robert Campbell, soon succeeded by Jim Bridger, Thomas "Broken Hand" Fitzpatrick, and Milton Sublette. No more obscure character in Western annals has been so widely commemorated as Jacques La Ramie, who gave his name to a fort, a city, and a mountain range. Almost nothing is known of him except his name. Fort Laramie became the most famous of stopping points on the Oregon Trail. Here came Dr. Marcus Whitman and John Charles Frémont, General Stephen Watts Kearny, the Mormon migration, the Pony Express. Here Portugee Phillips stumbled in one bitter cold night, breaking up a Christmas party at Old Bedlam with the news of the Fetterman command's destruction. The same Old Bedlam—still there—was the scene of Captain Charles King's novel *Laramie, or "The Queen of Bedlam."* It was occupied by troops until 1890. Many of the old buildings remain. It is on a paved road three miles southwest of the town of Fort Laramie on U.S. 26.

Continuing on U.S. 26 and U.S. 20 you are on the Oregon Trail to Casper. Here was the Mormon Ferry of 1847, the Platte River Bridge of 1858–59, and *Fort Casper,* a replica of which has been built. It was named for Lieutenant Casper Collins, killed here in a fight with the Sioux in 1865. North from Casper on U.S. 87, to the right you see *Teapot Dome,* which gave its name to the oil scandals of the Harding administration, and *Kaycee,* which figured in the Johnson County War. On past Buffalo are Lake De Smet and *Fort Phil Kearney* (rebuilt in replica). The turnout to the right leads over *Massacre Hill* where Lieutenant Col. W. L. Fetterman was killed in the fight the Sioux call the "Battle of the Hundred Slain" (it was eighty-one). Nearby Captain Powell fought off Red Cloud's circling Oglalas from his wagonbox corral.

West from Sheridan on U.S. 14 is *Cody,* founded by "Buffalo Bill," with its fine monument to him by Gertrude Vanderbilt Whitney, and a museum of his mementos. Up the roads are Independence Rock, Fort Bridger, Green River, the Wind River Canyon, Thermopolis of the hot springs, the Owen Wister country. There is much more to see in Wyoming than can be accomplished in one summer.

West on the Kitchen Range

EVERY DAY OF THE YEAR, Americans eat, wear, and use enough beef products to form a line of steers, cows, bulls, and calves extending from the Pentagon in Washington to City Hall in Philadelphia. Add the sheep and pigs to this "spread," and the head of the line grunts through Boston toward Maine.

We eat more beef per person, these days, than we ate during the heyday of the Chisholm Trail. The national average in 1956 was 83.5 pounds per person, with California, and other sections of the Far West, 25 to 30 pounds above that. Add the lamb and pork to that; we have American-appetite of 163.5 pounds of red meat per person per year. Much of it still comes from the West. Omaha, Denver, Fort Worth and Salt Lake City are, with Chicago and South St. Paul, the largest livestock markets, just as they were in the 1880's.

During the 1920's, meat packers financed the research to determine meat's role in building healthy human bodies. The scientists proved that meat not only provides fuels for daily energy but is rich in proteins, vitamins and minerals—the materials that build sturdy bodies, maintain that sturdiness and ward off many diseases.

These discoveries—that meat not only tastes good, but is good-for-you—opened a new era for the livestock producer, and at a time when national population whooped past all predictions. So the science era dawned in meat processing. Today the 4,000 meat packing firms in the United States maintain huge laboratories and research centers, each striving for better products and processing methods as well as supervising quality.

From sources such as these come the trail-herd's grand evolutionary pageant: son-of-a-bitch stew to filet mignon; pemmican to deep-freeze hamburgers; chuck wagon to pre-cooked, fresh-frozen dinner. And the trail winds on, with developments just as spectacular looming above the horizon.

This cowboy continuity led Madeline Holland and Zoe Coulson of American Meat Institute's Home Economics' staff to delve into some of the West's famous old recipes, adjust them to the habits of time-clock kitchens and back-yard grills, and set them down for readers of *This Is the West.* Here, in the following pages, you can go-West on the home-range any mealtime.

COWBOY'S DELIGHT

1 pound ground beef	2 cups thin cream
2 cups raw potatoes, diced	1½ teaspoons salt
2 small onions, chopped fine	¼ teaspoon pepper

Combine ingredients, turn into 2½ quart casserole. Bake, covered, one and one-half hours at 325°F. Remove cover last half-hour of cooking to brown top. Four servings.

APACHE SUNSET

2 pounds beef stew meat	½ teaspoon thyme
¼ cup flour	1 can tomato sauce
3 tablespoons melted lard	1 bouillon cube
2 teaspoons salt	2 cups water
¼ teaspoon pepper	6 whole carrots, sliced
½ clove garlic	6 small onions
½ teaspoon marjoram	

Cut meat into one and one-half inch cubes. Dredge meat in flour and brown thoroughly in hot lard. After browning, sprinkle on salt and pepper. Mince garlic and add to meat with herbs, tomato sauce, bouillon cube dissolved in water. Stir well, heat to boiling, then cook slowly two to two and one-half hours. About forty-five minutes before beef is done, add carrots and onions and more salt, if needed. Thicken drippings, if you like. Four to five servings.

HAMBURGER FLAPJACKS

Broil or pan-fry thin ground-beef patties. While they cook, bake flapjacks on a lightly greased griddle. Place hamburger between two flapjacks and eat with catsup, mustard or pickle relish.

BARBECUED POT ROAST

3 to 4 pound pot roast of beef	2 cloves garlic, minced
3 tablespoons fat	2 tablespoons brown sugar
2 teaspoons salt	½ teaspoon dry mustard
¼ teaspoon pepper	¼ cup lemon juice
½ cup water	¼ cup vinegar
1 8-ounce can tomato sauce	¼ cup catsup
3 medium onions, thinly sliced	1 tablespoon Worcestershire sauce

Brown meat in fat; add seasonings, water, tomato sauce, onions and garlic. Cover and cook over low heat one and one-half hours. Combine sugar, mustard, lemon juice, vinegar, catsup, and Worcestershire sauce and pour over meat; cover and continue cooking about one hour, or until meat is tender. Remove meat to hot platter. Skim off most of fat, dilute with water to suit taste, then thicken with two tablespoons flour mixed until smooth with one-quarter cup water. Four servings.

BEEF STEAK MEX

1 pound round steak	½ clove garlic, minced
2 teaspoons salt	1 medium onion, chopped
1 teaspoon chili powder	1 No. 303 can tomatoes
⅓ cup flour	
2 tablespoons lard	

Mix one-half teaspoon salt, chili powder, and flour and pound into steak. Cook garlic and onion in fat until tender; add meat and brown on both sides. Add tomatoes and remaining salt. Cover and simmer forty-five minutes, or until meat is tender. Prepare gravy from drippings. Four servings.

PORK PEPITA

Meat Balls	*Sauce*
1 small onion, chopped	⅔ cup grated cheddar cheese
1 clove garlic, chopped	1 teaspoon salt
Fat	¼ teaspoon pepper
1½ pounds ground lean pork	½ teaspoon oregano
2 cups fresh bread crumbs	2 eggs, beaten
½ cup minced parsley	Dash Tabasco
2 (8-ounce) cans tomato sauce	Dash Worcestershire sauce
1 cup water	

Brown onion and garlic in two tablespoons hot fat. Add to meat with remaining meat ball ingredients and mix well. Shape into balls (one-quarter cup mixture per ball.) Brown a few at a time in a few tablespoons hot fat over low heat. Drain off fat and place all meat balls in the pan. Combine sauce ingredients and pour over meat balls. Simmer, covered, one hour and forty-five minutes. Six servings.

DUDE RANCH PORK CHOPS

4 pork chops, cut 1 inch thick	½ teaspoon salt
Fat	⅛ teaspoon pepper
1 medium onion, sliced thin	1 cup chili sauce

Brown pork chops on both sides in a little hot fat. Place browned chops in shallow baking dish, cover with sliced onions. Stir salt and pepper into chili sauce, pour over chops. Cover baking dish, and bake at 325°F. one and one-half to two hours. Four servings.

TUCSON LUNCH

⅓ cup catsup
⅓ cup water
1 medium onion, shredded
1 tablespoon vinegar
1 tablespoon Worcestershire sauce
½ teaspoon chili powder
1 teaspoon salt

8 slices bacon
2 pounds ground lamb
1½ teaspoons salt
¼ teaspoon pepper
3 tablespoons melted lard

Prepare barbecue sauce by mixing catsup, water, onion, vinegar. Worcestershire sauce, chili powder and salt. Cover and simmer twenty minutes. Dice bacon and mix with lamb. Add salt and pepper. Shape into eight patties, brown on both sides in hot lard. Pour sauce over meat and simmer until sauce and meat are piping hot. Serve patties on toasted hamburger buns with a little of the sauce spooned over each. Eight servings.

LAMB IN A PAN

2 pounds lamb riblets
2 tablespoons melted lard
1 teaspoon salt
¼ teaspoon pepper
½ cup water

2 carrots, diced
2 medium potatoes, diced
1 large onion, diced
1 green pepper, diced

Brown lamb riblets in melted fat, turning meat to brown on all sides. Add seasonings and water. Cover and simmer one hour. Add vegetables and cook, covered, thirty minutes longer. Thicken gravy, if desired, and serve with meat and vegetables. Four servings.

QUICK SOURDOUGH BISCUITS

1 package compressed yeast
2 cups lukewarm water
5½ cups sifted enriched flour
⅓ cup melted shortening

3 tablespoons sugar
½ teaspoon salt
4½ teaspoons baking powder
¼ teaspoon soda
Milk

Soften yeast in water; stir in two cups of flour. Cover and allow mixture to stand about twelve hours or overnight; stir in shortening. Sift together two cups flour, sugar, salt, baking powder, and soda; add to batter with one and one-quarter cups flour or enough flour to make a moderately stiff dough.

Turn out on a floured pastry cloth or board and knead until smooth and satiny. Divide dough into two equal portions. Roll one portion of dough one-half inch thick and cut with a two-inch biscuit cutter. Form dough into balls and place on a greased baking sheet. Repeat with other portion. Brush with milk and let rise until doubled, about one hour. Bake in a 400°F. oven fifteen to twenty minutes.

RAMON ADAMS' OWN BEANS

Wash beans and put them to soak over night. Drain off the water the next morning, cover them with more cold water, and set them over a slow fire to cook. Cut a chunk of dry salt pork into pieces for seasoning but do not add more water during cookery. Hold back the salt until the beans are done. They should cook at least five hours and preferably all day; but only until tender; not until mushy.

Pemmican Pâté

Pemmican, the dried meat and tallow sausage of the Indians and mountain men, was the most famous food produced by the West. It became the standard ration for explorers in all the remote areas of the world during the eighteenth and nineteenth centuries. At Dartmouth College early in 1957, Dr. Vilhjalmur Stefansson gave the editor of *This Is the West* a modernized, kitchenette version of the mixture. Since the famous Arctic explorer lived on it for years at a time, his concession to the "store bought" substitutes is commendable.

One package of dried beef   One package of cream cheese
Two or three ounces of butter or oil   Herb or spice flavorings

Dehydrate dried beef in slow oven until it is crisp. Drop in Waring Blender or Osterizer with fat, cream cheese and other ingredients. Whip for a minute or two. Good tasty spread . . . preferably on crisped sourdough biscuits.

All-Time Books of the West

WESTERNERS ACROSS THE NATION were invited in 1954 to submit lists of ten books they thought to be outstanding. With members of all Corrals participating, the following ten received the most mentions:

1. Hiram M. Chittenden. *The American Fur Trade of the Far West.* 3 vols. 1902.
2. Reuben Gold Thwaites. *Original Journals of the Lewis and Clark Expedition of 1804–1806.* 7 vols. 1904–1907.
3. John G. Bourke. *On the Border With Crook.* 1896.
4. Walter Prescott Webb. *The Great Plains.* 1931.
5. Josiah Gregg. *Commerce of the Prairies.* 1844.
6. A. B. Guthrie. *The Big Sky.* 1947.
7. Stuart N. Lake. *Wyatt Earp, Frontier Marshal.* 1931.
8. Francis Parkman. *The Oregon Trail.* 1903 ed.
9. Mari Sandoz. *Crazy Horse.* 1942.
10. Owen Wister. *The Virginian.* 1902.

In all, 125 books were nominated. The list follows:

Adams, Andy. *The Log of a Cowboy.* Boston and New York: Houghton Mifflin Company, 1927.

Adams, Ramon. *Six Guns and Saddle Leather.* Norman: University of Oklahoma Press, 1954.

Alter, J. Cecil. *James Bridger.* Salt Lake City: Shepard Book Company, 1925.

Bandelier, Adolph. *The Delight Makers.* New York: 1890.

Barnes, Will C. *Western Grazing Grounds and Forest Ranges.* Breeders Gazette. Chicago: 1913.

Beebe, Lucius, and Clegg, Charles. *U.S. West—The Saga of Wells Fargo.* New York: E. P. Dutton & Co., 1949.

Billington, Ray A. and Hedges, J. B. *Westward Expansion.* New York: The Macmillan Co., 1949.

Bourke, John G. *On the Border with Crook.* New York: C. Scribner's Sons, 1891.

Brady, C. T. *Indian Fights and Fighters.* Garden City, N. Y.: Doubleday, Page & Company, 1927.

Brayer, Garnet M. and Herbert O. *American Cattle Trails 1540–1900.* Bayside, N. Y.: 1952. (With special separate map.)

Breckenridge, William. *Helldorado.* Boston: Houghton Mifflin Company, 1928.

Brimlow, George F. *Harney County, Oregon and Its Range Land.* Portland, Ore.: Binfords & Mort, 1951.

Brininstool, Earl A. *Fighting Indian Warriors.* Harrisburg, Pa.: Stackpole Co., 1953.

Bristow, Gwen. *Jubilee Trail.* New York: The Thomas Y. Crowell Co., 1950.

Burns, Walter Noble. *The Saga of Billy the Kid.* Garden City, N. Y.: Doubleday, Page & Company, 1926.

———. *Tombstone.* Garden City, N. Y.: Doubleday, Page & Company, 1927.

Calvin, Ross. *Sky Determines.* New York: The Macmillan Co., 1934.

Carver, Jonathan. *Travels Through the Interior Parts of North America in the Years 1766, 1767, 1768.* London: 1778.

Cather, Willa. *Death Comes for the Archbishop.* New York: A. A. Knopf, 1927.

———. *O Pioneers!* Boston and New York: Houghton Mifflin Company, 1913.

Catlin, George. *Letters and Notes of the Manners, Customs, and Conditions of the North American Indians. . . .* 2 vols. London: 1841.

Chittenden, Hiram M. *The American Fur Trade of the Far West.* 3 vols. New York: F. P. Harper, 1902.

Clark, Walter Van Tilburg. *The Ox-bow Incident*. New York: Random House, 1940.
———. *The Track of the Cat*. New York: Random House, 1949.
Clay, John. *My Life on the Range*. Chicago: priv. ptg., 1924.
Coe, George W. *Frontier Fighter*. Boston: Houghton Mifflin Company, 1934.
Coutant, V. G. *Coutant's History of Wyoming*. Laramie, Wyo.: 1899.
Cunningham, Eugene. *Triggernometry*. Caldwell, Idaho: Caxton Printers, 1941.
Custer, George A. *My Life on the Plains*. New York: Shelton & Co., 1874.
DeVoto, Bernard. *Across the Wide Missouri*. Boston: Houghton Mifflin Company, 1947.
Dick, Everett. *The Sod-House Frontier*. New York: D. Appleton-Century Co., Inc., 1937.
Dobie, J. Frank. *Guide to Life and Literature of the Southwest*. Dallas, Texas: Southern Methodist University Press, 1952.
———. *The Longhorns*. Boston: Little, Brown & Company, 1941.
———. *The Voice of the Coyote*. Boston: Little Brown & Company, 1949.
Downey, Fairfax Davis. *Indian Fighting Army*. New York: Charles Scribner's Sons, 1944.
Fee, Chester G. *Chief Joseph*. New York: Wilson-Erickson, 1936.
Ferris, Warren A. *Life in the Rocky Mountains*. Denver, Colo.: Old West Publishing Co., 1940.
Frémont, John C. *Exploring Expedition to the Rocky Mountains, Oregon and California*. Buffalo, N. Y.: 1851.
Frink, Maurice. *Cow Country Cavalcade*. Denver, Colo.: Old West Publishing Company, 1954.
Gard, Wayne. *The Chisholm Trail*. Norman: University of Oklahoma Press, 1954.
Garland, Hamlin. *A Son of the Middle Border*. New York: The Macmillan Co., 1917.
Garrard, Lewis. *Wah-to-Yah and the Taos Trail*. Cincinnati: 1850.
Garrett, Pat. *The Authentic Life of Billy the Kid*. Santa Fe, N. M.: 1882.
Gillett, James. *Six Years With the Texas Rangers*. Austin, Tex.: 1921
Graham, Col. William A., *The Custer Myth*. Harrisburg, Pa.: Stackpole Co., 1953.
Gregg, Josiah. *Commerce of the Prairies*. New York: H. G. Langley, 1944.
Grinnell, George Bird. *The Fighting Cheyennes*. New York: C. Scribner's Sons, 1915.
Guthrie, A. B. *The Big Sky*. New York: William Sloane Associates, Inc., 1947.
Hafen, LeRoy and Ann W. *Old Spanish Trail*. Glendale, Calif.: Arthur H. Clark Co., 1954.
Haley, J. Evetts. *Jeff Milton*. Norman: University of Oklahoma Press. 1948.
Hamilton, W. T. *My Sixty Years on the Plains*. . . . New York: Forest and Stream Publishing Co., 1905.
Hammond, George P., and Rey, Agapito. *The Narrative of Coronado's Expedition*. Albuquerque: University of New Mexico Press, 1941.
Hanson, Joseph Mills. *The Conquest of the Missouri*. Chicago: A. C. McClurg & Co., 1909.
Haycox, Ernest. *Bugles in the Afternoon*. Boston: Little, Brown & Company, 1944.
Hough, Emerson. *The Covered Wagon*. New York and London: D. Appleton & Company, 1922.
Hunter, Marvin and Rose, N. H. *An Album of Gunfighters*. Bandera, Texas: 1951.
Hunter, Marvin. *The Trail Drivers of Texas*. 2 vols., Cokesbury Press, 1924.
Hyde, George E. *Pawnee Indians*. Denver, Colo.: Brown Book, 1951.
Inman, Col. Henry. *Old Santa Fe Trail: The Story of a Great Highway*. New York: 1897.
Irving, Washington. *Astoria*. New York: G. P. Putnam's Sons, 1902.
Kantor, MacKinlay. *Warwhoop*. New York: Random House, 1952.
———. *Wicked Water*. New York: Random House, 1949.
Krakel, Dean. *The Saga of Tom Horn*. Laramie, Wyo.: 1954.

Kuhlman, Charles. *Legend into History*. Harrisburg, Pa.: Stackpole Co., 1951.

Lake, Stuart N. *Wyatt Earp, Frontier Marshal*. Boston: Houghton Mifflin Company, 1931.

Laut, Agnes. *The Story of the Trapper*. New York: D. Appleton & Company, 1902.

Lea, Tom. *The Wonderful Country*. Boston: Little, Brown & Company, 1952.

Linderman, Frank. *American*. New York: The John Day Co., 1930.

McCarter, Margaret Hill. *The Price of the Prairie*. Burt, New York: 1912:

McCoy, Joseph S. *Historical Sketches of the Cattle Trade of the West and Southwest*. Kansas City: 1874.

Mackenzie, Alexander. *Voyages from Montreal*. . . . New York: New Amsterdam Book Co., 1902.

McWhorter, L. V. *Hear Me, My Chiefs!* Caldwell, Idaho: Caxton Printers, Ltd., 1952.

Marriott, Alice. *The Ten Grandmothers*. Norman: University of Oklahoma Press, 1945.

Martin, Douglas D. (ed.). *Tombstone's Epitaph*. Albuquerque: University of New Mexico Press, 1951.

Masterson, W. B. "Famous Gun Fighters of the Western Frontier—Wyatt Earp," *Human Life*, Feb. 1907.

Maximilian zu Wied. *Reisen ins Innere von Nord-Amerika*. (Including the *Atlas* with the Bodmer prints.) Paris: 1836.

Mercer, Asa S. *Banditti of the Plains*. With a foreword by William H. Kittrell. Norman: University of Oklahoma Press, 1954.

Myers, John M. *The Last Chance: Tombstone's Early Years*. New York: E. P. Dutton & Co., Inc., 1950.

Neihardt, John G. *The Song of Hugh Glass*. New York: The Macmillan Co., 1915.

——. *Song of the Indian Wars*. New York: The Macmillan Co., 1925.

Nelson, Bruce. *Land of the Dacotahs*. London: Oxford University Press, 1946.

Nye, Col. W. S. *Carbine and Lance*. Norman: University of Oklahoma Press, 1937.

O'Conner, Richard. *High Jinks on the Klondike*. Indianapolis: Bobbs-Merrill Company, Inc., 1954.

Parkman, Francis. *The Oregon Trail*. Boston: Little, Brown & Company, 1903.

Pike, Zebulon M. *Exploratory Travels Through the Western Territories of North America*. Philadelphia: 1810.

Raine, William M. *Famous Sheriffs and Western Outlaws*. New York: Doubleday, Doran & Co., Inc., 1929.

Rascoe, Burton. *Belle Star*. New York: Random House, 1941.

Rhodes, Eugene M. *The Trusty Knaves*. Boston: Houghton Mifflin Company, 1933.

Richardson, Rupert. *The Comanche Barrier to South Plains Settlement*. Glendale, Calif.: Arthur H. Clark Co., 1933.

Rølvaag, Ole E. *Giants in the Earth*. New York: Harper & Brothers, 1929.

Root, F. A. and Connelley, W. C. *The Overland Stage to California*. Topeka, Kans.: 1901.

Russell, Charles M. *Trails Plowed Under*. Garden City, N. Y.: Doubleday, Page & Company, 1927.

Ruxton, George F. *Adventures in Mexico and the Rocky Mountains*. London: 1847.

——. *Life in the Far West*. Ed. by Le Roy A. Hafen. Norman: University of Oklahoma Press, 1951.

Sandoz, Mari. *The Buffalo Hunters*. New York: Hastings House, 1954.

——. *Cheyenne Autumn*. New York: McGraw-Hill Book Co., 1953.

——. *Crazy Horse*. New York: Alfred A. Knopf, Inc., 1952.

——. *Old Jules*. Boston: Little, Brown & Company, 1935.

Schaefer, Jack. *First Blood*. Boston: Houghton Mifflin Company, 1953.

——. *Shane*. Boston: Houghton Mifflin Company, 1949.

Sears & Roebuck Catalogue. Chicago: 1878.

Sherman, Gen. William T., Memoirs of. New York: D. Appleton & Company, 1875.

Siringo, Charles A. *A Texas Cowboy*. New York: H. W. Wilson Co., 1875.

Smith, Joseph. *The Book of Mormon*. 1830 (Salt Lake City, many editions).

Sonnichsen, C. L. *I'll Die Before I'll Run*. New York: Harper & Brothers, 1951.

Sprague, Marshall. *Money Mountain*. Boston: Little, Brown & Company, 1953.

Stanley, Henry M. *My Early Travels and Adventures*. New York: C. Scribner's Sons, 1895.

Strahorn, Carrie Adell. *Fifteen Thousand Miles By Stage*. New York: G. P. Putnam's Sons, 1911.

Stuart, Granville. *Forty Years on the Old Frontier*. 2 vols. Cleveland, Ohio: The Arthur H. Clark Co., 1925.

Thwaites, Reuben G. *Early Western Travels*. 32 vols. Cleveland, Ohio: The A. H. Clark Company, 1904–07.

——. *Original Journals of the Lewis and Clark Expedition of 1804–1806*. 7 vols. New York: 1904–05. (Actually all editions of these journals were nominated.)

Turner, Frederick Jackson. *The Frontier in American History*. New York: H. Holt & Company, 1920.

Van de Water, Frederick F. *Glory-Hunter: a Life of General Custer*. Indianapolis: Bobbs-Merrill Company, Inc., 1934.

Vestal, Stanley. *Sitting Bull*. Boston: Houghton Mifflin Company, 1932.

——. *Queen of Cowtowns—Dodge City*. New York: Harper & Brothers, 1952.

——. *New Sources of Indian History*. Norman: University of Oklahoma Press, 1934.

Webb, Walter Prescott. *The Great Plains*. Boston: Ginn & Company, 1931.

——. *The Texas Rangers*. Boston: Houghton Mifflin Company, 1935.

Wellman, Paul I. *Death in the Desert*. New York: The Macmillan Co., 1935.

Westerners Brand Book. Los Angeles Corral: 1947.

White, Stewart E. *Long Rifle*. Garden City, N. Y.: Doubleday, Doran & Co., Inc., 1932.

Wilson, Rufus R. *Out of the West*. New York: Press of the Pioneers, 1933.

Wissler, Clark. *Indians of the United States*. New York: Doubleday, Doran & Co., Inc., 1940.

Wister, Owen. *The Virginian*. New York and London: The Macmillan Co., and The Macmillan Co., Ltd., 1902.

Wood, Elizabeth L. *Pete French, Cattle King*. Portland, Ore.: Binfords & Mort, 1951.

The Westerners

THE WESTERNERS had its inception in March, 1943, when a group of Chicagoans interested in Western Americana met at the home of Elmo Scott Watson, professor of journalism at Northwestern University, to hear a discussion of a book, *The Sagebrush Dentist*, by its authors Herman Gastrell Seeley and Will Frackelton. However, no organization was effected and no further action taken for nearly a year.

Then, under the prodding of Leland Case, fourteen men, much the same group, met again in Watson's Winnetka home to hear Clarence Paine, librarian of Beloit College, discourse on *Calamity Jane*. That night the name *The Westerners* was adopted and the *Chicago Corral* was formed. The governing Posse appointed consisted of Watson, Case, and Franklin J. Meine. A meeting arranged for March 27, 1944, at the Cliff Dwellers club rooms, marked the actual birth of the Westerners. Twenty-three Charter Members were present to hear Don Russell discuss the legalistic status of *Jesse James*. The next month the late Dr. Irving S. Cutter spoke on another James boy, Dr. Edwin James. Since then, except for occasional barbecue sessions in July and occasional lapses in August, the Westerners have met monthly to hear an original paper by a member or a guest speaker.

The first scheduled meeting was reported by Elmo Watson in a ten-page mimeographed bulletin he called *The Brand Book*, after the books that recorded cattle brands in the West. Here, he believed, Westerners could record their brands, that is, their areas of interest in the West. The first issue was distributed in April; by June applications for subscriptions were being received from those too distant to attend meetings. Thus the Corresponding Membership was instituted. At the end of the first year a bound book, based on the lectures, was produced. Volume II appeared a year later. After that *The Brand Book* was printed. Monthly issues were assembled with an index and bound at a nominal cost for members.

Early in 1945 Leland Case was in Denver, where he talked with kindred souls. In March, Sheriff Watson gave the salutatory address at the founding of The Westerners there. A year later the Los Angeles Corral was founded. Others followed. Here is a roundup of chapters of the Westerners:

Chicago Corral, meets the fourth Monday of each month at Ireland's, 630 North Clark Street. Secretary, Arthur G. Murdock, 3050 W. Belmont Ave., Chicago 18, Ill. Publications: *The Westerners Brand Book*, monthly since March, 1944; Volume XIV began with March, 1957, issue; editor, Don Russell, 191 Clinton Ave., Elmhurst, Ill.; director of publications, Leigh P. Jerrard, 522 Willow Road, Winnetka.

Denver Posse, meets the fourth Wednesday at Denver Press Club, 1330 Glenarm Place; Secretary-treasurer, Erl H. Ellis, 730 Equitable Building, Denver 2, Colorado. Publications: *The Denver Westerners Monthly Roundup*, Volume XIII starts January, 1957; started as *The Brand Book*, mimeographed, 1945; printed, 1951; became *Roundup*, 1954. Books: *The Eleventh Annual Brand Book*, dated 1955, was published in 1956.

Los Angeles Corral, meets third Thursday at Costa's Grill, 525 Ord Street; Sheriff, Don Meadows, 640 Terraine Ave., Long Beach 14, California. Publications: *The Branding Iron*, quarterly. In 1947 five numbers of *Los Angeles Corral Westerners Brand Book* were published bi-monthly. *The Branding Iron* started in March, 1948, on an irregular schedule, supplemented by occasional *Keepsake* numbers; by the end of 1956 there had been 37 serial numbers of both. Books: *The Sixth Annual Brand Book* was published in 1956.

New York Posse, founded 1952, meets monthly. Address all communications to The Westerners, Room 1012, 51 East 42nd Street, New York 17, N.Y. Publications: *The Westerners New York Posse Brand Book* is published quarterly, printed. Books: *Landmarks on the Oregon Trail*, by Paul Henderson, 1955, limited to 250 copies at $25.

Potomac Corral, Washington, D.C., was organized December 16, 1954. Tally Man;

Bert Sheldon, 4827 43rd Place, N.W., Washington 16, D.C. Publication: *Corral Dust,* quarterly, since March, 1956.

Spokane Posse, organized March 17, 1955; meets third Thursday of month, 6 p.m., at Spokane Hotel. Tally Man, Franklin T. Curtis, 316 East Eighteenth Ave., Spokane 35, Wash. Publication: *The Pacific Northwester,* quarterly, first issue dated Winter, 1956–57.

Kansas City Posse, organized April 5, 1955, meets the second Tuesday of each month at Milleman's on the Plaza. Tally Man, James Anderson, 446 West 62nd Street, Kansas City 13, Missouri. Publication: *The Trail Guide,* "published occasionally," first issue dated September, 1955; fourth issue of Volume I dated December, 1956, printed.

Tucson Corral, organized 1953. Meets monthly, usually at Student Union, University of Arizona; Secretary: Don Bufkin, 902 S. Eli Drive, Tucson, Ariz.

Black Hills Corral, organized 1953. Meets monthly, usually at A & F Cafe, Rapid City; Secretary: Joe Koller, Box 469, Belle Fourche, S. Dak.

St. Louis Westerners. For information address Dr. Harold A. Bulger, 4405 West Pine Blvd., St. Louis 3, Missouri.

French Corral, organized 1956, has sessions on square dancing every Wednesday, on Indian dances every Tuesday, and classes in Western riding twice a week, also special sessions on Western motion pictures and fancy roping. Secretary: Gabriel Chen, 26, Rue Clisson, Paris, XIII°, France. Publication: *The Westerners French Corral,* Paris.

England. The English Corral of The Westerners was founded in 1954 with a membership scattered throughout the British Isles and abroad. No regular meetings are contemplated. Address: Editor, Frederick W. Nolan, "Kildare," 95 Albion Street, New Brighton, Cheshire, England. Publication: *The English Westerners Brand Book,* monthly, since November 1954. It has appeared in a variety of forms, mimeographed, printed, and by offset. Volume III started with November, 1956, issue.

Authors

Ramon Adams lives in Dallas, Texas, and is finishing the first complete Bibliography of Western Rangeland Literature. He is the author of *Come and Get It, The Story of the Cowboy Cook, Dictionary of Western Words,* and numerous other books on the West.

O. K. Armstrong, long a student of the Amerind, is a Missourian, a former congressman, a Roving Editor for the *Reader's Digest.*

Oren Arnold, headquarters in Phoenix, Ariz., can look from his study windows at some of the source material for his numerous books and articles on the West.

S. Omar Barker, a director of the Western Writers of America, lives in "the other" Las Vegas—the New Mexico one. His poems used in some of the chapter headings are from *Sunlight Through the Trees* (Highlands University Press, Las Vegas, N. Mex.) and *Songs of the Saddlemen* (Sage Books, Denver, Colo.).

Kenneth S. Bennion is a free-lance writer and advertising executive in Salt Lake City, Utah.

Stanley Vestal is the justifiably famous pen-name of Dr. W. S. Campbell, Professor of Journalism, University of Oklahoma, Norman.

Badger Clark, the beloved "poet laureate of South Dakota," lives in Custer, South Dakota. His lonely cabin is a summertime "College of Western Americana" for poets, writers and English Lit. majors.

Homer Croy, one of Missouri's most famous products, writes books, movies, articles, with the impudent glee of a leprechaun. His letterhead may identify him as Inspector 22 of the North Fenway Ironworks in Gallabismuhclaaara, Wales . . . but he lives across from the Palisades in uptown New York City.

Howard R. Driggs, native of Utah and son of one of the builders of the Union Pacific R. R., is president of American Pioneer Trails Association, Inc., Bayside, New York City. He is the author of dozens of books. Two of the latest are *The Old West Speaks* and *The Cowkid.*

Richard Dunlop, associate editor of *Home & Highway,* Skokie, Illinois, is a veteran magazine writer and a director of The Chicago Corral.

William B. Edwards is associate editor of *Guns Magazine* in Skokie, Illinois, and a director of The Chicago Corral.

Richard L. Evans, author and columnist, is internationally famous as "the voice" of the Salt Lake City Tabernacle Choir broadcasts from "The Crossroads of the West." He is a member of The Council of Twelve, The Church of Jesus Christ of Latter-day Saints.

Bert Fireman, a native of San Francisco, produces the "Under the Sun" column for *The Phoenix* (Ariz.) *Gazette,* authors and narrates the Arizona network show *Arizona Crossroads,* and is a contributor to *Arizona Highways.*

Wayne Gard, editorial writer for the *Dallas* (Tex.) *Morning News,* is the author of *Sam Bass, Frontier Justice, The Chisholm Trail,* and numerous magazine articles.

Walter Havighurst, professor of English, Miami University, Oxford, Ohio, is the author of *Wilderness for Sale, Annie Oakley of the Wild West, George Rogers Clark, the Long Ships Passing, Land of Promise,* etc.

James Horan is Special Events Editor of the New York *Journal American.* He is the author of twelve books of fiction and nonfiction about the Civil War and the West. He was cofounder of the New York Posse of the Westerners.

Robert West Howard, author of *Two Billion Acre Farm, The Real Book About Farms, Educational Planning by Communities,* etc., is currently Roving Editor, the American Meat Institute, Chicago, Illinois, and Chairman, Publications Committee, the Chicago Corral.

Alice Marriott, known to postal clerks of Santa Fe and Oklahoma City as "Roving

Lady," is author of *Hell on Horses and Women* and hundreds of magazine articles.

Don Russell, editor of *The Brand Book*, a veteran encyclopedia editor and authority par excellence on Western Americana, lives in Elmhurst, Illinois.

William P. Schenk, erstwhile secretary to Carl Sandburg, is associate editor, *Science Digest*, Chicago, Illinois.

Joseph Stocker, once a student in Stanley Vestal's journalism classes, resigned newspaper work in 1948 to free-lance—the day before he got married (!!!). Uniquely, this brashness paid off. He has since sold nonfiction to 75 magazines, plus the movie "Belly It In" and—so far—one book, *Arizona, a Guide to Easier Living*.

Reginald R. Stuart, author of *The Burrell Letters, San Leandro, a History, How Firm a Foundation, Fred Finch Children's Home* and *Tully Knoles of Pacific*, is director of California History Foundation, College of the Pacific, Stockton, California.

Charles W. Towne, youthful feature writer for *The Boston* (Mass.) *Herald*, went west as Buffalo Bill Cody's publicity man, managed the inn at Cody, Wyoming, became publicity director for Anaconda Copper in Butte, retired to Phoenix, Arizona, where he has youthfully partnered with cousin Ed Wentworth in the production of *Shepherds Empire, Pigs from Cave to Cornbelt, Cattle and Men*, and other classics of America's livestock history.

J. F. Weadock, associate publisher of *The Arizona Star*, has been a cowboy and a cavalryman. He is the author of *Dust of the Desert*.

Walter Prescott Webb, professor of history at the University of Texas in Austin, is one of the truly great names in Western writing. Authorities regard his *The Great Plains* as "the definitive book" on the area. He is currently finishing *The West: 1860–1950* for Harper's.

Colonel Edward N. Wentworth, known as "Colonel Ed" to stockmen and agricultural educators from the Everglades to the Olympias, was director of the Livestock Bureau of Armour & Co. until he retired to Chesterton, Indiana, two years ago. With "Cousin Charley" Towne, he researched and wrote some of the best histories of American livestock ever published. He is working, in 1957, on a definitive history of the horse in America.

Mitzi Zipf, president of the Arizona Press Women and the Mesa Archaeological and Historical Society, is an exceptional combination of housewife-newswoman-archaeologist. Both she and her husband are "staffers" on *The Arizona Republic*. An archaeology major at University of Arizona, she contributes the exciting searches for "The First Westerners" to *Arizona Highways, Desert Trails, The Kiva, Arizona Historical Review*, et al.

PRINTED IN U.S.A.